Contributions to Economics

More information about this series at http://www.springer.com/series/1262

Julia Köhn

Uncertainty in Economics

A New Approach

Springer

Julia Köhn
Berlin, Germany

ISSN 1431-1933 ISSN 2197-7178 (electronic)
Contributions to Economics
ISBN 978-3-319-55350-4 ISBN 978-3-319-55351-1 (eBook)
DOI 10.1007/978-3-319-55351-1

Library of Congress Control Number: 2017942769

Printed on acid-free paper

This Springer imprint is published by Springer Nature
The registered company is Springer International Publishing AG
The registered company address is: Gewerbestrasse 11, 6330 Cham, Switzerland

Preface

In mainstream economic theory, uncertainty is closely linked to the theory of economic choice. Particularly, since the 1950s the epistemic aspect of uncertainty dominates the intellectual debates and uncertainty became modelled as a subjective probability belief of a rational economic agent. Several attempts have been made to extend this approach and make it more realistic.[1] Yet, the ontological aspects of uncertainty are still not reflected in economic theory. The overarching goal of this book is to seek a comprehensive understanding of the economic theory of uncertainty and to appraise it critically. Based on this, I aim to develop a theory of economic uncertainty that integrates epistemological and ontological aspects of uncertainty. This book is based on my dissertation, which was supervised by Professor Birger Priddat (Department of Economics) at Witten/Herdecke University.

Therefore, I firstly should establish that ontological aspects of uncertainty are similarly important as epistemic ones. In Part I of this book, I therefore analyse the concept of uncertainty in economic thought and show that originally uncertainty was conceptualised as both epistemic and ontological. Only due to the economic professions' attempt to become acknowledged as a science, the more problematic aspect of ontological uncertainty became neglected and the subjective probability approach to uncertainty became dominant in economic theory.

Secondly, I will explore the ontological facets of uncertainty in Part II. Here, I critically appraise theories of uncertainty that emphasise the ontological character of uncertainty. It will become obvious that, even though, these theories are not part of the mainstream in economics, they contain significant critiques on the mainstream approach, which explain the blindness of modern economics to economic phenomena such as instability, slumps or excessive booms. Furthermore, these approaches suggest that the positivistic and instrumentalist philosophy of the science of economics inhibits a New Economic Uncertainty Paradigm, which

[1] For example, Simon (1955), Kahneman and Tversky (1979) or Gigerenzer (2002).

could reflect both the epistemic and ontological aspects of uncertainty and its implications for economic behaviour.

Based on these findings, I develop a new approach to the methodology of economics in Part III, which legitimises a New Uncertainty Paradigm in economics. The analysis suggests that taking uncertainty seriously in economics calls for a fundamental change in the methodology of economics, in which reasonable fiction replaces rational probabilities.

Berlin, Germany Julia Köhn

References

Gigerenzer G (2002) Bounded rationality: the adaptive toolbox. MIT Press, Cambridge

Kahneman D, Tversky A (1979) Prospect theory: an analysis of decision under risk. Econometrica 47(2):263–291

Simon HA (1955) A behavioural model of rational choice

Contents

Chapter 1
Introduction

> Uncertainty means, first of all, that no one ever knows how things will actually transpire. This framing posits, like the efficient markets hypothesis, that the central element is information. In this case, however, information is never perfect, nor should it be. The imperfection of information is not a defect (or a 'failure') of markets, and cannot be overcome with greater knowledge or better techniques. Imperfect information is the physiological condition and reason of markets. (Esposito 2013: 9)

This book is about the nature of uncertainty in economics and its implications for the science of economics. The concept of uncertainty is a fundamental of economic thought. We cannot understand meaningful economic phenomena, like the market, the price or profit without recognizing the centrality of uncertainty to the economy and economics. Yet, the modern positivist research principles have neglected the significance of uncertainty, to establish and defend an elegant economic science. The analysis shows that this is illegitimate both from a history of ideas perspective and from a methodological perspective. Positive economic theories are meaningless in the face of uncertainty. Furthermore, if uncertainty is a fundamental of economics, Positive Economic theories are meaningless per se. Therefore, I suggest new Research Principles for the Science of Economics, which acknowledge uncertainty as an economic fundamental. Based on the new principles of economics of coherence and believability I develop the fictional choice approach as a new theory of choice in an economy that is fundamentally uncertain to different degrees.

1.1 Many Faces of Uncertainty

Uncertainty has been one of the most controversial topics in economic philosophy and methodology. There is no consensus among economists what uncertainty actually means and how it is relevant for the advancement of economic theory (Lawson 1988). Uncertainty has many faces in economics.

J. Köhn, *Uncertainty in Economics*, Contributions to Economics,
DOI 10.1007/978-3-319-55351-1_1

When it comes to uncertainty, the economic discipline falls apart and debates become highly emotional (Rosenberg 2013). Uncertainty possesses an extraordinary brisance as it can be interpreted as a nail in the coffin of deterministic neoclassical economics (Dow 2008). Therefore, it is no surprise that most economist's opinions on uncertainty are highly political and dogmatic.[1] On the one hand there are those, who wish to save the Neoclassical Uncertainty Paradigm and on the other hand there are those outside the mainstream, who wish to pull it over and replace it with another Uncertainty Paradigm on which there no consensus has been reached (Hodgson 2009). The consequence is a passionate debate that began in the 1930s and continues. Since that time, the problem of uncertainty in economic philosophy and methodology had been discussed time and again, there were periods of silence and when the Millennium came the problem had been pushed to the margin, neglected and almost forgotten (Hodgson 2011a).

The financial crisis, drew back attention to this unsettled debate in the philosophy of economics and by the year 2007 uncertainty became identified as one, if not the cause of the crisis.[2] Yet, the authors, who drew back attention to the problem of uncertainty, neither explained how uncertainty caused the crisis nor what uncertainty actually means or implies for economic theory.

The new debate on uncertainty was thus similarly ambiguous as former debates and for this reason disappeared just as quickly as it came. As Hodgson's survey (2011a: 4–5) has shown, the problem of uncertainty had almost re-disappeared from scientific economic publications by 2010. I take this observation as a starting point of my analysis of the many faces of uncertainty in economics. I attempt to clear up the confusion and provide an analytical basis for the discussion of the problem of uncertainty in the following parts of this essay. Economic literature is replete with references to uncertainty. Each of these references, however, addresses different aspects of the problem. Without claiming comprehensiveness, I want to present some facets of uncertainty to the reader. First, I present the understandings of uncertainty, which take uncertainty to be fundamental to economics. Secondly, I introduce the Neoclassical Uncertainty Paradigm. Finally, I will delineate a Janus-faced conception of uncertainty in economics. On the one side, there is Neoclassical Uncertainty and on the other side there are a variety of Fundamental Uncertainty conceptions.

On the Fundamental Uncertainty side, there is most prominently Knightian Uncertainty, which is commonly referred to as a lack of probability distributions, which causes the immeasurability of risk.[3] Particularly, neoclassical economists

[1]Hodgson (2011b: 4) for example argued: "Economists often react to unpredictability with angst or even panic."

[2]E.g.: Daníelsson (2008), Dow (2008), Eichengreen (2008), Frydman and Goldberg (2008), Hodgson (2009), Arcemoglu (2009), Colander et al. (2009), Skidelsky (2010), Stiglitz (2010a, b), Turner (2010), Colander (2010), Nelson and Katzenstein (2010). This list is anything but exhaustive. The crisis literature is wide and most serious authors referred to the problem of uncertainty in some way and more or less explicitly.

[3]E.g.: McKinney (1977), LeRoy and Singell (1987), Langlois and Cosgel (1993), Runde (1998).

have criticised this view, as it implies that formal mathematical equilibrium models, which dominate neoclassical economics, fall apart. Arrow (1951: 417), for example, had argued, that without measurable probabilities "no theory can be formulated". And Lucas (1977: 15) claimed later for the case of Knightian Uncertainty that, "(i)n case of uncertainty, economic reasoning will be of no value".

A second face is Keynesian Uncertainty. In his General Theory Keynes (1936) discussed the problem of investment behaviour under conditions of uncertainty. He argued that investors confronted with uncertainty about the future do not and can not calculate the future value of some good. Therefore, in order to take action economic agents, rely on their animal spirits, which Keynes defined as an urge to action rather than inaction.[4] Choice under conditions of uncertainty, therefore, evades the rational choice framework. Instead choice is taken based on gut feeling and custom.[5]

The Behavioural Uncertainty interpretation draws back on Keynes' observations and analyses agent's real behaviour (in laboratory experiments) under conditions of uncertainty in order to reveal the behavioural strategies they apply in situations of uncertainty. The central thesis is that people do not behave rationally in the face of uncertainty. Instead people show biases[6] or apply fast and frugal heuristics.[7]

Also, the Realists interpretation of Uncertainty is rooted in Keynes analysis and emphasises agent's inability to form rational expectations in situations of uncertainty. Their argument is ontological in nature. They assume that economic reality is essentially open and therefore the future is yet to be created, when agents take action. This makes it impossible to make any reasonable prediction about future states and questions the deterministic world-view of neoclassical economics.[8]

Most recently, the Imperfect Knowledge interpretation of uncertainty has emerged.[9] Considering the realist critique, they argue, that the future is essentially open in economics. However, in the short run, the future is structured and some possible future states can be identified.[10] They therefore suggest, modelling uncertainty as non-routine change, which allows them to make imprecise predictions about the future developments. This interpretation therefore takes an intermediate position between Realist Uncertainty and the neoclassical interpretation.

---

[4]E.g.: Kregel (1976), Lawson (1985a), Greer (2000), Runde and Mizuhara. (2003), Skidelsky (1992, 2010).

[5]In the Post-Keynesian literature, however, Keynesian Uncertainty is often referred to as liquidity preference, which is the agent's preference to retain money rather than make investment decisions (Fontana 2000, 2001; Ferrari-Filho and Conceição 2005: 579).

[6]E.g.: Allias (1953), Simon (1955), Ellsberg (1961), Kahneman and Tversky (1979, 1982), Thaler (1992, 1999).

[7]E.g.: Gigerenzer (2001, 2002), Gigerenzer and Goldstein (2002), Gigerenzer et al. (2008), Gigerenzer and Gaissmaier (2011).

[8]E.g.: Lawson (1985a, b, 1987, 1988, 1989, 1995, 2003, 2009).

[9]E.g.: Frydman et al. (2007), Frydman and Goldberg (2008, 2010), Goldberg et al. (2013).

[10]Already in 1991 Katharina Juselius published a stochastic framework that allowed for routine change, which is underling most of the Imperfect Knowledge Models today (Juselius 1991).

Despite this variety of different facets of Fundamental Uncertainty, the Neoclassical Uncertainty came to dominate modern economics since the 1950s. Under the neoclassical conception, uncertainty is defined as subjective probability distributions. This paradigm is part of the neoclassical theory of choice. It is assumed that any agent possesses a complete utility function over all possible states and that (s)he always chooses the option with the highest expected utility. Whereas the utility of the options get calculated based on the subjective probability assigned to the option and the subjective probability for the occurrence of that option. Choice is thus conceptualised, like a game of chance, in which optimal decisions can be calculated.[11]

All in all, uncertainty has a Janus-face in economics. There is Neoclassical Uncertainty and there are different conceptions of Fundamental Uncertainty. Both types of uncertainty are entitled by strong arguments. They describe very different problems and therefore the theories formulated on the basis of different types of uncertainty also provide rather different conclusions. When it comes to the problem of uncertainty, there is no one fit all solution. Neither the Neoclassical Uncertainty Paradigm, which conceptualises uncertainty for methodological reasons as a form of risk, nor the Fundamental Uncertainty Paradigms allow for universal conclusions. The very nature of the problem, leaves economists with the challenge that uncertainty is a fundamental source of economic behaviour and at the same time its obstacle.

The Neoclassical Uncertainty Paradigm was a clever intermediate stage that allowed economists to integrate uncertainty and at the same time keep their theoretical achievements. However, this came at the price that the Fundamental Uncertainty Paradigm remained underexposed or even got rejected for methodological reasons. The success of the Neoclassical Uncertainty Paradigm fed the rumour that the Fundamental Uncertainty Paradigm would lead to a non-formal economic theory of "anything goes" (Coddington 1982), which fuelled fears among economists, that a scientific discussion of Fundamental Uncertainty Paradigm is not only impossible, but also would damage the still new scientific image of economics. For these reasons the Fundamental Uncertainty Paradigm almost got lost during the twentieth century developments in economic thought.

On the background of this diverse and heated struggle in the philosophy and methodology of economics, I aim to understand the complex nature of uncertainty and its implications for the principles of economics. I believe that a new understanding of the nature and implications of uncertainty is indispensable to reform modern economics.

[11]E.g.: Friedman and Savage (1948, 1952), Ellsberg (1954), Savage (1954), Elster (1979), Levi (1980, 1986, 1990), Sugden (1986), Machina (1987), Anand (1993), Binmore (2009), Riedel (2013).

1.2 Framing the Issue

This book stands in the tradition of economic philosophy. Starting in the 1970s and 1980s economics underwent an opening process. After almost three decades of pure and mainly mathematical economics and a high time of econometrics, economists started to rediscover the strong links between economics and other social sciences, the humanities and new fields. Also, the methodology of economics expanded. Particularly in Behavioural Economics and Game Theory, laboratory experiments started to gain importance. This trend expanded since then, so that methods as well as insights from psychology and neuroscience became integrated into economics. Beside these most recent mergers between economics and other disciplines, particularly the link between economics and history as well as economics and philosophy, became rediscovered by that time.[12] The opening procedure, which began in the 1970s still lasts and has intensified during the last years.

The financial crisis of 2007 and the following worldwide recession and national dept crisis both shocked economists all over the world. Almost nobody had seen this slump coming and dominant economic theories were unable to explain it.[13] Also, the economic methodology turned out to be inappropriate. Consequently, the opening process of economics pursued by a growing number of economists, among them opponents of the orthodoxy and groups of critical thought within economics, emerged at many places. Two of the most significant think tanks in economics, which have their origin in this new movement for plurality and critical thought are the "Institute for New Economic Thinking" (INET 2009) and the

[12]In 1963 the first modern academic journal in the History of Economics was established in Japan. In the early years the Journal of "History of Economic Thought" was mainly focused on particularly Japanese questions related to economic theory and its development. Only few years later the Journal of "History of Political Economy" got established in the U.S. This journal is still today highly relevant and discusses the emergence of economic ideas and its relevance for politics. One decade later the first European Journal in History of Economic thought was founded in the U.K. (Journal of the History of Economic Thought, 1979). Other still today leading journals were established in the following years in Australia (History of Economics Review, 1981) and continental Europe (History of Economics, 1983). Finally, the "European Journal of the History of Economic Thought" was first published in 1993 in the U.K. After this series of journal formations had come to an end a new branch of academic economics gained importance and attention. In 1985 the Journal of "Economics and Philosophy" was found. It is still today one of the leading journals at the intersection between economics and philosophy and discusses mainly methodological as well as ethical questions related to economic thought. In 1994 a second journal with a focus on economic methodology was established (Journal of Economic Methodology). In the same year we saw a second new journal with an emphasis on the political dimension of economics (Philosophy and Public Affairs). Most recently, two new journals emerged at the intersection between economics, philosophy and also politics (Erasmus Journal for Philosophy and Economics, 2008; Politics, Philosophy and Economics, 2009). Particularly, in the Erasmus Journal for Philosophy and Economics questions of history of economic thought get discussed frequently.

[13]Strong concerns on the role of economic theory in the becoming of the crisis were raised for example by, Eichengreen (2008), Colander et al. (2009) and Colander (2010).

"World Economic Association" (WEA 2011). On its website, the INET[14] justifies itself as follows:

> The Institute for New Economic Thinking was created to broaden and accelerate the development of new economic thinking that can lead to solutions for the great challenges of the twenty-first century. The havoc wrought by our recent global financial crisis has vividly demonstrated the deficiencies in our outdated current economic theories, and shown the need for new economic thinking—right now.[15]

Leading economists have joined the INET and considerable financial means allow them to set up new research programs, for example, in Imperfect Knowledge Economics, Banking History, New Thinking on Risk and Uncertainty, Economic History or even to set up a curriculum committee in order to change university education in economics.

Therefore, New Economic Thinking can be interpreted as a branch of economic philosophy that aims to rethink the philosophical foundations of economics in order to develop new economic theories, which go beyond the twentieth century paradigms and help to understand and prevent economic slump. To reach this aim, New Economic Thinking combines classical economic insights[16] with new lines of economic thought and new methods.[17]

In this monograph, I follow a similar research strategy and therefore, this piece can be classified as part of New Economic Thinking and Economic Philosophy. Critically rethinking the problem of uncertainty in economics, therefore, is not only state of the art in new economic thinking,[18] but also puts itself in a long and flourishing tradition of economic philosophy, which only lately has been rediscovered and demarcated by Seele (2011, 2014).

This book is about the problem of uncertainty in economics and its implications for economic theory. It analyses the origin, development and philosophical implications of the concept of uncertainty in economics. Furthermore, I go beyond the state of the art and ask, based on the findings of the analytical part of this book, what kind of Uncertainty Paradigm new economic thinking would need. Therefore, this book can be classified as a piece of *economic philosophy* under the definition of

---

[14]The WEA claims a similar commitment when they write: "The Association will encourage the free exploration of economic reality from any perspective that adds to the sum of our understanding. To this end it advocates plurality of thought, method and philosophy." (WEA Manifesto) Furthermore, in 2012 the WEA had established two new online Journals (WORLD ECONOMIC REVIEW and Economic Thought), which reflect the new pluralism in economics and emphasise the interrelation of economics and philosophy. Though INET and WEA are organised and funded differently, they have similar aims and use similar means. Pluralism and Economic Philosophy are at the forefront of the modernisation of economics. http://www.worldeconomicsassociation.org/journals (2013-06-21).

[15]http://ineteconomics.org/about (2013-06-21).

[16]Classical economic insights by Alfred Marshall, Friedrich A. von Hayek, J. M. Keynes, Carl Menger seam to be still relevant. They need to be reread and reinterpreted in the light of the economy of the twenty-first century.

[17]E.g.: Kirman (2011a, b, 2014).

[18]http://ineteconomics.org/key-topics/uncertainty-and-risk (2014-06-11).

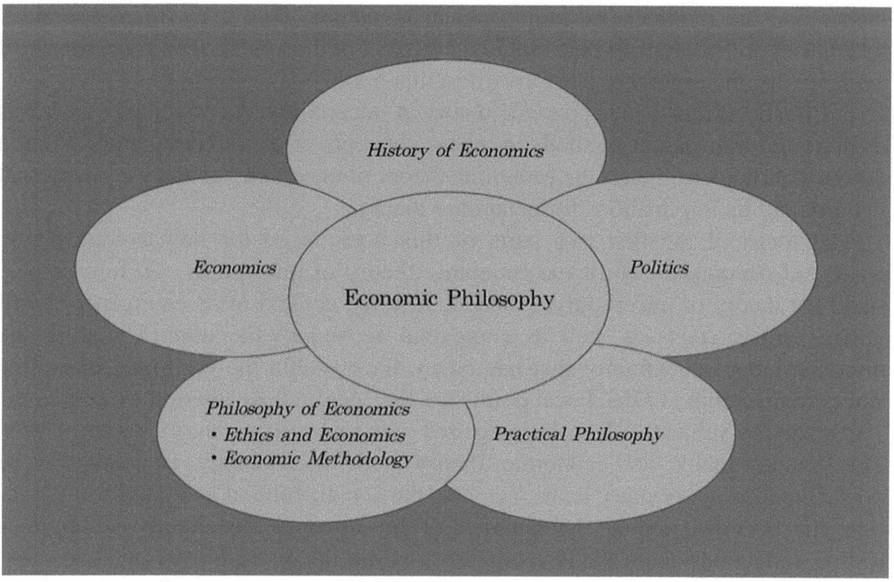

Fig. 1.1 Economic philosophy, authors' own figure

Peter Seele (2011, 2014). Figure 1.1 shows the different subjects, which belong to the field of economic philosophy according to Seele.

Seele argued that Economic philosophy analyses the historic, methodological and practical or ethical foundations of economic problems. It uses an archaeological and philosophical methodology and is located at the intersection between history of economics, philosophy of economics, politics and economics. Furthermore, economic philosophy discusses and reflects the theoretical and practical consequences of economic thought or theory.[19]

Some parts of this monograph are about the past, yet it is not a book in the history of economic thought or any other kind of historical work. It is a philosophical study about the economic concept of uncertainty. The subject of my analysis is economic

[19]Political and ethical questions play a minor role in this analysis. Though, I belief that these normative aspects are highly relevant I will not discuss them here. I am convinced, that a normative discussion would go beyond the scope of this dissertation for two reasons. First of all, since the beginning of the twentieth century the economic discipline is undecided, whether normative questions can be tackled by economists (Keynes 1890; Friedman 1953; Hausman and McPerson 1996; Hands 2001: 70ff; Chaplin and Schotte 2008). Therefore, discussing the normative implications of the already highly controversial problem of uncertainty would provoke an emotional discussion that would outshine the analytical problems discussed here. Secondly, I am committed to an educational goal. In that way I want to provide an analytical basis for evaluating and bettering the theory of uncertainty, however, it is on the society to judge, which way forward to take. In my opinion the economist, while having private political and ethical convictions has the duty to shed light on the problems of economics in order to reach a better understanding of them, which then can be used for better politics.

theory and my methods are philosophical in nature. This is a critical appraisal, which uses archaeology to understand the subject of the appraisal and as a source of evidence for the argument put forward in this book.

I critically appraise the economic theory of uncertainty. A critical appraisal uses explicit and transparent methods to assess concepts or data (Young and Solomon 2009). This book evaluates the economic theory of uncertainty. I analyse its internal validity and its implications for economic theory.

The focus of the first two parts of this book is on the archaeological and analytical decomposition of the economic theory of uncertainty. To fully understand the theory of uncertainty, I analyse it in the context of its emergence. I will utilize primary texts as well as contextual secondary literature. I analyse the discourse about uncertainty that has taken place within the economic discipline since Adam Smith (1776). Focal points are the Marginal Revolution as well as the 1920s and the Subjective Revolution paired with formalism in the 1950s and 1960s. The transformation of economic theory and methodology is going to be documented using primary texts. Yet, also the social, cultural and historical conditions that accompanied the development of the economic Uncertainty Paradigm as well as reflections about the developments within the discipline and the historiography about it will be of similar interest. My aim is not to write an all-encompassing history of the economic Uncertainty Paradigm. Instead, I use fragments from the past, to identify and understand paradigm shifts. I therefore place myself in the tradition of Michel Foucault's archaeological method (1969, 1972) about which Ian Hacking (2006: xiii) writes:

> Archaeology organises the past to understand the present. It lifts the dust-cover off a world that we take for granted. It makes us reconsider what we experience as inevitable.

Based on a systematic philosophical analysis of the emergence and development of the Uncertainty Paradigms in economics I will deduce conditions for a modern Uncertainty Paradigm and discuss its implications for the principles of economics and economic methodology in particular in third part.

1.3 A Readers Guide: Outline and Structure of the Argument

This book is organized in three parts. The First Part analyses the origins and development of uncertainty in economics and delineates the Neoclassical Uncertainty Paradigm. *Uncertainty and the History of Economic Thought* (Chap. 2) is the first chapter of the first part. Here I argue in more detail than in the introduction that, although, uncertainty is one of the oldest and most substantial parts of economic thought, there is no consensus among economists, what uncertainty is and what it implies for the study of economic phenomena. Uncertainty has a Janus-Face in economics. On the one side uncertainty is defined as a calculable subjective probability belief. On the other side uncertainty is an economic fundamental that causes economic phenomena and hinders scientists from understanding them, which implies that the future is necessarily unknowable.

The third chapter is *Truth, Probability and Uncertainty* (Chap. 3). The scientific study of uncertainty is commonly associated with probability calculus. However, the meaning of probability had changed fundamentally in the course of time. Probability reasoning has its origin in the emazipation of men from the power of the church. It is a truth-constructing instrument with no link to reality and therefore a dubious foundation for a modern science. The apparent calculability of truth created an illusion of certainty and scientific accuracy.

The next chapter is an analysis of the *The Principles of Economics* (Chap. 4). Economics, once a low science was particularly vulnerable for the illusion of certainty and accuracy created through the use of probabilistic and mathematical instruments. Once Economics was a science that strived to understand economic phenomena in order to give policy advice for the good of the whole society, it became a science that defines itself by the methods it uses. Particularly, the stochastic and mathematical methods became constructive for economics, which lead to neglecting non-calculable and therefore Fundamental Uncertainty. If one includes Fundamental Uncertainty in the economic analyses one necessarily leaves the mainstream of the discipline.

The first part ends with a critical appraisal of *Probability and Neoclassical Uncertainty* (Chap. 5). In the 1950th economic uncertainty became defined as a subjective but rational probability expectation. The apparent dichotomy between subjective and rational belief was overcome by an integration of the theory of rational choice, expected utility theory and subjective probability theory. This Neoclassical Uncertainty Paradigm is still today underlying modern macroeconomics and financial economic models. Nevertheless, the usability of this account is limited as its axiomatic foundations are rather strong. Consequently, the applicability of the theory to real world problems is restrictive. Neoclassical Uncertainty Models create internal validity and yet no truth.

The Second Part turns to the older and more substantial tradition of Fundamental Uncertainty Approaches. I begin with Frank H. Knight's account of Fundamental Uncertainty, which he developed, while he was investigating *The Origin of Profit* (Chap. 6). Uncertainty is fundamental to economic phenomena and explains the emergence of profits and losses. Furthermore, probability beliefs formulated in the face of uncertainty are estimations. Therefore, they build no foundation for rational choice. Choice in the face of uncertainty is based on an entrepreneurial spirit and faith.

J. M. Keynes, therefore, emphasises the acquaintance of *Uncertainty and Economic Instability* (Chap. 7) in his theory of economic behaviour under conditions of uncertainty. In the face of uncertainty economic decision makers have only limited knowledge, which implies that they have to use the power of reason in order to take reasonable decisions. Uncertainty, therefore neither implies ignorance, nor does it allow for rational choice. Decision makers have to rely on indirect forms of knowledge, which can only be reached based on logical reasoning and which are necessarily biased by the social and psychological nature of the economic agent.

Animal Spirits strongly influence reasonable economic choice in the face of uncertainty and evades rationality analysis.

Friedrich A. von Hayek and G. L. S. Shackle discuss *The Division of Knowledge and Unknowledge* (Chap. 8) as instruments for managing the limits of knowledge in the face of uncertainty. In a market economy knowledge is necessarily scattered and uncertainty is therefore omnipresent. No matter how hard one tries it cannot be overcome, as new knowledge creates new uncertainty. Only the market mechanism uses uncertainty as recourse for novelty, progress and temporarily optimal allocations (Witt 2007). Uncertainty is the source of the free market economy, freedom and surprise. Individual probabilistic reasoning is insufficient in such a situation. Besides being logically invalid, it excludes the knowledge, which is scattered in society when knowledge is scarce anyway. Only human imagination can be used to come up with similarly reasonable images of the future as the price mechanism could produce. Human imagination can imitate a hypothetical price mechanism and eliminate all impossible solutions to get close to an unattainable optimal choice.

Thus, the second part shows that Uncertainty is fundamental to *The Nature of Economics* (Chap. 9) and ignoring it or misrepresenting it as a type of subjective probability per se, leaves out important aspects of economic reality and economic problems. The ninth chapter, uses a realist perspective on the nature of uncertainty in economics and defines the conditions for Fundamental Uncertainty based economics. This type of economics distinguishes between different degrees of uncertainty and assumes non-randomness and performativity, which can be used as means of explanation.

Finally, Part III turns to the methodological implications of uncertainty for the science of economics. I argue that *Extending the Boundaries of Economics* (Chap. 10) is obligatory if one aims to integrate Fundamental Uncertainty into economic analysis. Besides questioning the power of purely stochastic economic models, this new turn in the philosophy of economics allows for much more differentiated and ontology based analytical instruments along the Uncertainty Corridor. Furthermore, the analysis suggests that reflexivity can be used for manipulation and it calls for the normative responsibility of the economist. In a fundamentally uncertain economy, economic theories and models are not meaningless, but powerful.

Nevertheless, the character of economic analysis changes fundamentally under conditions of Fundamental Uncertainty. Probability theory is no longer the key to the management of the limits of knowledge. *Uncertainty and Fiction* (Chap. 11) replaces uncertainty and probability. Instead of creating apparent precision, the theory of fiction can be used to explore an uncertain future in order to take reasonable decisions. Fictional choice theory is presented as a meta-theory of choice under conditions of different degrees of uncertainty and reflexivity.

Economics and economists are *Human after All* (Chap. 12). Uncertainty points to this assessment und shows that the science of economics needs reorientation and reformation. Uncertainty is often presented as the nail in the coffin of modern analytical economics. It is not. Acknowledging uncertainty is the key for new methods and pluralism in economic analysis. Furthermore, it points to the human nature of the science. There is no economy out there that only needs to be discovered by some positivistic economist. It rather is the case that we are creating the economy and its conditions. Economics is a reflexive procedure that creates economic realities. The advancement of this science of human cohabitation is essential.

References

Acemoglu D (2009) The crisis of 2008: structural lessons for and from economics. MIT Working Paper

Allais M (1953) Le Comportement de l'Homme Rationnel devant le Risque, Critique des Postulats et Axiomes de l'Ecole Americaine. Econometrica 21(4):503–546

Anand P (1993) Foundations of rational choice under risk. Oxford University Press, Oxford

Arrow KJ (1951) Mathematical models in the social sciences. In: Lerner D, Lasswell H (eds) Policy Sciences in the United States. Stanford University Press, Stanford, pp 129–154

Binmore K (2009) Rational decisions. Princeton University Press, Princeton

Chaplin A, Schotte A (2008) The foundations of positive and normative economics: a handbook. Oxford University Press, Oxford

Coddington A (1982) Deficient foresight: a troublesome theme in keynesian economics. Am Econ Rev 72(3):480–487

Colander D (2010) The economics profession, the financial crisis, and method. J Econ Methodol 17(4):419–427

Colander D, Föllmer H, Haas A, Goldberg M, Juselius K, Kirman A, Lux T et al (2009) The financial crisis and the systemic failure of academic economics. Institute for the World Economy, Kiel

Daníelsson J (2008) Blame the models. J Financ Stab 4:321–328

Dow SC (2008) Mainstream methodology, financial markets and global political economy. Camb J Econ 27(1):13–29

Eichengreen BJ (2008) Origins and responses to the current crisis. Working Papers

Ellsberg D (1954) Classic and current notions of "measurable utility". Econ J 64:528–556.

Ellsberg D (1961) Risk, ambiguity, and the savage axioms. Q J Econ 75(4):643–669

Elster J (1979) Ulysses and the sirens. Cambridge University Press, Cambridge

Esposito E (2013) The structures of uncertainty: performativity and unpredictability in economic operations. Econ Soc 42(1):102–129

Ferrari-Filho F, Conceição AC (2005) The concept of uncertainty in Post Keynesian Theory and in Institutional Economics. J Econ Iss XXXIX(3):579–594

Fontana G (2000) Post Keynesians and circuitists on money and uncertainty: an attempt at generality. J Post Keynesian Econ 23(1):27–48

Fontana G (2001) Keynes on the "Nature of economic thinking": the principle of non-neutrality of choice and the principle of non-neutrality of money. Am J Econ Sociol 60(4):711–743

Foucault M (1969) L'archéologie du savoir. Gallimard, Paris

Foucault M (1972) The archaeology of knowledge. Pantheon Books, New York

Friedman M (1953) The methodology of positive economics. In: Friedman M (ed) In positive economics. Chicago University Press, Chicago

Friedman M, Savage L (1948) The utility analysis of choices involving risk. J Polit Econ 56:279–304

Friedman M, Savage L (1952) The expected-utility hypothesis and the measurability of utility. J Polit Econ 60:463–474

Frydman R, Goldberg M (2008) Macroeconomic theory for a world of imperfect knowledge. Capital Soc 3(3):1–76

Frydman R, Goldberg MD, Phelps ES (2007) Imperfect knowledge economics: exchange rates and risk. Princeton University Press, Princeton

Gigerenzer G (2001) Simple heuristics that make us smart. Oxford University Press, Oxford

Gigerenzer G (2002) Bounded rationality: the adaptive toolbox. MIT Press, Cambridge, MA

Gigerenzer G, Gaissmaier W (2011) Heuristic decision making. Annu Rev Psychol 62:451–482

Gigerenzer G, Goldstein DG (2002) Models of ecological rationality: the recognition heuristic. Psychol Rev 109(1):75–90

Gigerenzer G, Hoffrage U, Goldstein DG (2008) Fast and frugal heuristics are plausible models of cognition: reply to Dougherty, Franco-Watkins, and Thomas (2008). Psychol Rev 115 (1):230–239

Goldberg MD, Frydman R, Phelps ES (2013) Rethinking expectations: the way forward for macroeconomics. Princeton University Press, Princeton

Greer W (2000) Ethics and uncertainty: the economics of John M. Keynes and Frank H. Knight. Edward Elgar, Cheltenham

Hacking I (2006) The emergence of probability: a philosophical study of early ideas about probability, induction and statistical inference. Cambridge University Press, Cambridge

Hands WD (2001) Reflection without rules: economic methodology and contemporary science theory. Cambridge University Press, Cambridge

Hausman DM, McPerson MS (1996) Economic analysis and moral philosophy. Cambridge University Press, Cambridge

Hodgson GM (2009) The great crash of 2008 and the reform of economics. Cambridge J Econ 33:1205–1221

Hodgson GM (2011a) The eclipse of the uncertainty concept in mainstream economics. J Econ Iss 45(1):159–176

Hodgson GM (2011b) On the limits of rational choice theory. World Econ J 17:1–16

Juselius K (1991) Long—run relations in a well—defined statistical model for the data generating process. Cointegration analysis of the PPP and the UIP relations for Denmark and Germany. In: Gruber J (ed) Econometric decision models, Lecture notes in economics and mathematical systems, vol 366. Springer, Berlin Heidelberg, pp 336–357

Kahneman D, Tversky A (1979) In: Kahneman D, Tversky A (eds) Prospect theory: an analysis of decision under risk Econometrica 47(2):263–291

Kahneman D, Tversky A (1982) Judgement under uncertainty: heuristics and biases. Cambridge University Press, Cambridge

Keynes JN (1890) The scope and method of political economy. Batoche Books, Kitchener

Keynes JM (1936) The general theory of employment, interest and money. Palgrave Macmillan, London

Kirman A (2011a) The crisis in economic theory. Rivista Italiana degli Economisti, SIE—Societa' Italiana degli Economisti 16(1):9–36

Kirman A (2011b) Complex economics: individual and collective rationality. Routledge, London

Kirman A (2014) Is it rational to have rational expectations? Mind and Society 13(1):29–48

Kregel JA (1976) Economic methodology in the face of uncertainty: the modelling methods of Keynes and the post-Keynesians. Econ J 86:209–225

Langlois RN, Cosgel M (1993) Frank knight on risk, uncertainty, and the firm: a new interpretation. Econ Inquir 31(3):456–465

Lawson T (1985a) Uncertainty and economic analysis. Econ J 95(380):909–927

Lawson T (1985b) Keynes' economics: methodological issues. Croom Helm, London

Lawson T (1987) The relative/absolute nature of knowledge and economic analysis. Econ J 97 (388):951–970

Lawson T (1988) Probability and uncertainty in economic analysis. J Post Keynesian Econ 11 (1):38–65

Lawson T (1989) Realism and instrumentalism in the development of econometrics. Oxford Econ Pap 41:236–258

Lawson T (1995) A realist perspective on contemporary "Economic Theory". J Econ Iss XXIX (1):1–32
Lawson T (2003) Reorienting economics. Routledge, London
Lawson T (2009) Contemporary economics and the crisis. Real-World Econ Rev 50:122–131
LeRoy S, Singell L (1987) Knight on risk and uncertainty. J Polit Econ 95:394–406
Levi I (1980) The enterprise of knowledge. MIT Press, Cambridge
Levi I (1986) The paradoxes of Allais and Ellsberg. Econ Philos 2:23–53
Levi I (1990) Pareto unanimity and consensus. J Philos 89:481–492
Lucas RE (1977) Understanding business cycles. University of Chicago, Chicago
Machina M (1987) Choice under uncertainty: problems solved and unsolved. J Econ Perspect 1:121–154
McKinney J (1977) Frank H. Knight on uncertainty and rational action. South Econ J 43 (4):1438–1452
Nelson S, Katzenstein P (2010) Uncertainty and risk and the crisis of 2008. Paper presented for the "Politics in the New Hard Times" Workshop, University of California, San Diego
Riedel F (2013) Die Schuld der Ökonomen. Econ, Berlin
Rosenberg A (2013) Reflexivity, uncertainty and the unity of science. J Econ Methodol 20 (4):429–438
Runde J (1998) Clarifying Frank Knight's discussion of the meaning of risk and uncertainty, (1921). Camb J Econ 22:539–546
Runde J, Mizuhara S (eds) (2003) The philosophy of Keynes' economics: probability, uncertainty and convention. Routledge
Savage L (1954) The foundations of statistics. Dover Publications, New York
Seele P (2011) Ökonomische Philosophie: Ein programmatisches Vorwort. Ökonomie, Politik und Ethik in der praktischen Philosophie der Antike. De Gruyter, Berlin
Seele P (2014) Ökonomische Philosophie. Ein Plädoyer für die Rehabilitierung einer alten Disziplin. Inform Philos 14(1):30–36
Simon HA (1955) A behavioural model of rational choice. Q J Econ 69(1):99–118
Skidelsky R (1992) John Maynard Keynes: the economist as saviour 1920-1937s. MacMillan
Skidelsky R (2010) Keynes: the return of the master. Publicaffairs
Smith A (1776) Wealth of nations: an inquiary into the nature and causes of the wealth of nations. Prometheus Books, New York
Stiglitz J (2010a) Freefall: America, free markets, and the sinking of the world economy. W. W. Norton, New York
Stiglitz J (2010b) The Stiglitz report: reforming the international monetary and financial systems in the wake of the global crisis. New Press, New York
Sugden R (1986) New developments in the theory of choice under uncertainty. Bull Econ Res 38:1–24
Thaler RH (1992) The winner's curse: paradoxes and anomalies of economic life. Princeton University Press, Princeton
Thaler RH (1999) Mental accounting matters. J Behav Decis Mak 12:183–206
Turner A (2010) The future of finance: the LSE report. London School of Economics & Political Science, London
Witt U (2007) Novelty and the bounds of unkowledge in economics. Papers on Economics and Evolution 7
Young JM, Solomon MJ (2009) How to critically appraise an article. Nat Clin Pract Gastroenterol Hepatol 6(2):82–91

Part I
Uncertainty in Economic Thought

Uncertainty has various facets in economic thought and a history that goes back to the founding fathers of political economy. David Hume and Adam Smith emphasised the importance of uncertainty for the economic development and explained the existence of economic allocation problems both with scarcity of resources and ambiguity, which originates from uncertainty and limited human knowledge. Furthermore, they have identified uncertainty to be a serious challenge to the aspired scientificness of economics. Particularly, Hume demanded for idealistic and abstract mathematical reasoning in economics, because uncertainty impedes any realistic science. This plea for abstract theories in the face of uncertainty has been followed up by William Stanley Jevons (1863, 1871), Carl Menger (1871) and Léon Walras (1874) during the so-called marginal revolution. They developed the theory of the utility maximizing economic agent under conditions of certainty. Later, Jevons extended this theory to conditions of risk, by assigning objective probabilities to the utilities of some agent. However, in most economic decision-making no objective probabilities can be assigned, so that this economic theory of rational choice was rather limited at the beginning of the twentieth century.

New developments in the theory of probability during the 1920s and their integration into the economic theory of choice during the 1950s and 1960s, allowed for the extension of the rational choice framework to situations in which objective probabilities were missing. These situations became defined as situations of uncertainty in Neoclassical Economics. From that time on, uncertainty was equivalent to subjective probabilities in economics (also called the Baysian theory of uncertainty, I call this the Neoclassical Uncertainty Paradigm).

The first part traces the emergence and development of the Neoclassical Uncertainty Paradigm and discusses its underlying methodology. Particularly, the different theories of probability underlying the economic theory of choice under conditions of imperfect knowledge, such as risk and uncertainty are analysed critically. Also, the emergence and development of the concept of probability is presented in detail. This analysis allows understanding the concept of probability on the background of its emergence and shows that probability is originally a measure of ignorance, which was later turned into a measure of belief. Nevertheless, it is used in economics as if it would allow for a rational and unambiguous analysis of economic decision-making. The analysis shows that rational choice theory and the different theories of probability were originally designed as analytical instruments with limited scope and limited applicability to real economic problems. They are devices of an abstract and elegant, idealistic and closed body of theory. The Neoclassical Uncertainty Paradigm was originally neither designed to be the basis of modern economic theories that operate under conditions of uncertainty, nor does it cover the problem of uncertainty in economics by any means. The theory is analytically brilliant and at the same time fundamentally flawed, as it misrepresents the problem of uncertainty in economics by all means and therefore leads to a structural underestimation of its impact on the economy.

References

Jevons WS (1863) A general mathematical theory of political economy
Jevons WS (1871) The theory of political economy. Palgrave Macmillan, London
Menger C (1871) Grundsätze der Volkswirtschaftslehre. Mohr Siebeck, Tübingen
Walras L (1874) Éléments d'économie pure ou théorie de la richesse sociale

Chapter 2
Uncertainty in the History of Economic Thought

Uncertainty as many faces in contemporary economics. These different faces emerged since the 1950s. They are the consequence of an historical debate in the science of economics, which dates back to the early days of modern economics in the eighteenth century. Since then, economists have an ambivalent relation to the problem of uncertainty, which expresses itself in a Janus-face definition of uncertainty. On the one hand, there is the Fundamental Uncertainty Paradigm, which acknowledges uncertainty as a fundamental source of economic phenomena and which perceives the economy as a not perfectly determined system and economic action as not purely random. Therefore, the knowledge problem is argued to be insurmountable in economics. On the other hand, there is what I call the Neoclassical Uncertainty Paradigm, which assumes that the knowledge problem can be overcome on the basis of rational choice theory combined with subjective probability beliefs. The opponents of this concept are aware that it is unrealistic and hypothetical, yet they argue that it is the only way forward in a modern science of economics. This chapter delineates the emergence of this Janus-face conception of uncertainty. I begin with a critical discussion on the knowledge problem in economics and the early desire for general laws and rational economic action. Then, I discuss the methodological and theoretical advancements of the marginal revolution, which lead to the evolution rational choice theory, which will be discussed in the third section. In the fourth section, I concentrate on the classical distinction between risk and uncertainty in the 1920s. Afterwards I briefly introduce the becoming of the concept of subjective probability theory, which allowed economists to reinterpret uncertainty as a form of quantifiable risk. As a consequence, the Janus-face concept of uncertainty evolved. The last section summarizes my findings.

J. Köhn, *Uncertainty in Economics*, Contributions to Economics,
DOI 10.1007/978-3-319-55351-1_2

2.1 The Uncertain Fundament of Economics

We will start our investigation into the origins of the Neoclassical Uncertainty Paradigms in the eighteenth century. By that time the Scottish enlightenment provided a fruitful breading-ground for a rational analysis of the economy. During this time religion and moral convictions still played an important role in economic thought, yet, critical thought, reason and the observations of reality (evidence) gained importance in the sciences (Backhouse 2002). Scientific objectivity became the ideal of economic reasoning. Inspired by Montesquieu's Spirit of the Laws (1793), economic thinkers like Hume and Smith started to search for "constant and universal principles of human nature" (Wertz 1975: 482). The rise of secularism was the starting point of classical economics and it became the aim of economists to identify the laws that govern human welfare (Backhouse 2002: 111). Most prominently, David Hume argues for the ideal of abstract mathematical reasoning. He writes:

> There remain, therefore, algebra and arithmetic as the only sciences, in which we can carry on a chain of reasoning to any degree of intricacy, and yet preserve a perfect exactness and certainty. We are possessed of a precise standard, by which we can judge of the equality and proportion of numbers; and according as they correspond or not to that standard, we determine their relations, without any possibility of error. When two numbers are so combined, as that the one has always a unite answering to every unite of the other, we pronounce them equal; and it is for want of such a standard of equality in extension, that geometry can scarce be esteemed a perfect and infallible science. Hume (1738: III)

Though, the mathematical and statistical techniques of this time were not satisfactory sophisticated, Hume acknowledged their analytical precision. He furthermore argued that these techniques could be used in order to identify cause and effect of a certain phenomenon. His Treaties on Human Nature, for example can be interpreted as an attempt to identify the causes of human action. Though he used no mathematical techniques, he did a critical analysis of the potential causes of human nature to identify the laws that govern human action.

Beside his theoretical economic achievements, Hume contributed to the philosophy of science and particularly epistemology. He argued that there are three forms of human reason:

> For this reason, it would perhaps be more convenient, in order at once to preserve the common signification of words, and mark the several degrees of evidence, to distinguish human reason into three kinds, viz. THAT FROM KNOWLEDGE, FROM PROOFS, AND FROM PROBABILITIES. By knowledge, I mean the assurance arising from the comparison of ideas. By proofs, those arguments, which are derived from the relation of cause and effect, and which are entirely free from doubt and uncertainty. By probability, that evidence, which is still attended with uncertainty.[1] (Hume 1738: III)

To Hume, reason is generally reached either by argument or by proof (Hepfer 2011). Whereby it is necessary to distinguish between different types of arguments

---

[1]Bold is in the original.

(varying in the supportive evidence and the way of logical inference), which are associated with different levels of uncertainty. If there is no uncertainty, Hume speaks of knowledge, while he speaks of probabilities (meaning weightings), if there is uncertainty. Consequently, arguments are either based on knowledge or probabilities depending on the level of certainty or uncertainty. Proofs on the other hand, are not dependent on arguments, but on definitions. Reason, which can only be reached by argument, is not opposite to uncertainty.[2] Instead reason is inseparably linked to different levels of uncertainty. Only few arguments are based on knowledge, while in most cases probabilities get used to build arguments.

Particularly, inductive reasoning, which implies a stable causal relation between cause and effect, is inseparably linked to uncertainty. Hume, pointed out, that even though it appears to the observer that some cause brings about some effect, because one could observe this relation several times, it neither needs to be the case that there actually is this relation in reality, nor that it will also hold in the future. For this line of thought Hume became associated with the problem of induction, even though he had never referred to it himself in this way. Instead it was John Maynard Keynes who drew the connection between the problem of induction and Hume's philosophy. In Chap. 18 of his "Treaties on Probability" Keynes draws the reader's attention to the following quote from Hume (1772: Part I):

> Nothing so like as eggs; yet no one, on account of this apparent similarity, expects the same taste and relish in all of them. 'This only after a long course of uniform experiments in any kind, that we attain a firm reliance and security with regard to a particular event. Now there is that process of reasoning, which from one instance draws a conclusion, so different from that which it infers from hundreds of instances that are no way different from that single? This question I propose as much for the sake of information, as that with any intention of raising difficulties. I cannot find, I cannot imagine any such reasoning. But I keep my mind still open to instruction, if any one will vouchsafe to bestow it on me.

Hume points to the problem that conclusions derived from induction cannot be demonstrated with the same certainty as conclusions derived from deductive arguments. No matter how many apparently similar eggs one examines, there is no certainty that any egg, will be like the eggs examined sofar (Hepfer 2011). Put in more general terms, Hume identified that there is no necessity from observation that causal relations in the future will resemble causal relations in the past.[3]

[2]Today, uncertainty is often interpreted as a lack of reason. To Hume uncertainty and reason belong inseparable together.

[3]Keynes, therefore, suggests in his discussion of Hume's Problem of Induction pretty much in line with Mill (1848) and Popper (1990, 2002) that one should not discriminate between good and bad or more or less certain conclusions derived from induction on the basis of analogous instances. Instead one should try to analyse the underlying causal structure by conducting crucial experiments or using methods of difference. E.g.: "In an inductive argument, therefore, we start with a number of instances similar in some respect AB, dissimilar in others C. We pick out one or more respects A in which the instances are similar, and argue that some of the other respects B in which they are also similar are likely to be associated with the characteristic A in other unexamined cases: The more comprehensive the essential characteristics A, the greater the variety amongst the non-essential characteristics C, and the less comprehensive the characteristics B which we seek to

This scepticism about the state of human knowledge can also be found in Adam Smith's reasoning about economic choice. Smith recognized that economic decision makers were in most cases confronted with imperfect knowledge. According to him economic knowledge is neither sharp nor clear, instead it is cloudy, amorphous, ambiguous or even not available or existent. Furthermore, he doubts the significance or possibility for probabilistic knowledge. Smith attached much greater value to the use of wise human reasoning and the use of moral rules as a basis for action in situations of uncertainty, than for the application of probability calculus. Whereby, he did not deny that decision makers have some probable knowledge of how the future may turn. Instead of forming calculating chances the form probability beliefs based on trends and argument from analogy (Bardy 2013: 9).[4] Bardy (2013: 1) summarizes Smith's position as follows:

> Instead of sharp, definite, determinate, calculated, and exact probabilistic estimates or distributions, inexact, indefinite, indeterminate, and imprecise estimates of probabilities could be derived and used so that decision makers were able to make choices among different possible options that concerned the future in a rational fashion.

His dislike for the use of probability calculus was rooted in his doubt about the most fundamental assumption underlying conventional theories of probability. He had argued: "The world neither ever saw, nor ever will see, a perfectly fair lottery; or one in which the whole gain compensated the whole loss; because the undertaker could make nothing by it" (Smith 1776: 45).

Smith strengthens his argument against the ergodicity[5] of economic events, by an analysis of the insurance market. He argues, that if, economic reality was purely random, it would be possible to insure (based on probability calculations) against any type of risk and there would be no potential for profits in the insurance market.[6]

---

associate with A, the stronger is the likelihood or probability of the generalisation we seek to establish" (Keynes 1921: 219–220).

[4]Smith (1776: 99) argues, that although "[. . .] the risk [. . .] cannot [. . .] be calculated very exactly [. . .]. [It] admits [. . .] of such a gross estimation, as renders it, in some degree, reducible to strict rule and method".

[5]Ergodicity is used to describe a system or pattern that has the same average behaviour over time. The term is derived from the Greek words ergon and odos and describe a particular work-path. In 1969 Paul A. Samuelson (p. 12) has written that if economists hope to move economics from "the realm of history" into "the realm of science" they must impose the "ergodic hypothesis". A similar argument has been put forward by Lucas (1972) and Lucas and Sargent (1982). See also Samuelson (1947).

[6]E.g.: "The lottery of the law, therefore, is very far from being a perfectly fair lottery; and that as well as many other liberal and honourable professions, is, in point of pecuniary gain, evidently under-recompensed." (Smith 1776: 107). And he (pp. 107–107) continues: "That the chance of loss is frequently undervalued, and scarce ever valued more than it is worth, we may learn from the very moderate profit of insurers. In order to make insurance, either from fire or sea-risk, a trade at all, the common premium must be sufficient to compensate the common losses, to pay the expense of management, and to afford such a profit as might have been drawn from an equal capital employed in any common trade. The person who pays no more than this, evidently pays no more than the real value of the risk, or the lowest price at which he can reasonably expect to insure it. But

Both conditions do not hold in the real economy, and therefore Smith concludes that first of all human knowledge is limited, and secondly, that economic events do not happen randomly. Consequently, probability calculus is of little relevance to economics from Smith's point of view.

Both Hume and Smith, thus were well aware of the limits of human knowledge and rejected probability calculus as a reasonable instrument to handle them. Instead they identified an insurmountable uncertainty accompanying economic problems. This uncertainty has two fundamental sources. First, humans are facing epistemological challenges. One of them is the problem of induction, which states that no matter how much effort one spends, knowledge can never be proofed with certainty based on evidence and human observation. Secondly, economic phenomena such as profit show that economic reality is not characterised by randomness. Consequently, epistemological instruments such as theories of probability, which assume an underlying ergodic ontological structure, are of limited use in economic contexts (they can be used in that part of the economy, which is almost ergodic and therefore insurable). Because of this uncertainty surrounding economic action Hume and Smith both observed that economic actors do not always act rationally (Ashraf et al. 2005). As they only possess limited knowledge, they often behave according to customs and moral rules and show behavioural biases, such as over-enthusiasm (Akerlof and Shiller 2009; Johnson and Fowler 2011: 317). Consequently, classical economics was aware of the problem of uncertainty for both epistemological and ontological reasons and virtue ethics, instead of probability calculus, were used to handle the problem. Furthermore, it becomes obvious that the existence of markets and profits presuppose uncertainty. Without uncertainty, there would be no need for economic reasoning nor action and the science of economics. Adam Smith showed during the eighteenth century, that free trade in a free market is much more efficient in handling the forces of uncertainty for the good of society, than a mercantile or centrally planned economy.

However, only few years later, inspired by Hume's and Smith's plea for more scientific economics, probability calculus gained importance in the economic assessment of uncertainty. In this process, fundamental uncertainty and its necessity for the economic problem became less important. Instead of acknowledging Fundamental Uncertainty and investigating its implications for the science of economics, economists concentrated on the development of probabilistic methods that allowed ignoring the fundamental character of uncertainty in economics. The applied probabilistic methods suggested that the problem of Fundamental Uncertainty, as it had been identified by Hume and Smith can be overcome and that optimal choice was even possible in the face of uncertainty. Benthamite Utilitarianism (1781) provided the intellectual basis for utilitarian calculus of decision-making and which is the methodological point of departure for the calculability and apparent control of uncertainty in economics.

---

though many people have made a little money by insurance, very few have made a great fortune; [. . .]."

2.2 The Marginal Revolution and Probabilistic Utility Maximization

As indicated in the previous part of this chapter, the Smithian interpretation of uncertainty did not become dominant in economic thinking. Instead of virtue ethics, probabilistic reasoning gained importance in the economic discourse on the imperfection of human knowledge. In order to substantiate this point, we have to go deeper into the theoretical developments of that time. Jevons (1863, 1871), Menger (1871), and Walras (1874) brought marginal utility theory to the core of economics independent of each other. Based on Bentham's utilitarian idea of pleasure maximization (1781), according to which political decisions should be taken on the basis of the utility or pleasure the policy could provide for the public, they argued that any economic action should be evaluated based on its utility for the individual. Before we discuss theoretical developments in utility theory during the marginal revolution and its mathematical and probabilistic foundations, let us briefly consider Bentham's idea of pleasure maximization.

In 1781 Jeremy Bentham in his "Introduction to the Principles of Morals and Legislation" brought the idea of utility to the forefront. He suggested the measurement of quantities of pleasure as something positive and pain as something negative. The utility of something is the difference between the positive and the negative effects of it. Consequently, the utility of an action or policy can be positive or negative. Furthermore, the utility of one and the same thing can be different for two persons. While one person may like ice-cream, another person may hate it. For the first person getting a bowl of ice-cream would have a positive utility, while the same event would have a negative utility for the second person. Individual preferences determine how someone evaluates something. Yet, Bentham argued that the utility judgements of one person can be compared to the judgements of the other person. This allows for an overall measurement of utility. Bentham was the first who made an attempt to formalize this idea and use it as a scientific basis for social policy (Stigler 1950: 309). To Bentham, legislations should be judged on the basis of the utility it provides for the members of society. J. B. Say (1880: 138f), then was the first person, who applied utility reasoning to economic problems in the 1820s (Viner 1925). He integrated both the concept of utility as well as the concept of marginal analysis into economic theory and thereby the principle of diminishing marginal utility found its way into economics. Still, marginal utility theory was not applied in economics before the 1870s. By that time the key ideas of the marginal revolution condensed. Jevons unified marginality, utility, maximization and individualism, in a mathematical equilibrium concept. Figure 2.1 shows the formula:

$$\frac{MU_1}{MU_2} = \frac{p_1}{p_2}.$$

Fig. 2.1 Utility function, Jevons (1871)

He (1871: 231) explains his equation as follows:

> Production in a market governed by free competition is an operation by which the (productive) services may be combined in products of appropriate kind and quantity to give the greatest possible satisfaction of needs within the limits of the double condition that each service and each product have only one price in the market, at which supply and demand are equal, and that the prices of the products are equal to their costs of production.

The marginal utility and the marginal costs of a good or service, or taken even more generally, of any action are assumed to be equal to its price. Thereby, utility became measurable in terms of money values. Furthermore, Jevons assumes, following Bentham, that each individual aims to maximize his or her utility. If any market participant is following these principles, equilibrium prices will be reached and overall utility will be maximized. From the level of policy choice this theory was transferred to the individual level. If any individual follows the logic of the theory, overall utility will be maximized. Therefore, it was reasonable to take individual choices on the basis of this originally rather general theory.

Marginal utility theory became a new guide to action in a time in which sensible choice became more and more difficult. Compared to earlier times, a flood of information overwhelmed decision makers in the late nineteenth century. The amount of information available increased significantly, while moral or Christian values crumbled as a basis for reasonable choice (Hacking 1990; Bernstein 1998; Esposito 2007; Ferguson 2009). Quantification became the new guide to action in different areas of life and politics. Jevons was proud of his achievements and introduced a new era for the science of economics and politics. He (1871: Chap. 1) writes:

> Previous to the time of Pascal, who would have thought of measuring doubt and belief? Who would have conceived that the investigation of petty games of chance would have led to the creation of perhaps the most sublime branch of mathematical science-the theory of probability? Now, there can be no doubt that pleasure, pain, labour, utility, value, wealth, money, capital, etc. Are all notions admitting of quantity; nay, the whole of our actions in industry and trade certainly depend upon comparing quantities of advantage and disadvantage.

Jevons's and other economist's enthusiasm for quantitative theories and models reflects the spirit of the time. During the nineteenth century more and more aspects of human life became measured. Statistical data was collected increasingly and statistics got used during the industrial revolution more and more extensively. Bernstein (1998: 191) even writes of an 'explosion' of scientific (meaning statistical) research. These quantitative surveys got used in the growing insurance industry as well as in politics. Fire insurances and trade insurances became used on a larger scale. The insurance companies used statistics as a basis for calculating the insurance rate. In this way, the risk of a house burning down became quantifiable for the first time; it was no longer a matter of bad luck.

At the same time safety and certainty became purchasable. People were bestowed the opportunity to hedge against risks, and thereby escape the wheel of fortune. Purchasing a security did not change the possibility for a house burning down, yet it eliminated the risk of becoming homeless. The price of the insurance therefore was the price for the risk avoidance. Consequently, some uncertainty was turned into certainty. The possibility of becoming homeless was eliminated and thereby one part of the future predefined and some uncertainty eliminated. Yet, the way in which the future will actually unfold, was still uncertain. Only the potential consequences of potential future developments became certain. One possibility was taken from the future and risk became tangible. However, uncertainty about the development of the future was not turned into certainty about the future. This opened up the possibility for riskier individual behaviour and thereby led to an increase in foreign trade (Willett 1901; Bernstein 1998). The use of statistical methods and probability theory in everyday life strengthened the belief in a free market economy, in which anybody is free to insure against any kind of risk. The introduction of probability theory allowed for the liberation from old social and economic structures and at the same time contributed to a more scientific image of economics, which before had been associated with moral philosophy rather than science. This optimism, brushed away Smith's and Hume's doubts about the uncertainty and incalculability of economic reality.

At that same time, statistics about social measures also got used for policy legitimization. Measures of unemployment, crime rates like income statistics or health measures were collected and policies got evaluated on the basis of the development of these measures. Bentham would have been pleased by these developments. In a way his ideas about the measurement and use of utility were executed in practice. However, also in theory his utility concept gained importance. Both the leading economists and mathematician Francis Edgeworth (1894) and the brilliant young mathematician Frank Ramsey developed concepts of utility measurement machines. Edgeworth's 'hedometer' even found its way into the hard core of economic theory. However, Ramsey's (1926: VII)[7] idea of the creation of a 'psychogalvanometer' remained an ideal. Though these ideas gained no practical relevance in the first place, they can be understood as pre-theories or tools to rational choice theory (Mirowski 1994).

2.3 From Reason to Rational Choice Theory

As already indicated, the ideal of rational choice changed fundamentally at the end of the eighteenth century.[8] Ideas of the free individual replaced clerical and moral ideas about the good life. This increased the experienced uncertainty and ambiguity

[7]For a detailed discussion of Ramsey's concept see Gillies (2012: 53ff).

[8]Yet, in the period between 1870 and 1925 stochastic theory and the development of neoclassical economic theory were not linked. Neither the marginalists, such as Jevons and Edgeworth or pioneers in statistics and economics like Bowley and Allen (1935), Bowley (1939), Keynes (1921, 1936, 1937), Slutsky (1937) and Wald (1939) stressed or emphasised a link between economics and statistics (Mirowski 1989: 222, 1994; Barnett 2011: 190). Though, Jevons used graphical techniques to discuss the price level, whereas Edgeworth worked with index numbers and Bowley (1939) published empirical work on wages and the distribution of income, "none of the first two

of reality significantly. Decisions became more complex and moral evaluation standards vanished. Therefore, the nature of choice changed fundamentally. The new disorientation led to the development of a new actor or decision-making model. Originally, it was the reasonable housefather, who took decisions in advantage of his family (Priddat 2014). Only men had transaction rights during that time, while women were responsible for the internal housekeeping. It was the duty of men to care for their families. Already in the ancient world with its oicos tradition, housekeeping was associated with prudencia, meaning wisdom. The ideal of the rational actor emerged and got revitalised in the nineteenth century. During the dark ages and at the beginning of modern times, moral rules had predetermined choice. However after the dominance of the church crumbled, a new model of choice was needed. The ancient ideal of the oikosdespotes (lat. pater familias) or rational actor, who was making careful decisions based on reason and wisdom with the aim to maximize the wellbeing of his family was rediscovered.[9]

During the marginal revolution, rational action became an individual subjective concept. Instead of acting according to some general rules or morals, action was assumed to be rational, if the actor makes a choice that best satisfies the actors needs or utility. Consequently, selfishness became reinterpreted as behaving reasonably or rationally. While the oikosdespotes was taking care of his family, the new rational actor was satisfying one's own needs. This also implies that anything that goes beyond individual need satisfaction was irrational. The meaning of rationality thus turned from a moral and social connotation to a subjective and individual concept.

Supported by the developments in economic theory rationality became associated with measurability and probability theory was found to be an appropriate tool to create measurability. The general desire for measurability and reason-based choice was also reflected in economics. Economics was aiming to become acknowledged as a science during the late nineteenth century. The marginal revolution had led to an increasing formalism and mathematical orientation in economics (Blaug 1998). Scientificness was then associated with measurability and the economics adopted these mathematical instruments to increase its scientific status (Mirowski 1992, 2002; Schnellenbach 2002). Therefore, the measurable concept of utility got used to operationalize the individual level of need satisfaction. The preferences, needs and desires of one actor determine how much utility a certain action and their consequences cause for that person. Consequently, maximizing the utility of each

generations of innovators of neoclassical price theory such as Jevons, Walras, Marshall, Edgeworth, Bowley and so forth felt compelled to link that particular theory to explicit empirical evidence or to pollute their value theory with stochastic concepts" (Mirowski 1989: 224). Darnell (1981) for example had shown that these economists purposefully rejected applying statistics. Edgeworth on the other hand labelled the hope of obtaining demand curves with statistical methods "criminal" (Edgeworth 1894: 473, 1925: 8). E.g.: "There is really only one theorem in the higher part of the calculus (of probabilities), but it is a very difficult one, the theory of errors, or deviation from an average. The direct application of this theory to human affairs are not very considerable" (Edgeworth 1925: 287).

[9] Described more detailed also in Priddat (2014).

action implies that the needs of the actor can be met as best as possible. The concept of utility already integrates balancing costs and benefits. Thus a utility-maximizing actor always acts to its individual benefit given any potential constrains. Therefore, that actor was assumed to act rationally. Finally, Jevons integrated these trends in society and economics and developed a mathematical model of rational choice. This rational actor model integrated the idea of wise decisions by one oicosdespotes and the idea and utility maximization in favour of one individual and thereby reflects the key ideas of the marginal revolution: methodological individualism, maximization and rationality in the form of calculability (Williamson 1993). The new model builds the fundamental unit of choice in economic theory. Furthermore, maximizing the utility of a choice became the new criteria for reasonable choice as it restored decidability. Due to its formal and objective appearance, utility theory provided a scientific criterion for choice. This new scientific concept replaced moral rules of choice.

It was Jevons, who first integrated probability reasoning into economics. Inspired by the use of probability calculus in the insurance industry as well as in politics, Jevons argued that the theory of probability was a sufficient basis for calculations about the future. Based on the idea of normality and average, Jevons assumed that certainty about the future could be reached based on sufficient historical data. Bernstein (1998: 190) even argued that, "He brushed off the problem of uncertainty by announcing that we need simply apply the probabilities learned from past experience and observation". Quotes like the following suggest that Jevons assumed probabilistic knowledge to be a reasonable basis for rational action.[10]

The new quantitative model of choice eliminated some uncertainties and ambiguities, which characterised the problem of choice. The theory of rational choice under conditions of perfect information, which includes statistical knowledge, transformed subjective choice into an objective numerical measure. The development of statistics was essential for the emergence of the statistical concept of knowledge in economics (Schnellenbach 2002; Bilboa 2008).[11]

The concept of imperfect knowledge re-enters into the economic discourse around 1870, during the so-called Marginal Revolution. It was the Austrian Carl Menger, who argued in his "Grundsätze der Volkswirtschaftslehre" (1871) that the imperfection of human knowledge about the quantity and quality of goods as well as about agent's own needs initially requires economic action. Put the other way around, Menger argues that if human knowledge were perfect, there would be no need for economic action. Menger's argument is similar to that of Smith. Consequently, he concludes similarly to the classical economists, that economic relations

[10] The test of correct estimation of probabilities is that the calculations agree with the fact of the average. [. . .] We make calculations of this kind more or less accurately in all ordinary affairs of life (Jevons in Bernstein 1998: 190).

[11] This certainly included the findings of Laplace (1814), Gauss, Bernoulli (1738) and Louis Bachelier (1900). See also Bernstein (1998) and Hacking (1990, 2001, 2006, 2014).

are characterized by the uncertainty of quantities and qualities of production as well as by the unintended consequences of human action (Beckert 1996: 806). This presumption also builds the foundation for the Austrian theory of the entrepreneur, as a risk-taking agent, who is better informed or has more courage than other market participants.[12]

Acknowledging the limits of human knowledge, however, was a serious challenge to contemporary theoretical economics. Léon Walras in his pioneering 1874 work "Elements of Pure Economics" had developed an equilibrium model of a perfect market, which was built on the assumptions of perfect knowledge, no time lag and no monopolistic competition. Walras showed that under these perfect conditions markets always reach Pareto-efficient[13] allocations. Now, the introduction of imperfect information endangered this analytically elegant general equilibrium theory. Menger's emphasis on the imperfection of human knowledge sank into oblivion until Frank Knight (1921) and John Maynard Keynes (1921, 1936, 1937) revitalised the discussion about the problem of uncertainty in economic theory and entrepreneurial practice.

2.4 Separating Uncertainty

Since the beginning of economic reasoning about uncertainty there were two competing schools. One the one side there were the uncertainty purists, who acknowledge uncertainty as an important force in the economy as well as a serious challenge to knowledge about the functioning of the economy and economic theorizing. On the other side, there were those economists, who were well aware of the problem of uncertainty and argued that utility maximizing choice on the basis of probabilistic knowledge is the rational economic way to manage this economy endogenous uncertainty. Between 1920 and 1950 these two schools of thought split up completely. From then on we can distinguish between the Fundamental Uncertainty Paradigm and the Neoclassical Uncertainty Paradigm, which reinterprets uncertainty as risk and thereby neglects its fundamental significance for the economy and economics.

The common starting point of the division was Chicago economist Frank H. Knights dissertation "Risk, Uncertainty and Profit" (1921). He distinguished most prominently between risk and uncertainty. While there was unity about his definition of risk, his conception of uncertainty was interpreted in exclusionary ways. The first interpretation was inspired by Hume, Smith and Menger and defined

---

[12]As we shall see later, also Friedrich A. von Hayek (2007) bases his fundamental criticism against socialism on this insight. He, similar to other Austrians argued, that central planning is necessarily insufficient, due to the lack of knowledge of the planning agency.

[13]Pareto efficiency is a state of market allocation in which it is impossible to make any one individual better off without making at least one individual worse off (Sen 1970).

uncertainty as a fundamental force underlying all human and economic action. The second, inspired by the probabilistic utility maximizing theories of the Marginalists and particularly Jevons, interpreted uncertainty as a problem of subjective probability theory. The later interpretation became dominant in economics, in the form of the Neoclassical Uncertainty Paradigm, which developed in the 1950s (Lawson 1985a, b; Esposito 2007; Beckert 2011). However, contemporary textbooks, such as Marshall's "Principles of Economics" (1890), already reflect the spirit of the Neoclassical Paradigm in the 1920s.

Underlying Knight's distinction between risk and uncertainty is the assumption that economic choice and entrepreneurial action is only possible if human knowledge is imperfect. In his study on the origin of profit, Knight shows, that profits can only arise in imperfect markets. Beckert (1996: 807) summarises Knight's fundamental rejection of the perfect market model and rational choice theory in this way:

> Under the assumption of perfect markets economic theory cannot explain profits, because the market will attract new suppliers until the price of the good equals the marginal costs of the product. [...] Agents are uncertain about the future state of affairs and therefore cannot, in a dynamic economy, make decisions that lead to equilibrium outcomes.

Consequently, Knight rejected a utility maximizing approach to economic choice. In his book, he discussed how entrepreneurs actually make decisions in situations of uncertainty, instead of providing an elegant mathematical theory. *Risk, Uncertainty and Profit* is a scientific study of entrepreneurial practice rather than a book on economic theory (Runde 1998). In analysing entrepreneurial behaviour, Knight found fundamental differences in the stages of knowledge economic decision makers may possess. Thereby he laid the foundation of our modern understanding of the limits of human knowledge in economics. Knight distinguishes three stages of human knowledge; certainty, risk and uncertainty. And according to him economics is particularly concerned with the later two.

Consequently, it was Frank H. Knight (1921), who distinguished risk from uncertainty. In this way uncertainty became defined in contrast to risk and not independently. Based on the assumption that human knowledge, particularly about the future, but also about past and present is imperfect,[14] Knight argues that any economic theory, which assumes full knowledge, is insufficient. In order to understand the workings of the economic system the meaning and significance of the imperfection of human knowledge needs to be examined (Knight 1921: 199). This is his starting point for an inquiry into the nature and function of knowledge and its interrelation with economics. His investigation into the relation between knowledge and economics, leads him to the conclusion that most of the knowledge used in economics is probabilistic knowledge.

He distinguishes between three types of probabilistic knowledge used in economics. First of all, there is a priori probabilistic knowledge, which can be derived

[14]Cf. Knight (1921: 202): "We do not perceive the present as it is and in its totality, nor do we infer the future from the present with any high degree of dependability, nor yet do we accurately know the consequences of our own actions."

from logical principles. A priori probability can be derived from "(a)bsolutely homogenous classification of instances completely identical except for really indeterminate factors." And he (1921: 224) continues that "(t)his judgment of probability is on the same logical plane as the propositions of mathematics." A priori or logical probabilities are therefore applicable to games of chance.

The second type of probabilistic knowledge is based on statistical probabilities, which can be derived from the analysis of empirical data. Naturally, these probabilities are weaker than those derived from a priori principles, as they are based on the conviction that "[...] the proportions found in the past will hold in the future." (Knight 1921: 225) Already, Hume (1738, 1772) had argued convincingly, that tough it might be wise for reasonable men to make this assumption, in order to gain insights, there is no certainty that the future will be like the past.

And thirdly, knowledge used in economics is based on estimates. In situations in which estimates are used "there is no valid basis for any kind for classifying instances.[15]" (Knight 1921: 225) In these situations common knowledge or intuitions get used for making economic decisions.

Based on these three types of knowledge in economics, we can now derive the classical dualist conception of risk and uncertainty. To Knight, any situation in which a priori or statistical probabilities are attainable is a situation of risk, whereas situations of uncertainty are those in which only estimates can be used. By the time, Knight was writing his dissertation the third type of knowledge was neglected in economics (Knight 1921: 231). Yet, to him it was the key to understanding the need for economic reasoning as well as for making sense of the origins of profit. Knight, thus, comes to similar conclusions as Menger, even though the two had very different backgrounds.

> It is this true uncertainty which by preventing the theoretically perfect outworking of the tendencies of competition given the characteristic form of "enterprise" to economic organization as a whole and accounts for the peculiar income of the entrepreneur. (Knight 1921: 232)

From this analysis of knowledge in economics Knight (1921: 233) distinguishes between "[...] the measurable uncertainty and an immeasurable one [...]". The measurable uncertainty, which can be quantified by either a priori or statistical probabilities, he calls "risk". Whereas situations in which no objective probability calculus can be applied and only estimates are available are termed "uncertainty".

Almost as if he had anticipated the upcoming developments in probability theory, he argues that one can also distinguish risk from uncertainty on the basis of objective and subjective probabilities. The difference between the two categories being, that the former are based on objective or interpersonal evidence, whereas the later are based on personal judgement. By the time, Knight was writing there was also a technical difference between the two. While objective probabilities where quantifiable, subjective probabilities were not yet. In the course of time, the details of Knight's theory were neglected, so that his distinction often got restated in an

[15] Italic is in the original.

incomplete way.[16] As a consequence, risk got defined in economics as any kind of measurable imperfection of human knowledge. Risk in economics is thus a case in which agents possess statistical or stochastic knowledge. While uncertainty got defined as a situation, in which agents do not have access to any kind of statistical or stochastic knowledge. Consequently, choice in situations of uncertainty is rather random guess, than rational choice. Yet, Menger (1871) and Knight (1921) had argued that, particularly situations of uncertainty are crucial in economic theory and still they were not compatible to the theory of rational choice and perfect markets, and therefore lay outside of scientific economics.

In the same year (1921) in which Frank Knight's famous book appeared, J. M. Keynes also published his PhD Dissertation "Treaties on Probability". Unlike Knight's book, Keynes' was not a piece of economic research; instead it was a philosophical inquiry into the epistemological foundations of the theory of probability. However, Keynes reached a similar conclusion, namely that there are highly unique situations, about which no numerical probability beliefs can be formed. He (1921: 32) argues, probability "[...] is unknown to us through our lack of skill in arguing from given evidence. The evidence justifies a certain degree of knowledge, but the weakness of our reasoning power prevents our knowing what the degree is." Later, in his economic inquiries (1936, 1937), he concludes, like Menger and Knight, that economic situations are in most cases characterised by risk and uncertainty. Therefore, idealistic analyses of market allocations in the tradition of Walras (1874) are according to his view, in most cases, meaningless. Most important economic phenomena, like profit, recession, or investment, can only be explained under the assumption of imperfect knowledge, rather than perfect knowledge (Bateman 1998).

However, by the time Keynes was writing his magnum opus, the neoclassical school of thought dominated economics. There was a joint attempt of economists to become acknowledged as a science similarly precise and mathematically sophisticated as physics. General equilibrium analysis and rational choice theory were particularly suitable for this endeavour. Both theories could be formalised in mathematical terms (Mirowski 1980, 1992, 2002; Weintraub 2002). In the course of time, the two theories, not only became fundamental theories of economics, but also prototypes, of how economic theories have to be in terms of mathematical sophistication and analytical abstraction and elegance. One could even argue, that these theories became constitutive for economics. Any case that could be analysed by these theories was a phenomenon of interest for the science of economics. Any case that could not be approached on the basis of this theory and the applied mathematical methodology, fell outside the interest space of economics.[17] As

[16]Later on, in this dissertation, I will argue that this representation of Knight's classical distinction misrepresents Knight's key ideas. Yet, he is used in the way presented here to legitimize the probabilistic management of uncertainty in economics since the 1950s.

[17]For a more detailed discussion of this thesis, please see Chap. 4. Here, I unfold the argument that shows, that economics became defined on the basis of its methodology and theory, rather than on the basis of real economic problems.

Fundamental Uncertainty did not fit the mathematical economic approach, while being an obvious challenge in economic reality, it became necessary to integrate uncertainty into the rational general equilibrium framework of the newly developing neoclassical scientific economics. New developments in the theory of probability made this integration possible. The newly developed theory of subjective probabilities allowed for the rational calculation of subjective probabilities. This was the starting point of the separation of the uncertainty fundamentalists and the neoclassical subjective probability interpretation of uncertainty.

Opponents of the former interpretation are Chicago Economist Frank H. Knight, Cambridge Economist J. M. Keynes, the Austrian Friedrich A. von Hayek and his student G. L. S. Shackle. They argued that uncertainty is a fundamental characteristic of economic ontology and a serious challenge to economic knowledge. We will discuss their approaches to Fundamental Uncertainty in length in the next part of this book, as their thoughts are diverse and highly relevant for the development of a profound understanding of the problem of uncertainty in economics. Nevertheless, economics was dominated by the neoclassical stochastic Uncertainty Paradigm. The emergence and development of this paradigm is closely linked to the subjective theory of probability and the growing importance of mathematical models and a scientific ethos in economics. One could even argue that the economic mainstream was scared by fundamentalist views on uncertainty. Lucas (1977: 15) for example, noted: "In case of uncertainty, economic reasoning will be of no value." And Arrow's (1951: 417) doubts, when he said that without measurable probabilities "no theory can be formulated" underlines my argument that, Fundamental Uncertainty got neglected due to the fact, that it makes mathematical modelling highly problematic, if not impossible.

2.5 Subjective Probability Theory and Uncertainty

Before the 1920s, the objective view on probability, according to which probabilities can either be calculated based on frequencies from past data or based on logical inference was dominant. Characteristic for both types of objective probabilities is that the state of past or possible events needs to be defined in total. However, Knight had argued that this is impossible in situations of uncertainty. This led him to the conclusion that no probabilities can be calculated in situations of uncertainty. However, only few years after Knights Magnum Opus, Frank P. Ramsey (1926, 1927, 1929, 1931), a British mathematician and philosopher at Cambridge University, who was a close friend to Ludwig Wittgenstein and John M. Keynes, developed the idea of subjective probabilities, which can be defined without a perfectly defined state space. The same idea had also been put forward by the Italian mathematician Bruno De Finetti (1929). Independently of each other, they argued that degrees of belief can be measured in terms of probability relations. Particularly, Ramsey (1926: 166) admits, that some degrees of belief can be measured more accurately than others, and yet he argues that any kind of subjective degrees of belief about the future can be expressed in terms of numerical probabilities. He reached this conclusion by combining the ideas of utility and probability. To him (1926: 166) the non-objective theory of probability is a branch of formal logic that allows individuals to measure degrees of belief:

> We must therefore try to develop a purely psychological method of measuring belief. It is not enough to measure probability; in order to apportion correctly our belief to the probability we must also be able to measure our belief.

Ramsay's theory of subjective probability is thus a concept that allows for the measurement of rational degrees of belief. And it is based on the assumptions that (1) agents act to their benefit (utility maximising), (2) hold beliefs about everything, (3) beliefs are consistent and therefore rational, (4) an agent's actions reveals their beliefs.[18]

Subjective degrees of beliefs, which can be measured in terms of subjective probabilities, can be derived from hypothetical bets. The concept of betting is key to Ramsey's subjective probability theory. It is based on his view (p. 183), that life "[...] is based fundamentally on betting, but this will not seem unreasonable when it is seen that all our lives we are in a sense betting. Whenever we go to the station we are betting that a train will really run, and if we had not a sufficient degree of belief in this we should decline the bet and stay at home. The options God gives us are always conditional on our guessing whether a certain proposition is true."

Ramsey insists that the theory of probability is a part of logic; the logic of partial belief. As a part of formal logic, the theory of probability also underlies the laws of logical reasoning. Consistency of partial belief, is therefore similarly important in the subjective theory of probability as it is in formal logic. If probability beliefs are consistent, they can be classified as rational degrees of belief. This idea of rationality

[18]Consider Ramsey's own words (1926: 176–177): "Let us now discard the assumption that goods are additive and immediately measurable, and try to work out a system with as few assumptions as possible. To begin with we shall suppose, as before, that our subject has certain beliefs about everything; then he will act so that what he believes to be the total consequences of his action will be the best possible. If then we had the power of the Almighty, and could persuade our subject of our power, we could, by offering him options, discover how he placed in order of merit all possible courses of the world. In this way all possible worlds would be put in an order of value, but we should have no definite way of representing them by numbers. There would be no meaning in the assertion that the difference in value between α and β was equal to that between γ and δ. Suppose next that the subject is capable of doubt; then we could test his degree of belief in different propositions by making him offers of the following kind. Would you rather have world α in any event; or world β if p is true, and world γ if p is false? If, then, he was certain that p was true, simply compare α and β and choose between them as if no conditions were attached; but if he were doubtful his choice would not be decided so simply. I propose to lay down axioms and definitions concerning the principles governing choices of this kind. This is, of course, a very schematic version of the situation in real life, but it is, I think, easier to consider it in this form."

interpreted as consistency emerged conjointly with the Neoclassical Uncertainty Paradigm and survived until today. Following Ramsey (1926: 182) rationality in economics of imperfect information, means consistency of beliefs. These beliefs neither need to bet true nor in any way wise, yet they do not contradict the consistency axiom. He writes (1926: 182):

> We find, therefore, that a precise account of the nature of partial belief reveals that the laws of probability are laws of consistency, an extension to partial beliefs of formal logic, the logic of consistency. They do not depend for their meaning on any degree of belief in a proposition being uniquely determined as the rational one; they merely distinguish those sets of beliefs which obey them as consistent ones.

This idea of rationality departs fundamentally from that of classical economics, which interpreted rationality as a way of wise reasoning in the interest of the community. Since the beginning of the twentieth century, however rationality became defined in economics as valid logical reasoning, regardless of its connection to economic reality or truth and independent of its benefits for the economy as a whole. Economic action lost its orientation towards the public welfare.

In 1933 the Russian mathematician Andrey N. Kolmogorov followed this idea in his 'Foundations of the Theory of Probability' and provided a mathematical proof of the subjective theory of probability and thereby described axioms of subjective probability theory still valid today. The theory can be applied to situations, in which objective probability calculus fails. No matter how subjective and weak these numerical measures of subjective belief are, the gap in the measurability of probabilities to which Knight's definition had been pointing was closed.[19]

The flowing quotes from Marshall's The Principles of Economics (1890) already indicate this development. Marshall describes the intersubjective calculability of probabilities in situations of uncertainty (p. 100): "The different uses between which a commodity is distributed need not all be present uses; some may be present and some future. A prudent person will endeavour to distribute his means between all their several uses, present and future, in such a way that they will have in each the same marginal utility. But in estimating the present marginal utility of a distant source of pleasure a twofold allowance must be made; firstly, for its uncertainty (this is an objective property which all well-informed persons would estimate in the same way); and secondly, for the difference in the value to them of a distant as compared with a present pleasure (this is a subjective property which different people would estimate in different ways according to their individual characters, and their circumstances at the time)."

[19]The developments in the theory of probability will be discussed in more detail later in this dissertation. For the historical overview of this chapter it is sufficient to note that probabilities became measurable in situations of uncertainty in the basis of the newly developed subjective theory of probability.

To Marshall a probability measure is an objective property in situations of uncertainty, which can be calculated by well-informed and rational men. Marshall continues in the footnotes (p. 102):

> We may however consider here how to measure numerically the present value of a future pleasure, on the supposition that we know, (i) its amount, (ii) the date at which it will come, if it comes at all, (iii) the chance that it will come, and (iv) the rate at which the person in question discounts future pleasures. If the probability that a pleasure will be enjoyed is three to one, so that three chances out of four are in its favour, the value of its expectation is three-fourths of what it would be if it were certain: if the probability that it will be enjoyed were only seven to five, so that only seven chances out of twelve are in its favour, the value of its expectation is only seven twelfths of what it would be if the event were certain, and so on. [This is its actuarial value: but further allowance may have to be made for the fact that the true value to anyone of an uncertain gain is generally less than its actuarial value (see the note on p. 135).] If the anticipated pleasure is both uncertain and distant, we have a twofold deduction to make from its full value. We will suppose, for instance, that a person would give 10 s. for a gratification if it were present and certain, but that it is due a year hence, and the probability of its happening then is three to one. Suppose also that he discounts the future at the rate of twenty per cent per annum. Then the value to him of the anticipation of it is $3/4 \times 80/100 \times 10$ s. i.e. 6 s.

In this way, Marshall, had adopted Jevon's idea of rational choice based on probabilistic knowledge. Even before the subjective theory of probability had been developed, Marshall introduced the ideas of intersubjective probabilities in the face of uncertainty as a basis for rational choice.

2.6 The Janus-Face of Uncertainty in Economics

From this point on, we have to distinguish two types of uncertainty in economics. Firstly, there is the Fundamental Uncertainty proposed by Knight (1921) and Keynes (1921, 1936, 1937), in line with Hume (1738), Smith (1776), and Menger (1871). This Paradigm turns against the idea of complete determinism and randomness in economics. Instead Knight and Keynes suggest, that uncertainty is an unquantifiable fundamental in economics that brings about surprise and the need for reasonable economic decisions. We will discuss this type of uncertainty more deeply in the second part of this essay.

Secondly, there is the Neoclassical Uncertainty Paradigm, which assumes that any economic situation can be treated "*as if*" it was a situation of risk, even though, there is no option to assign objective numerical probabilities to possible future events. This concept ignores the possibility, that there might be future events, which are unknown to the individual. The original conception of risk merged in the Neoclassical Uncertainty Paradigm. Underlying this concept are the assumptions of complete determinism and randomness of economic events (Beckert 2011).

References

Akerlof GA, Shiller RJ (2009) Animal spirits: how human psychology drives the economy, and why it matters for global capitalism. Princeton University Press, Princeton

Arrow KJ (1951) Mathematical models in the social sciences. In: Lerner D, Lasswell H (eds) Policy Sciences in the United States. Stanford University Press, Stanford, pp 129–154

Ashraf N, Camerer C, Lowenstein F (2005) Adam smith, behavioral economis. J Econ Perspect 19 (3):131–145

Bachelier L (1900) Théorie de la spéculation. Ann Sci École Norm S 3(17):21–86

Backhouse RE (2002) The Penguin history of economics. Penguin, London

Bardy ME (2013) Adam Smith's theory of probability and the roles of risk and uncertainty in economic decision making. Working Papers California State University—Department of Operations Management

Barnett V (2011) E.E. Slutsky as economist and mathematician: crossing the limits of knowledge. Routledge, London

Bateman BW (1998) Keynes' uncertain revolution. University of Michigan Press, Ann Arbor

Beckert J (1996) What is sociological about economic sociology? Uncertainty and the embeddedness of economic action. Theory Soc 25(6):803–840

Beckert J (2011) Imagined futures fictionality in economic action. Max-Planck-Institut für Gesellschaftsforschung Discussion Paper 8, pp 1–30

Bentham J (1781) Introduction to the principles of morals and legislation. Batoche Books, Kitchener

Bernoulli D (1738) Expositions on the new theory on the measurement of risk

Bernstein PL (1998) Against the gods: the remarkable story of risk. Wiley, New York

Bilboa I (2008) Rational choice. MIT Press, Cambridge, MA

Blaug M (1998) The problems with formalism: interview with Mark Blaug. Challenge 41(3):35–45

Bowley AL, Allen RDG (1935) Family expenditure. A study of its variation. Staples

Bowley AL (1939) Three studies in national income. Cambridge University Press, Cambridge

Darnell A (1981) A. L. Bowley, 1869–1957. In: O'Brien DP, Presley JR (eds) Pioneers of modern economics in Britain. MacMillan, London

de Finetti B (1929) L'invenzione della verità. R. Cortina

Edgeworth F (1894) The measurement of utility by money. Econ J

Edgeworth F (1925) Papers relating to political economy

Esposito E (2007) Die Fiktion der wahrscheinlichen Realität. Suhrkamp, Berlin

Ferguson N (2009) The ascent of money: a financial history of the world. Penguin Books, London

Gillies D (2012) An objective theory of probaility. Routledge, London

Hacking I (1990) The taming of chance. Cambridge University Press, Cambridge

Hacking I (2001) An introduction to probability and inductive logic. Cambridge University Press, Cambridge

Hacking I (2006) The emergence of probability: a philosophical study of early ideas about probability, induction and statistical inference. Cambridge University Press, Cambridge

Hacking I (2014) Why is there philosophy of mathematics at all? Cambridge University Press, Cambridge

Hayek FA (2007) The road to serfdom: text and documents. University of Chicago Press, Chicago

Hepfer K (2011) Die Konstruktion der Erkenntnis: 'Imagination' im Treatise on Human Nature. Archiv für Geschichte der Philosophie 9:349–365

Hume D (1738) A treatise of human nature. Biblio Bazaar, Charleston

Hume D (1772) An enquiry concerning human understanding. Hackett, Indianapolis

Jevons WS (1863) A general mathematical theory of political economy.

Jevons WS (1871) The theory of political economy. Palgrave Macmillan, London

Johnson DPD, Fowler JH (2011) The evolution of overconfidence. Nature 477(11):327–320

Keynes JM (1921) A treatise on probability. Rough Draft Printers, New York

Keynes JM (1936) The general theory of employment, interest and money. Palgrave Macmillan, London

Keynes JM (1937) The general theory of employment. Quart J Econ 52(3):209–223

Knight FH (1921) Risk, uncertainty and profit. Nabu Press, Charleston
Kolmogorov A (1933) Foundations of the theory of probability. Chelsea Publishing Company, New York
Laplace PS (1814) Philosophical essay on probabilities. Wiley
Lawson T (1985a) Uncertainty and economic analysis. Econ J 95(380):909–927
Lawson T (1985b) Keynes' economics: methodological issues. Croom Helm, London
Lucas RE (1972) Expectations and the neutrality of money. J Econ Theor 4:103–124
Lucas RE (1977) Understanding business cycles. University of Chicago, Chicago
Lucas RE, Sargent TJ (1982) Rational expectations and econometric practice. University of Minnesota Press
Marshall A (1890) Principles of economics. Prometheus Books
Menger C (1871) Grundsätze der Volkswirtschaftslehre. Mohr Siebeck, Tübingen
Mill JS (1848) Principles of political economy with some of their applications to social philosophy. Hackett, Indianapolis
Mirowski P (1980) The birth of the business cycle. J Econ Hist 40(1):171–174
Mirowski P (1989) The probabilistic counter-revolution, or how stochastic concepts came to neoclassical economic theory. Oxf Econ Pap 41:217–235
Mirowski P (1992) More heat than light: economics as social physics, physics as nature's economics. Cambridge University Press, Cambridge
Mirowski P (1994) Edgeworth's writings on chance, economic hazard, and statistics. Rowman & Littefield, Lanham
Mirowski P (2002) Machine dreams: economics becomes a cyborg science. Cambridge University Press, Cambridge
Montesquieu C, Baron de. (1793) De L'esprit Des Loix (The spirit of laws). Cambridge University Press, Cambridge
Popper KR (1990) World of propensities. Thoemmes Continuum
Popper KR (2002) The logic of scientific discovery. Psychology Press
Priddat BP (2014) Economics of persuasion. In: Ökonomie zwischen Markt, Kommunikation und Überredung. Metropolis, Marburg
Ramsey FP (1926) Truth and probability. Ramsey (1931) The foundations of mathematics and other logical essays. Harcourt, Brace, New York, pp 156–198
Ramsey FP (1927) Facts and propositions. Harcourt, Brace, New York
Ramsey FP (1929) On a problem in formal logic. Harcourt, Brace, New York
Ramsey FP (1931) In: Braithwaite RB (ed) Mathematics and other logical essays. Harcourt, Brace, New York
Runde J (1998) Clarifying Frank Knight's discussion of the meaning of risk and uncertainty, (1921). Camb J Econ 22:539–546
Samuelson PA (1947) Economics. McGraw-Hill Irwin, New York
Samuelson PA (1969) Classical and neoclassical theory. Penguin Books, London
Say JB (1880) A treatise on political economy or the production, distribution, and consumption of wealth. Batoche Books, Kitchener (This is an English translation of Say's Traité d'economie politique, first published in 1803)
Schnellenbach J (2002) New political economy, scientism and knowledge: a critique from a Hayekian perspective, and a proposal for an extension of the research agenda. Am J Econ Soc 61(1):193–214
Sen AK (1970) Collective choice and social welfare. Holden-Day, San Francisco
Slutsky E (1937) The summation of random causes as the source of cyclic processes. Econometrica 5(2):105–146
Smith A (1776) Wealth of nations: an inquiary into the nature and causes of the wealth of nations. Prometheus Books, New York
Stigler GJ (1950) The development of utility theory I. J Polit Econ 58(4):307–327
Viner J (1925) The utility theory and its critics. J Polit Econ XXXIII: 369–387

Wald A (1939) Contributions to the theory of statistical estimation and testing hypotheses. Ann Math Stat 10(4):299–326
Walras L (1874) Éléments d'économie pure ou théorie de la richesse sociale
Weintraub ER (2002) How economics became a mathematical science. Duke University Press, Durham
Wertz SK (1975) Hume, history, and human nature. J Hist Ideas 36(3):481–496
Willett AH (1901) The economic theory of risk and insurance. Columbia University Press, New York
Williamson O (1993) Calculativeness, trust, and economic organization. J Law Econ 36:543–486

Chapter 3
Truth, Probability and Uncertainty

The Neoclassical Uncertainty Paradigm is a probabilistic concept. It allows for the calculability of uncertainty by means of probabilities. Furthermore, it is the basis of rational choice in situations of uncertainty. Probability has become a widely-accepted concept in economics and other sciences. Yet, the foundations of probability reasoning are found in the ordinary business of everyday life and theology. Only later, probability calculus became associated with science.

The chapter is organized in three sections. The first section examines the development and changing meanings of the probability concept. I argue that probability theory is an epistemological concept that guides peoples' reasoning and action in a contingent reality, in which certainty, knowledge and truth are only ideals. In Sect. 3.2 I turn to the scientific credibility of probability calculus and argue that the numerical appearance of probability calculus supported its acceptance in the sciences. Finally, I turn to the problem of induction.

3.1 The Changing Meanings of Probability

The formalisation of probability theory narrowed the application space of probabilistic reasoning and at the same time increased the level of confidence in probabilistic conclusions. It is a formal tool that helps people to take actions and legitimizes those on the basis of the internal validity that the axioms underlying probability theory provide. Nevertheless, it does not change the character of reality. Therefore, it does neither produce security nor truth. Any probability, needs to be seen as a temporal degree of belief, or opinion that is reasonable to hold in that particular situation, given a certain amount of information. Yet, there is no guarantee that things could not be different (Ramsey 1926; Carnap 1950; Shackle 1955; Daston 1987; Spencer-Brown 1996; Hacking 2006; Esposito 2007).

In the middle of the seventeenth century human interaction became more and more complex. Even though the nature of reality did not change, people started to

J. Köhn, *Uncertainty in Economics*, Contributions to Economics,
DOI 10.1007/978-3-319-55351-1_3

acknowledge that reality is not absolute. Depending on what perspective one takes, one and the same element of reality can have different meanings or consequences. The concept of an absolute truth was put into question and people saw themselves confronted with growing complexity, ambiguity and the uncertainty of reality (Hacking 2006: 73ff).

Before the age of enlightenment, the problems of uncertainty and ambiguity were non-existent. In fact, the phenomenon of chance or fortune was well known since the ancient world. The goddess Fortuna had the power of destiny. Neither chance or luck nor people's own choices determined success or defeat. People believed that the course of events happened at Fortuna's will (Esposito 2007: 22). Even though the mathematical foundations of probability calculus were already known at the end of the fifteenth century (Hacking 2006) it did not get used, because people still believed that the course of events was a god's will (the Christian God like Fortuna some 100 years earlier was believed to control the wheel of fortune) and not in the hands of the people. The church had an absolute monopoly on truth. The people of the renaissance had limited self-determination. The good life and the choices to be taken to live a good life were predefined by the church and a generally accepted code of ethics (Esposito 2007: 23ff.). Furthermore, there was also no need for individual choice, regarding their careers or businesses. Society was organized around strict rules of behaviour, which gave no space for individual considerations. All in all, reality by the time of the renaissance was not very complex and the need for individual choice was rather limited. Reality was not contingent, yet. Anything of importance was a matter of fact, which was unquestionably true. Opinion, belief or guess played no meaningful role during this period (Esposito 2007: 21).

The enlightenment, however, led to a decline of security. More and more absolute truth collapsed and gave way for ambiguity. Still, people desired truth and security. They were looking for guidance in a more and more uncertain world. The renaissance mode of choice via first principles provided by church or monarchy was not helpful in this new uncertain world, began breaking away from clerical authority. Though certainty was out of reach now, people still had to act and to decide. Therefore, they were looking for guidance. How could a reasonable choice be generated, if reality is ambiguous and the future uncertain and yet not arbitrary? The loss of security and guidance brought about the desire for a new reasonable basis of choice. Under these circumstances people had the desire to calculate the reasonable (Esposito 2007: 20). There was not yet the idea of rational choice, however, people were looking for conventions and symbolic systems (Foucault 1971) that could be accepted as a basis for reasonable choice in an uncertain environment (Daston 1988: XII). Numerical probabilities served this desire and provided a basis for calculating the reasonable, which neither need to bet true nor provable. Probability calculus offered hope at a time, when people were exploring the space between absolute certainty and complete doubt. It did not remove ambiguity and uncertainty, yet, it allowed people to handle it wisely. The level of confidence was enhanced by the development and use of probability calculus.

3.2 Probabelism, Credibility and the Formalization of Science

A new philosophical trend emerged, today called “constructive scepticism”, who’s opponents (such as Pascal (1623–1662), Fermat (1607–1665), Hygens (1629–1695), Leibniz (1646–1716) and members of the Port Royal Society) argued that incomplete knowledge does not imply ignorance (Hacking 2006). When the space for absolute truth shrank, opinion, estimation and belief gained importance. These concepts are classical parts of rhetoric and as such they were devalued during the middle ages. When people acknowledged their ignorance, these concepts became respectable again. Probability calculus combines logic as the art of truth producing valid reasoning with rhetoric. Instead of producing absolute truth, it became the aim to provide guidance for logical reasoning on the basis of opinions and beliefs, rather than facts. Probability calculus was therefore designed as an instrument for people to act reasonable (which meant in accordance with the laws of logic), when absolute truth is out of sight. Esposito (2007: 21) therefore argues that probability calculus was about the incapacities of human beings and not about nature. It never promised to bring back security. It instead created a fiction of security and spent confidence, in order to overcome people’s incapacity to act consciously and reasonably, when confronted with uncertainty. Illustrating this dimension of probability calculus, Esposito (2007) draws an analogy between fiction and the theory of probability. She (p. 21) argues that a fiction is not just a lie, even though its subject matter is neither real nor true. A fiction describes a possible and also plausible world. Based on the underlying assumptions about the nature of this factious realm, the fiction itself is a possible realisation of this factious reality. The fiction does not violate the assumptions. Therefore, it is a valid logical conclusion of the factious realm. Still, it is untrue. The fiction is a valid story, created by some author.[1] In the same way probability theory classifies imperfect knowledge neither as truth nor as falsity. Instead probability theory describes possible realities, about which we do not know and cannot know, which one is true and which one is false. The only guidance probability theory provides us with, is that the possible worlds we think about are valid. Based on the underlying assumptions of probability theory, it allows us to draw logically valid conclusions about the possible states of the world. In this way probability theory provides rational conventions as a basis for the management of the imperfection of our knowledge (Smithson 1989: 51). Probability theory covers the space between apodictic knowledge and pure subjective conviction or guess. This is a space in which it is not irrational to be uncertain and doubtful (Daston 1988: 61).

Naturally, uncertainty had been observed way before the development of probability theory. Ever since gambling and trade were part of social interaction, games of chance already played an important role in ancient societies. And international

[1] See also Chap. 11.

trade already began way before probability theory was developed. However, if it was believed that the course of events was determined by heavenly order and not by people's actions, there was no need for a theory of probability. Only the change in people's attitudes towards reality, brought about by the enlightenment changed their views on chance (David 1962: 23; Dacunha-Castelle 1997: 21; Esposito 2007: 22). Randomness and regularity became important categories of observation on the way to systematise uncertainty. Byrne argues that this led to the development of a "mathematics of contingency". It was the aim of this new type of mathematics to uncover order, regularity and necessity in areas in which people believed there was only chaos or God's will.

The term probability is much older than the theory of probability or probability calculus. It was first used to describe credibility. Ian Hacking (2006: 18) dates back the first numerical interpretation of probability to 1662. Esposito (2007: 23) argues that this credibility was particularly used to describe moral integrity and not to describe whether something was a fact or not. Thus, at first, probability was a subjective and social category. The term probability was used to describe whether and to what degree the opinion or belief of an individual was in line with the social code of ethics or some generally accepted authority of morality. It was a hermeneutic category rather than a logical concept, which could be provable and true. However, it also had an interpersonal or social element, as a probable belief is one, which in principle other individuals could agree upon, too. The probability of a belief was dependent on the credibility and number of supporters of this particular belief (Esposito 2007: 23). Kneale (1949: 169), therefore, had argued that, "[...] if we heard a man speak in ordinary life of the equal probability of various alternatives, we should understand him to mean that they are equally approvable as bases for action".[2] And Hacking (2006: 18) underlines this early subjective credibility meaning of the word probability, when he shows the interrelation of the word probable with the approbation of a doctor. He argues, that a 'probable doctor' was one who could be trusted and only 'probable doctors' got approbation.

The concept of probability was used as a testimony or measure of confidence that showed the credibility of a person or idea. In this way probability can be understood as a measure of quality and a point of orientation in an ambiguous reality. The unit of evaluation of this measure of quality was opinion not evidence. Reasonableness and degree of belief, rather than truth became the new points of orientation in the newly recognised contingent reality. This epistemological strategy of 'probabilism' was built on the assumption that both knowledge and certainty are impossible (Hacking 2006: 25).

Probabilism has its intellectual roots in theology. Thomas von Aquin had argued that a probable opinion, which is by definition neither universally true nor logically provable, is one that is shared by other wise men of church. Later the concept was used in criminology. The testimony of a witness was evaluated on the basis of probability reasoning. The more support there was by other witnesses or experts for

---

[2]Also quoted in Hacking (2006: 18).

a certain statement, the more probable was the testimony and the more weight it gained in finding a judgement.

First probability calculations were made for gambling. The question that provoked Galileo and others in the middle of the sixteenth century to develop probability calculus was: "How many equal alternatives arise in tossing three dice?" (Hacking 2006: 51). Probability thus was a concept that emerged and developed in the social sciences and due to practical consideration, rather than in the hard sciences.

The probabilistic concept of opinion needs to be seen opposed to the concept of knowledge. In medieval times, knowledge was associated with evidence and universal truth, which implies that something is true by necessity. Knowledge was a category of science. Therefore, it is no surprise, that probabilistic reasoning was not used in the physical sciences in the beginning. Though empirical data was already collected in the ancient world, it was not used as evidence to support one's opinion (Hacking 1990, 2006). Statistics got used for epistemological reasons only in the eighteenth century. During this time the meaning of probability changed fundamentally. As an example, Hacking (2006) cites Galileo, who had argued that Copernicus' theory of the earth revolving around the sun was 'improbable'. By 'improbable' Galileo meant that this theory was on the one hand not approvable and on the other hand it was contradicted by observations. The widely-observed evidence was (everybody could see it with their own eyes) that the sun is revolving around the earth and not the other way around. Using the term evidence, which belongs to the scientific vocabulary, again changed the meaning of probability. So that probability became accepted as a scientific category in the early nineteenth century. Leibnitz for example used the terms as if probability was defined by reason and evidence (Hacking 2006: 44). And Bernstein (1998: 48) adds that the German word 'wahrscheinlich' means translated literary "with the appearance of truth".

Blaise Pascal and Pierre de Fermat developed the mathematical foundations of statistics. Besides the changing meaning of the word probability, the calculability of probability supported the scientific appearance of probabilities. Applying mathematical calculus, which was already then highly respected and closely associated with ideal inference, fundamentally changed the image of probability.[3]

[3]Not until the late 1920s probability was treated as a mathematical and scientific subject (Doob 1953, 2001; Cramér 1999; Hamouda and Rowley 1996). Although, various types of probability concepts were already used in the sciences and also in everyday life, the concept of probability had no generally accepted formal theoretical basis since Kolmogorov (1933) launched his theoretic approach to probability theory. Von Mises (1950: vii) for example argued: "The essentially new idea which appeared about 1919 was to consider the theory of probability as a science of the same order as geometry and theoretical mechanics."

Kolmogorov established six axioms, which build an idealized basis for calculating probabilities for random processes. Summarized briefly, Kolmogorov (1933) had defined that any probability space has three fundamental components: Initially, there needs to be a sample space of random events. Secondly, there has to be a subset in the sample space that is closed. Finally, any probability space has a probability measure, which is non-negative, normalized (the probability of a certain event is unity and therefore 1) and continuous (Fine 1973; de Finetti 1964; Hamouda and Rowley 1996).

Still, probability reasoning always kept its double meaning. On the one hand the concept of probability was built on opinion, and on the other hand it was formed based on evidence. Another aspect of this development is, that probability reasoning was originally used to guide people in an ambiguous environment. Later the scientific use of the term suggested that probability reasoning could be used to establish truth and therefore support the epistemological endeavour of acquiring knowledge. The change in meaning and the formalization of probability theory conjointly build the foundation of a probabilistic concept of knowledge as it is commonly underlying neoclassical economic theories.

3.3 The Problem of Induction

In economics, as well as in all other sciences, we aim to reach knowledge about a particular subject matter. Knowledge is assumed to be both certain and true. Opposed to that opinion or belief, which are non-scientific epistemological categories neither need to be certain nor universally true. Yet, there seems to be a consensus that both opinion and belief need to be more or less justified. Thus, there is a fundamental difference between knowledge and belief or opinion, which also typically marks the line between science and non-science. As economics aims to be a predictive science (Backhouse and Medema 2009), it needs to be based on knowledge. On the other hand, it is obvious that the science of economics is in some way special as it deals with social humans (Hodgson 2001; Fine 2002). Because of this social dimension in economics the line between knowledge and belief or opinion is necessarily not as sharp as it should be. Different than in the natural realm, economic knowledge for the most part cannot be acquired directly by observation or intuition. Instead, economic knowledge is conditional and time-dependent and therefore needs to be inferred. If economics, aims to be acknowledged as a science, we have to ask ourselves, what constitutes knowledge in economics.

In the general philosophical discussion, certainty and truth are the sufficient conditions for knowledge. Bertrand Russell's definition is exemplary for this position: "We firmly believe, if it is true, is called *knowledge*, provided it is either intuitive or inferred (logically or psychologically) from intuitive knowledge from which it follows logically." (Russell 1912: 139) Frank Ramsey underlines this position, when he argued that knowledge is a belief, which is true, certain and formed in a reliable way (1926). Both philosophers underline the processual character of truth, which is constitutive for knowledge. On the one hand, there is direct or intuitive knowledge, which we know, is true. Definitions, for example, fall under this category of truth. They are true per se. On the other hand, (which is the most part of our knowledge) we possess indirect knowledge. This part of our knowledge can only be reached indirectly through a truth generating process, which is oriented towards qualitative criteria. Ramsey suggests that true beliefs need to be formed on a reliable basis and therefore are demonstrable and consequently objective.

Induction and deduction are two dominant processes for reaching demonstrable knowledge. In the case of deductive inference, knowledge in the form of a conclusion is derived in a logically valid form from premises. To reach a true conclusion and therefore knowledge under the definition of Russel and Ramsey, the premises need to be true, too. Though, there are different types of deductive inference, which should not be discussed in detail here, the process of deduction is incapable of reaching or establishing new knowledge. No new knowledge can be gained from deduction, since the conclusions derived from the premises are themselves contained in the premises. One could even argue that the conclusions are nothing but restatements of the premises (Salmon 1967: 8; see also Salmon 1963). This, however, does not imply that deduction is useless. Instead it allows us to uncover the hidden structure of an argument and to apply old knowledge to similar contexts. Furthermore, deductive logic defines a both valid and demonstrable process to use our knowledge. As such, it is a knowledge transformation tool. Thereby, it establishes truth and certainty, which is constitutive for knowledge. However, the process of deduction is useless for constituting new knowledge.

Induction on the other hand is an epistemological instrument, which can be used to establish new knowledge. Therefore, inductive reasoning is particularly important in the sciences, which aim to discover new knowledge about their subject matter. The philosophy of induction defines under which conditions beliefs are true and certain, so that a belief can become knowledge. The concept of probability gets used to carry out this transmission. Under this conception probability is defined as the degree of belief one can reasonably hold, which is certain and true. What, however, is defined to be reasonable, depends on the different theories of probability.[4] So one and the same belief may be accepted as knowledge under one definition of probability, while it is not accepted under another. Knowledge thus becomes a relative category and we can also speak of it as 'probable knowledge'. In this way, absolute deductive knowledge is fundamentally different from probable inductive knowledge. Inductive knowledge is less certain or absolute as it is not derived from true premises. Yet, inductive knowledge is also not arbitrary, as it is reached in accordance with well-defined logically valid principles. Still, one can argue that inductive knowledge is uncertain and not necessarily true and therefore no valid basis for scientific inference. Most prominently David Hume (1738: 231) had criticised the attempt of acquiring knowledge through induction:

> In all demonstrative sciences, the rules are certain and infallible; but when we apply them, our fallible and uncertain faculties are very apt to depart from them, and fall into error. We must, therefore, in every reasoning form a new judgement, as a check or control on our first judgement or belief; and must enlarge our view to comprehend a kind of history of all the instances, wherein our understanding has deceived us, compared with those, wherein its testimony was just and true [...]. By this means all knowledge degenerates into probability; and this probability is greater or less, according to our experience of the veracity or

[4]See also Sect. 5.1 of this dissertation.

deceitfulness of our understanding, and according to the simplicity or intricacy of the question.

According to Hume, we cannot assume that any knowledge, perhaps except of deductive knowledge, can be certain and universally true. Only probable knowledge could be reached, no matter how valid, certain and true the underlying rules of thought and inference are.

For induction to establish valid knowledge, which could be used as a scientific principle, it is necessary to infer new knowledge, which goes beyond the premises, from established premises according to some logically valid principles. And it is Hume, who had argued that this process could only bring about probable knowledge, which is necessarily uncertain and not necessarily true. New knowledge therefore is necessarily ambiguous and the concept of probability gets used to objectify this ambiguity. The concept of probability allows us to distinguish between more certain and therefore more probable knowledge and less certain and therefore less probable knowledge. Theories of probability are therefore theories of valid induction and at the same time the probability measure, serves as a quality measure of inference (McCann 1994: 25).

In economics, inductive reasoning is particularly important, as actors need to make decisions or take actions before it is even possible to possess complete, certain and true knowledge about some situation. Decision makers are operating in a dynamic environment. They are even changing the environment by their actions so that economic actors are confronted with a constant flow of information. Unlike the natural sciences, economic decisions cannot be repeated like experiments, so, for the most part, it is impossible to test or falsify new knowledge in the realm of economics. Probabilistic reasoning therefore became particularly important in economics, as "[...] economics is primarily convened with the decision-making process, involving the individual in maintaining a necessary uncertain belief as to the composition of the future" (McCann 1994: 26).

3.4 Conclusion

The meaning of the concept of probability changed fundamentally since its emergence. While probabilistic reasoning was first associated with credibility it later became connected with gambling and reason, before it got used in business and finally in the sciences. Though, probability gained reputation over the centuries, we have to acknowledge that it still is a measure of belief, which does not inform us about what will actually happen in the future. Probability calculus of any sort falls short on the problem of induction. Consequently, probability calculations, no matter how sophisticated and elegant they are, have no truth-value (Cf. Ayache 2010).

References

Ayache E (2010) The black swan: the end of probability. Wiley, Chichester
Backhouse RE, Medema SG (2009) On the definition of economics. J Econ Perspect 23 (1):221–233
Bernstein PL (1998) Against the gods: the remarkable story of risk. Wiley, New York
Carnap R (1950) Logical foundations of probability. Chicago University Press, Chicago
Cramér H (1999) Mathematical methods of statistics. Princeton University Press, Princeton
Dacunha-Castelle D (1997) Spiele des Zufalls: Instrumente zum Umgang mit Risiken. Gerling-Akademie-Verlag, München
Daston L (1987) The probabilistic revolution. MIT Press, Cambridge
Daston L (1988) Classical probability in the enlightenment. Princeton University Press, Princeton
David FN (1962) Games, gods and gambling. The origins and history of probabilities and statistical ideas from the earliest times to the Newtonian era. Charles Griffin, London
De Finetti B (1964) Theory of probability. Wiley, New York
Doob JL (1953) Stochastic processes. Wiley, New York
Doob JL (2001) Classical potential theory and its probabilistic counterpart. Springer, Berlin
Esposito E (2007) Die Fiktion der wahrscheinlichen Realität. Suhrkamp, Berlin
Fine T (1973) Theories of probability. Academic, New York
Fine B (2002) Social capital versus social theory: political economy and social science at the turn of the millennium. Springer
Foucault M (1971) L'ordre du discours: Leçon inaugurale au Collège de France prononcée le 2 décembre 1970. Gallimard, Paris
Hacking I (1990) The taming of chance. Cambridge University Press, Cambridge
Hacking I (2006) The emergence of probability: a philosophical study of early ideas about probability, induction and statistical inference. Cambridge University Press, Cambridge
Hamouda OF, Rowley R (1996) Probability in economics. Routledge, London
Hodgson GM (2001) How economics forget history. The problem of historical specificity in social science. Routledge, London
Hume D (1738) A treatise of human nature. Biblio Bazaar, Charleston
Kneale W (1949) Probability and induction. Oxford University Press, Oxford
Kolmogorov A (1933) Foundations of the theory of probability. Chelsea Publishing Company, New York
McCann C (1994) Probability foundations of economic theory. Routledge, New York
Ramsey FP (1926) Truth and probability. Ramsey (1931) The foundations of mathematics and other logical essays. Harcourt, Brace, New York, pp 156–198
Russell B (1912) The problems of philosophy. Cosimo Classics, New York
Salmon W (1963) On vindicating induction. Philos Sci 30(3):252–261
Salmon W (1967) Foundations of statistic inference. University of Pittsburgh Press, Pittsburgh
Shackle GLS (1955) Uncertainty in economics and other reflections. Cambridge University Press, Cambridge
Smithson M (1989) Ignorance and uncertainty. Emerging paradigms. Springer, Berlin
Spencer-Brown G (1996) Wahrscheinlichkeit und Wissenschaft. Carl-Auer-Verl, Heidelberg
von Mises L (1950) Human action: a treatise on economics. Liberty Fund, Indianapolis

Chapter 4
The Principles of Economics

Drawing back on John Neville Keynes' distinction between positive or regulative (normative) science, Milton Friedman (1953), had developed the methodology of positive economics, which still today dominates economic research all over the globe. Then, the question was, whether economics is a science or rather political economy, which was interpreted as an art. If economics were a science, it had to bring about a systematized knowledge about the economy, according to Friedman's view. Whereas, if economics were an art it would be concerned with identifying rules for attaining some given end. Friedman ended the dispute and established the view that economics is a positive science, which consisted of "a body of tentatively accepted generalizations about economic phenomena that can be used to predict the consequences of changes in circumstances" (Friedman 1953: 25).

In this chapter I show, how economics had become a science and extract, what today is constructive for the positive science of economics. It will become obvious that uncertainty may not play any role in positive economics as it violates the constructive principles of positive economics and thereby puts into question the scientificness of economics under the positive view.

I proceed in four steps. First, I introduce competing interpretations of the science of economics, in order to show that there have been many alternative convictions to positive economics in the course of time. The analysis will show, that there was agreement that scarcity is constitutive for the economic problems. Then, I turn to the methodology appropriate to analyse problems of scarcity. We find that rationality is the prime framework to analyse economic problems and predictability its aim. In order to exemplify my argument, I briefly discuss the emergence and development of econometrics as an ideal economic science. Before I conclude my analysis, I give a definition of positive economics in the fourth section. All in all, the chapter shows that the science of economics that includes uncertainty is only possible if economics steps aside from the positive research agenda.

J. Köhn, *Uncertainty in Economics*, Contributions to Economics,
DOI 10.1007/978-3-319-55351-1_4

4.1 Becoming the Science of Economics

Since its formation in the eighteenth century, economics has become a science of optimization, which is essentially constituted by its applied methodology, rather than by certain subject matters. In the early days of economics, it was the other way around. Economics then was differentiated from other subjects, by its subject matter. Economists studied the elements of the economy and the economy as a whole. The methodology applied was not predefined and transitions to philosophical and political questions were rather liquid. Inherent to these early economic investigations was an interest in the nature of economic problems. Today, the science of economics is methodology driven and focuses on optimization problems of scarce resources in idealised environments.

In a recent paper, Backhouse and Medema (2009) show that economists are in disagreement about what economics is. Different standard economic textbooks highlight different aspects of the discipline, which are even contradictory.

D1 "Economics is the study of how households and firms make decisions choices regarding production and consumption, when the outcome (pay-off) of today's decisions occurs at a significantly later date." (Davidson 2012: 2)
D2 "Economics is the study of economies, at both the level of individuals and of society as a whole." (Krugman and Wells 2004: 2)
D3 "Economics is the study of how human beings coordinate their wants and desires, given the decision-making mechanisms, social customs, and political realities of the society." (Colander 2006: 4)
D4 "Economics is the study of how society manages its scarce resources." (Mankiw 2001: 4)
D5 "Economics is the social science that studies the choices that individuals, businesses, governments, and entire societies make as they cope with scarcity." (Bade and Parkin 2002: 5)
D6 "Economics is the study of human behaviour, with a particular focus on human decision making." (Gwartney et al. 2006: 5)

The examples, which in part have also been given by Backhouse and Medema (2009: 221–222) show impressively that there is no unity within the discipline. It is therefore for the purpose of this book impossible to use one "standard" definition of economics, as there is none. This fact makes it necessary to spend some lines finding out what economics is and what economists do. I believe that this short excursion into the history of economic thought and economic methodology will pay off.

It is commonly assumed that Adam Smith's "Inquiry into the Nature and Causes of the Wealth of Nations" (1776) is the hour of the birth of economics. Actually, the history of economics dates back to the ancient world. Plato's idea of an ideal State similar to Aristotle's "Nichomachean Ethics and Politics" contain basic ideas about the economy and how it should be organised.[1] Also, the word economics dates back to the fourth century before Christ. It had been invented by the ancient Greek writer Xenophon. According to his definition, economics is the art of household management. This meaning of the word is still in use today and it is the basis for what Adam Smith had called political economy. He defines (1776: 428) political economy as "[...] a branch of the science of a statesman or legislator, [...]". The art of housekeeping or as Smith, who was once a professor of moral philosophy (Fontaine 1996; Winch 1996; Rothschild 2001), had put it the "branch of the sciences" is oriented towards the wealth of the nation, which is according to Smith the central aim of political economy. The idea that the government of a country has the duty to implement politics that fosters the wealth of the nation is embedded in his moral philosophy. Backhouse and Medema (2009: 223) therefore argue that "[...] Adam Smith's work was only one facet of a large system of moral philosophy and so cannot be understood apart from his concern with morality and with society as a whole, [...]". The origin of our modern concept of economics therefore lies in moral philosophy and in the moral duty to manage the economy for the sake of the wealth of the nation.

In the early nineteenth century, political economy moved away from philosophy and started to become more oriented towards the sciences, while its subjects matter for the time being was still oriented towards the wealth of the nation (O'Brien 2004). In 1803 Jean-Baptist Say defined political economy as the "science" that treats "the production, distribution and consumption of wealth" (Backhouse and Medema 2009: 223). This definition had been developed under the impression of the industrial revolution and the emergence of new forms of industrial organization and production. Say and David Ricardo (1817) aimed to create a new and separate science of political economy based on general laws and not on moral concerns.

Decades later, John Stuart Mill (1848: 323) aimed in a similar direction and defined political economy as, "[t]he science which traces the law of such of the phenomena of society as arise from the combined operations of mankind by the pursuit of any other object". According to Mill's view, the accumulation of (national) wealth is dependent on some true universal laws. Backhouse and Medema (2009: 223) argue, "Mill defined the subject as dealing with the results of certain motives, thereby linking it to the methods that were appropriate for it, and categorizing other motivations as outside of political economy. But his definition of these motives were tied to a specific subject matter: wealth. In Mill's view, the accumulation of wealth depended on certain laws that were known to be true, like the law of diminishing returns and the 'population principle': that population would multiply faster than food supply." Mill was a supporter of the logical deductive method. According to him, conclusions in the science of political economy have to be drawn from true universal laws. Whereby Mill admits that there are disturbing causes in reality that might interfere with the laws at work, so that only statements

[1]For a detailed discussion of the Ancient History of Economics please, see Schumpeter (1954: Part II, Chap. 1) Betsy (1997) and Backhouse (2002).

of tendencies were possible. In order to explore the general laws that govern the generation and distribution of wealth, Mill suggests using historical investigations.

In the following years, the scientific status of political economy become more widely accepted. However, the subject matter of political economy distanced more and more from the national level. The individual element of the economy gained importance and finally political economy became replaced by economics, in order to demonstrate the professionalism and scientific neutrality of the discipline. As a consequence, economics moved away from politics and from its original aim managing the economy for the sake of the wealth of the nation. Also the methods of economics became more scientific and oriented towards the individual. The same is true for the subject matter of economics. The focal point of economics shifted from the wealth of the nation to the interactions between the individuals within a larger society. Richard Whately (1832) even suggested renaming the subject "catallactics", which means the science of exchange. The Austrian Economists Ludwig von Mises (1950: 3) and F. A. Hayek (1998: 108–109) and later Buchanan (1964) used the term to emphasise the evolutionary and communicative aspect of economic interactions. The classical definition of the individual basis of economics, however, is found in Alfred Marshall's Principles of Economics (1890: 111–112):

> Political Economy or Economics is a study of mankind in the ordinary business of life; it examines that part of individual and social action which is most closely connected with the attainment and with the use of the material requisites of well-being. [. . .]. Thus it is on the one side a study of wealth; and on the other, and more important side, a part of the study of man.

By 1900, political economy turned from a study of the wealth of nations to economics as a study of men in their ordinary business of life. At the same time the concept of wealth was extended to the concept of utility. Which includes both material wellbeing and subjective concepts of pleasure and pain (Jevons 1871: vi). Methodology wise it became the aim to explain macro phenomena based on individual action (methodological individualism). Some economists of the time, among them Alfred Marshall (1890), Knut Wicksell (1901) and Philip Wicksteed (1910) even emphasized other individual elements such as psychology, character and belief as sources for explaining economic phenomena.

One of today's most frequently used definitions is the one put forward by Lionel Robbins' in his "Essay on the Nature and Significance of Economic Science" (1932). Robbins (p. 15) defined economics as "the science, which studies human behaviour as a relationship between ends and scarce means which have alternative uses". Though this is the basis for the most common currently accepted definition of economics, Robbins' view on economics initially was not accepted by the majority of the discipline. Backhouse and Medema (2009: 225) argue that the definition was too broad and too narrow at the same time. It was too broad in the way that it failed to distinguish economics sufficiently from other social sciences. And it is too narrow in the way that it overemphasizes theory. The definition leaves only little room for empirical analysis, history, institutions and completely denies the ethical and political dimension of economics.

The standard economic textbooks of the 1930s were reluctant to use Robbins' definition. Instead Alfred Marshall's definition dominated the English economic literature, whereas the wealth[2] based definitions and institutionalism could be found in the leading U.S. textbooks. In the heydays of American institutionalism, the Harvard professor Slichter (1931: 11) wrote: "The subject matter of economics is industry, the processes by which men get a living [...] economics studies industry, not as a technological process, but as a complex human practice and relationship." This definition goes far beyond the Robbins' definition and integrates a variety of works in the field of economics. Legal history, social studies, the theory of the firm, similar to labour economics and Alfred Marshall's view on economics could be integrated under this definition. Others, among them the Chicago professor Frank H. Knight (1933: 4) proposed a narrower definition: "[Economics] deals with the social organization of economic activity" via the price system or under free enterprise (Backhouse and Medema 2009: 226). He argued that economics has a rather narrow scope and that both Marshall and Robbins' definitions tend to suggest to apply the concept of rationality to far too broad a range of activities. For Knight, economics is a study of economic activity, which is characterized by the use of the price mechanism, the free market and the concept of rationality. Economics was not yet the study of human behaviour in general on the basis of these concepts.

These few examples show already, that there was no agreement of what economics is in the 1930s. Particularly Robbins' definition, was at the time of its emergence, against Robbins own claim that his definition only summed up the way economists thought about and practiced their discipline during that time, not able to reach consensus. The 1930s and the post-World War II years were characterized by diversity about what economists thought economics is or should be about. According to Backhouse and Medema (2009: 226) at least four definitions of economics, which emerged in earlier years could be found in the professional economic journal literature:

1. Economics is what economists do.
2. A scarcity definition in the style of Lionel Robbins.
3. A wealth definition, which was consistent with the scarcity definition.
4. A rationality definition, according to which economics is mainly concerned with the subject of rationality.[3]

These different aspects still today can be found in definitions of economics. Particularly the last three subjects seem to be the fundamental building blocks of economics and are therefore the classical subjects of economic reasoning: wealth, scarcity and rationality. The moral and political aspects, which have dominated the

[2]This idea had been put forward by Jacob Viner in 1932 and 1933 in a conversation as reported by Kenneth Boulding (1941: 1). See also Backhouse and Medema (2009: 222).

[3]See Parsons (1937: 757–775) and Spengler (1948: 2–3).

perception of economics in the beginning, have almost disappeared. Furthermore, the way, however, in which these subjects are approached changed fundamentally. Particularly, the Robbins' definition supported by Milton Friedman's (1953) "The Methodology of Positive Economics", emphasized the analytical and scientific side of economics and reflects the new focus on individual behaviour that characterizes marginalist microeconomic analysis. Whereas history, ethics, empirical studies, institutional analysis, political philosophy and philosophy of economics were pushed to the margins of the discipline.

4.2 Rationality and Prediction

During the Marginal revolution in the 1870s a new scientific standard for economics came into being. Before that paradigm shift, economics was associated with philosophy, politics, hermeneutics and case based research. However, large parts of the discipline did not adopt the new more scientific approach quickly. It took at least 50 years for marginalism to become the core of economics.

> [T]he so-called Marginalist Revolution in the 1870s consisted largely of engineers directly appropriating the newly developed formalism of nineteenth century physics, changing the names of the variables, and renaming the result 'mathematical economics'. (Mirowski 1989: 218, see also Mirowski 1994)

Fundamental concepts of economics such as rationality, equilibrium, and perfect competition as well as the concept of uncertainty, which is of particular interest in this essay, have been developed during this period of time. Paul Samuelson, who was a leading MIT economist, condensed this scientific movement in his 1948 textbook 'Economics'. The textbook was based on his ideas laid out in his dissertation 'Foundations of Economic Analysis—The operational significance of economic theory' (1947). He advocated mathematical economics and pointed to the fact that economics is primary about maximization or minimization (Backhouse 1994, 2010: 106), which renders the mathematical method particularly beneficial. His textbook was the first presentation of the fundamental concepts of mathematical economics that introduced scientific economics to the post-war generation of economists.

Though, Friedman had a different view on the nature of scientific economics and economic policy as Samuelson, he came to advocate scientific economics (Backhouse 2010: 107). In his widely read essay 'The Methodology of Positive Economics' Friedman (1953: 7) argues:

> The ultimate goal of a positive science in the development of a 'theory' or 'hypothesis' that yields valid and meaningful [...] predictions about phenomena not yet observed.

Friedman's argument was a defence of the highly idealistic concepts of rationality, perfect competition and profit maximization that have come to dominate scientific economics. His argument suggests, that the realism of the theory's assumptions did not matter. Instead of empirically testing the assumptions of an economic theory, the conclusions or predictions drawn based on the theories should be tested on empirical grounds. His line of argument was used by Friedman himself as well as by other economists to defend the unrealistic assumptions underlying most of modern economics. Friedman's essay therefore marks a turning point in economics becoming a theoretical and empirically based quantitative science, comparable to the natural sciences. Theory gained more importance and the realisticness of economic theories and its assumptions lost ground. Friedman had legitimized highly abstract theory, preferring very simple models that could be analysed graphically. He even draws back on verbal logical analysis and by any means the mathematics he used were not very advanced. In this way, Friedman simplified scientific economics and cut off the last remaining bit of connection between the method of scientific economics, which came to be constitutive for the subject of economics, and economic reality.

Mark Blaug (1962) therefore has written about the time following Friedman's essay:

> [T]he discipline of economics was never so confident as it was in the late 1950s and early 1960s: we *knew* that general equilibrium theory was the last world in theoretical elegance, that input—output analysis and linear programming would soon make it not just elegant but operational, and that 'the neo-classical synthesis' had successfully joined Keynesian macroeconomics to Walrasian (general equilibrium) microeconomics; in short, that true economics was one church and that the full truth was at any moment to be revealed to us.[4]

From that time on formal models dominate economic thinking, even though the scope of economic theory had been expended during the 1970s–1980s. Statistical techniques were advanced. Game theory became a vital area of research. Public Choice Theory similar to the New theory of the firm applied the concept of rationality to other areas of study. Also, empirical research in the form of experimental and later also behavioural economics was reintroduced into economics. Yet, mathematical modelling, abstract and unrealistic assumptions and formal statistical data analysis remained constitutive for economics, which finally had become a science.

It can therefore be concluded, that it was the aim of economics to become acknowledged as a scientific discipline. In order to reach this aim after World War II, economists applied methods used in the natural sciences to economics. In this way methodology gained importance in economics and finally became constitutive for the discipline. The idea that economists use of rigorous methodology, not unlike physicists and mathematicians would produce predictions similar to the natural science, and economics would be acknowledged as a science. It is therefore not a surprise, that any problem such as uncertainty, which could not be analysed with this methodology, were left aside. The economist's ignorance about the problem of uncertainty, which goes beyond the stochastic treatment of it, therefore must be seen as a result of economics becoming a science. The rhetoric of not being scientific was used against any form of non-formal economic reasoning since the 1950s.

---

[4]Also, quoted in Backhouse and Middleton (2000: 207) and Backhouse (2010: 108). Italic is in the original.

4.3 Econometrics

During the marginal revolution, Jevons (1863, 1871), Edgeworth (1894, 1925) and Menger (1871) have dreamed of a science of economics based on empirical research and mathematical models. Yet, by the end of the nineteenth century "(i)t may be doubted whether Jevons's hope of constructing demand curves by statistics is capable of realisation" (Edgeworth 1894: 543). However, the new century brought higher statistics and structural estimations to economic research. Individual economists, like Henry L. Moore, Henry Schultz working in America and Jan Tinbergen, Ragnar Fischer and Tjalling Koopmanns in Europe and leading economic think tanks like the National Bureau of Economic Research (NBER) and the Cowles Commission in the United States built the foundation of a new statistical era in economics during the first half of the twentieth century.[5] Though, statistical economics or econometrics, is not directly linked to the economic Uncertainty Paradigm, this emerging field of economics contributes to the breeding ground of the uncertainty axiom in economics. Louca (2007) suggests that the emergence of econometrics opened a new era in economics.

The Econometrics Society was founded in 1930 in order to support statistical and mathematical reasoning in economics. As Backhouse (2010: 99) points out this attempt is echoed in the constitution of the Society, where it says:

> Its main object shall be to promote studies that aim at a unification of the theoretical-quantitative and the empirical-quantitative approach to economic problems and that are penetrated by constructive and rigorous thinking similar to that which has come to dominate in the natural sciences.[6]

This declaration points to two constitutive characteristics of modern economics. On the one side, the declaration puts the focus on the mathematical and statistical methods. These methods were supposed to be more precise and rigorous than the verbal methods used by classical economists in previous decades. Additionally, there was an attempt to unify the already existing theoretical concepts, like that of the equilibrium, with empirical results. In this way, economists integrated not only the methods, but also imitated the research strategy of the natural sciences in the way that economists were encouraged to build theories and test them on the basis of empirical evidence. Particularly appreciated were theories that employed rigorous, and compared to the standards of that time, advanced mathematics. The aim was to simplify a problem in such a way that it could be expressed in mathematical terms. In order to reach that goal, it was often necessary to make arbitrary, abstract and often unrealistic assumptions. Yet, the results derived from these equations were rigorous in a logical sense (Backhouse 2010: 99).

---

[5]For a detailed discussion of the emergence and development of econometrics please see Epstein (1987) and Louca (2007).

[6]http://dev.econometricsociety.org/publications/quantitative-economics (2014-11-25).

On the other side, the declaration clearly sets the goal for economics to become a science like natural science. Natural scientists and particularly physicists and mathematicians have helped to win World War I and II. Furthermore, new theories like that of mechanics, relativity theory, quantum mechanics have proven the successfulness of the formal methods. By the end of World War II physics and mathematics have become two stereotypes of ideal science. Also, economists, and particularly those with a background in mathematics and statistics have played an important role in the war period. Economists were employed in agencies such as the Federal Trade Commission, the Treasury and the office of Price Administration. Like other social sciences they were also directly involved with military services, for example in the office of Strategic Service or the Central Intelligence Agency. Backhouse (2010: 102) argues that they were employed as general problem solvers working alongside mathematicians, physicists and engineers in order to provide intelligence on the enemy's military capacity as well as to assess the impact of Allied bombing. They also became involved in what had come to be called Operations Research. It was their aim to plan efficient air strikes or plan and control economic production. Their efforts in planning the wartime economy as well as the effective use of war material via newly developed methods, such as linear programming, have been appreciated. All in all, this fostered admiration for the natural sciences and their methods after World War II. Therefore, it became the aim of economics to become acknowledged as a science with the same status as that of the natural sciences.

This attempt of economics becoming a science similar to the natural sciences after the war, which is already spelled out in the declaration of the Econometrics Society of 1930, was contra to what most of classical economists did and also against the views held by the Institutional Economists in the United States, as well as leading figures of economic thought in Europe such as John M. Keynes and Friedrich A. von Hayek. Their theories were rooted in an interest in real world economic problems and preparation of transforming the war economy in a market economy after the war. Therefore, moral social and political ideas influenced their economic thinking in large parts. Their interest did not include the rigour and positivity of mathematical models were anything but in their interests. Neither, Keynes nor Hayek would have ever doubted that mathematical techniques, such as linear programming could be of help for solving particular economic problems, yet they denied that abstract reasoning about the economy is useful for solving the questions of their time.

Nevertheless, economics from the 1930s onwards came to be seen as a technical discipline centred on abstract modelling. While, rigor by the time of Henri Poincaré and Albert Einstein meant that mathematical modelling was supposed to be constrained to empirical data, soon rigour became associated with formal reasoning in general. Realisticness and empirical groundedness of theory became less and less important (Backhouse 2010: 100). Thus, for economists to become acknowledged as rigorous scientists, similar to their idols in the natural sciences, mathematical modelling became compulsory. Non-mathematical work was debunked for not being scientific and therefore pushed to the margin. Consequently, economics became a mathematical discipline in the period from the 1930s to the 1960s, and therefore also acknowledged as a scientific discipline.

By that time the image of economics and training of economists changed fundamentally (Fourcade and Khurana 2011). Mathematical techniques, advanced statistics and applied mathematics came to dominate the curriculum (Bowen 1953). Prior to the war, law, history of economic thought and the economy, institutional studies, philosophy and particularly political thought had dominated the economics curriculum. By the 1960s, hardly any non-formal subject could be found in the economist's curriculum. This is not only true for economics but also for associated fields of study, such as management. This trend in higher education combined with the wartime experience and the use of economics in organizing the war fostered the trend of formalisation and scientific modality in economics and management. Some of the wartime economists such as Milton Friedman or John von Neumann (who is, beside his work in expected utility theory in the field of economics, particularly known for his work on the atomic bomb and for designing the architecture of the modern computer as a device, which was supposed to be used in military services) became leading figures in economic thought after the end of World War II. Also, war time think tanks such as the Cowles Commission and RAND promoted the idea of a science of economics and fostered the development of new mathematical and statistical techniques. Leading figures in this movement were Tjalling Koopmanns, a Dutch economist trained originally in mathematics and statistics, and Trygve Haavelmo, who was a Norwegian economist that had worked for his government in the U.S. during war time. They advanced the mathematical framework and introduced the formal statistical framework into economics. According to Backhouse (2010: 104) this opened up the prospect that the testing of abstract economic theories could become even more rigorous. Statistic methods were applied to decide which theory fitted the empirical evidence best. It can be concluded, that even though economics became even more rigorous since the 1950s, it also became less relevant for economic problems, which are, according to the argument presented in this book, problems that arise from different degrees of uncertainty.

4.4 The Principles of Modern Economics

Following Backhouse (2010) and Weintraub (2002), which are leading intellectual figures in the analysis of the methodology and philosophy of economics, economics is today a science that defines itself on the basis of the applied methods and aims at identifying general laws and theories. The intellectual legitimacy for this was provided by the positivistic philosophy of science promoted by Milton Friedman and others.

This shift of economics to a narrower and technically (mathematically) more sophisticated scientific discipline after World War II was supported by the wartime activities of leading economists. Many economists had worked alongside scientists, engineers and mathematicians (Backhouse and Medema 2009: 226). Operations research similar to modern financial economics have their roots in wartime co-developments of economists and scientists from other disciplines (Fox 2009; Fourcade and Khurana 2011).

By the 1960s and 1970s, Robbins' definition had become widely accepted, similar to the axiomatic deductive research approach of economics, mathematical methods and a focus on theory development. The significance of Robbins' definition can also be seen in the textbook literature. In 1976 Paul Samuelson for the first time defined in his leading textbook "*Economics*", what economics is. His definition is rather close to that of Robbins (Samuelson 1947: 3):

> Economics is the study of how people and society end up choosing, with or without the use of money, to employ scarce productive resources that could have alternative uses, to produce various commodities and distribute them for consumption, now or in the future, among various persons and groups in society. It analyzes the costs and benefits of improving patterns of resource allocation.

From the quote it can also be seen that economics is about choice, on the individual as well as on the social level. Choice is the fourth fundamental subject of economics, which started to gain importance from the 1950s onwards and which has strong interconnections to scarcity and rationality. The very idea of scarcity implies choice. And choice in economics is commonly referred to as a rational process of either maximizing payoffs or utility. Whereby, the idea of rationality or bounded rationality or consistency may differ fundamentally among the different approaches. For the purpose of this essay, however, it is important to note that the new focus on choice (either individual or social) allowed economics to expand is borders, while staying focused. Economics as a science of choice (rational or not)[7] focused on solving problems "[...] whenever *scarce* means are used to satisfy *alternative ends*" (Friedman 1976: 6; see also Johnson 1947). The types of choice problems, which apply to this definition, however, do not only come from the economic sphere. Questions about religion, marriage, and criminality are according to this understanding of economics, as economic as questions about income, monetary growth rates or taxation. Backhouse and Medema (2009: 229) therefore argue that economics became an *approach* rather than a *subject matter*. Since the 1970s the subject matter of economics is diverse and therefore does not serve as a basis to define economics, whereas the economic approach is at least in the neoclassical mainstream of the discipline not diverse. The economic approach is the scientific study of individual and social choice under scarcity with the aim to maximize utility (and therefore following the concept of rationality. Gary Becker (1976: 5) famously summarized it as follows: "The combined assumption of maximizing behaviour, market equilibrium and stable preferences, used regardless and unflinchingly, form the heard of the economic approach as I see it."

[7]E.g.: Backhouse and Medema (2009: 228).

4.5 Conclusion

Our short historical journey through the development of economics, has shown that the constituting element of economics shifted from a concrete subject matter to a certain methodological approach, which constitutes economics and distinguishes it from other social sciences. There were no methodological constraints in the early days of modern economics. Today, however, economists in the mainstream follow a particular methodological agenda, which presumes a certain understanding of the discipline of economics, as well as a certain point of view and a moral attitude. As Becker (1976) had put it, the economic approach assumes rationality, equilibrium or a least a tendency towards equilibrium and aims at predictions made based on general laws or theories. These theories ought to be developed based on empirical analyses of historical data, experiments and case studies. The approach thus assumes a stable nature of economic problems and regularities. It is assumed that the same laws hold in the future, which have been explored in the past and present. Furthermore, it is assumed that the relevant laws could be discovered. This however is contradictory to the essential element of scarcity, which constitutes economics. There are economic problems, because knowledge and recourses are scarce and because the future will be different than the past in a way we cannot know. The economic methodology, which had become dominant after World War II and constitutive for economics does not take account of this paradox. Political management and moral considerations, which were the starting point of economics, no longer play a role in economics. It is my hypothesis that this is the case, because economists have overlooked or willingly ignored the nature of economic problems in order to keep the economic methodology. Under this definition of economics there is no space for uncertainty, in the way I discussed it in Part II of this book. Consequently, if we aim to integrate uncertainty in the economic analysis, we should change the Economic Research Paradigm.

References

Backhouse R (1994) The fixation of economic beliefs. J Econ Methodol Taylor Francis J 1(1):33–42

Backhouse RE (2002) The Penguin history of economics. Penguin, London

Backhouse RE (2010) The puzzle of modern economics: science or ideology? Cambridge University Press, Cambridge

Backhouse RE, Medema SG (2009) On the definition of economics. J Econ Perspect 23(1):221–233

Backhouse RE, Middleton R (2000) Exemplary economists: Europe, Asia, and Australia. Edward Elgar, Cheltenham

Bade R, Parkin M (2002) Foundations of microeconomics. Addison Wesley, Toronto

Becker GS (1976) The economic approach to human behaviour. The economic approach to human behaviour. Chicago University Press, Chicago, pp 3–14

Betsy P (1997) Ancient economic thought. Taylor & Francis, London

Blaug M (1962) Economic theory in retrospect. Cambridge University Press, Cambridge

Boulding K (1941) Economic analysis. Harper, New York

Bowen HR (1953) Graduate education in economics. Am Econ Rev 43(4):201–223

Buchanan JM (1964) What should economists do? South Econ J 30(3):213–222

Colander D (2006) Economics. McGraw-Hill, New York

Davidson P (2012) Post-Keynesian theory and a policy for managing financial market instability and its relevance to the great recession. Turk Econ Assoc 1(3):1–24

Edgeworth F (1894) The measurement of utility by money. Econ J

Edgeworth F (1925) Papers relating to political economy

Epstein LG (1987) A simple dynamic general equilibrium model. J Econ Theor 41(1):68–95

Fontaine P (1996) The French economists and politics, 1750–1850: the science and art of political economy. Can J Econ 29(2):279–293

Fourcade M, Khurana R (2011) From social control to financial economics: the linked ecologies of economics and business in twentieth century America. Harvard Business School, Boston

Fox J (2009) The myth of the rational market: a history of risk, reward, and delusion on Wall Street. Harper Business, New York

Friedman M (1953) The methodology of positive economics. In: Friedman M (ed) In positive economics. Chicago University Press, Chicago

Friedman M (1976) Inflation and unemployment. Nobel memorial lecture, December 13, 1976. The University of Chicago, IL

Gwartney JD, Stroup RL, Sobel RS, MacPherson DA (2006) Microeconomics. Thomson, Mason

Hayek FA (1998) Law, legislation and liberty: a new statement of the liberal principles of justice and political economy. Routledge, London

Jevons WS (1863) A general mathematical theory of political economy.

Jevons WS (1871) The theory of political economy. Palgrave Macmillan, London

Johnson G (1947) Notes from Milton Friedman's course in economic theory. In: Johnson M, Samuels WJ (eds) Research in the history of economic thought and methodology, vol 26-C. University of Chicago Press, Chicago, pp 63–117

Knight FH (1933) The economic organization. University of Chicago Press, Chicago

Krugman P, Wells R (2004) Microeconomics. Worth, New York

Louca F (2007) The years of high econometrics: a short history of the generation that reinvented economics. Routledge, London

Mankiw GN (2001) Principles of economics. Harourt, New York

Marshall A (1890) Principles of economics. Prometheus Books

Menger C (1871) Grundsätze der Volkswirtschaftslehre. Mohr Siebeck, Tübingen

Mill JS (1848) Principles of political economy with some of their applications to social philosophy. Hackett, Indianapolis

Mirowski P (1989) The probabilistic counter-revolution, or how stochastic concepts came to neoclassical economic theory. Oxf Econ Pap 41:217–235

Mirowski P (1994) Edgeworth's writings on chance, economic hazard, and statistics. Rowman & Littefield, Lanham

O'Brien DP (2004) The classical economists revisited. Princeton University Press, Princeton

Parsons T (1937) The structure of social action. McGraw-Hill, New York

Ricardo D (1817) On the principles of political economy and taxation. John Murray, London

Robbins L (1932) An essay on the nature and significance of economic science. Macmillan, London

Rothschild E (2001) Economic sentiment; Adam Smith, Condorcet and Enlightenment. Harvard University Press, Cambridge

Samuelson PA (1947) Economics. McGraw-Hill Irwin, New York

Schumpeter JA (1954) History of economic analysis: with a new introduction. Oxford University Press, Oxford

Slichter S (1931) Modern economic society. Holt, New York

Smith A (1776) Wealth of nations: an inquiry into the nature and causes of the wealth of nations. Prometheus Books, New York

Spengler JJ (1948) The problem of order in economic affairs. South Econ J 15(7):1–29

von Mises L (1950) Human action: a treatise on economics. Liberty Fund, Indianapolis

Weintraub ER (2002) How economics became a mathematical science. Duke University Press, Durham
Whately R (1832) Introductory lectures on political economy. B. Fellowes, London
Wicksell K (1901) Lectures on political economy. Routledge, London
Wicksteed P (1910) The common sense of political economy. MacMillan, London
Winch D (1996) Riches and poverty. An intellectual history of political economy in Britain, 1750–1834. Cambridge University Press, Cambridge

Chapter 5
Probability and Neoclassical Uncertainty

The chapter is organised in two sections. The first part of the chapter is dedicated to the theories of probability. I briefly present the classical and frequency theory of probability. Then I turn to the logical theory of probability, which points to the intersection of the theory of probability with ethics, logic and the theory of knowledge. Finally, I turn, based on Ramsey's criticisms on the logical theory of probability, to the subjective theory of probability, which is the fundament for the Neoclassical Uncertainty Paradigm. The emergence and development of this Paradigm is the subject of the second part of this chapter. I delineate the evolution of the paradigm based on the theories of expected utility and rational expectations. In the last section of this part I show the actual relevance of the Neoclassical Uncertainty Paradigm for Modern Economics with examples from finance and macroeconomics.

5.1 Between Objective and Subjective

Like the concept of uncertainty in economics, the philosophy of probability is Janus faced. On the one side, there are objective theories of probability and on the other, there are subjective concepts of probability. Hacking (2006: 12) writes:

> [...] probability [...] is Janus-faced. On the one side, it is statistical, concerning itself with stochastic laws of chance processes. On the other side, it is epistemological, dedicated to assessing reasonable degrees of belief in propositions quite devoid of statistical background.

This distinction can be traced back to the 1840s (Daston 1988: 191). First, the distinction was made by Poisson in 1837 and only few years later Ellis and Cournot (1843) define that *objective probabilities* denote "the existence of a relation which subsists between things themselves", while *subjective probabilities* concern "our

J. Köhn, *Uncertainty in Economics*, Contributions to Economics,
DOI 10.1007/978-3-319-55351-1_5

manner of judging or feeling, varying from one individual to the next"(Gillies 2000: 87). A similar interpretation can be found in Popper (1934: 148–149). He writes:

> A *subjective interpretation* of probability theory [...] treats the degree of probability as a measure of the feeling of certainty or uncertainty, of belief or doubt, which may be aroused in us by certain assertions or conjectures. [...] the *objective interpretation*, treats every numerical probability statement as a statement about *relative frequencies* with which an event of a certain kind occurs within a *sequence of occurrences*.[1]

The problem with this distinction between objective and subjective interpretations of probability is that it is not unambiguous. Furthermore, different authors use the classification in a different way (McCann 1994; Gillies 2000). Nevertheless, it points to an important difference in modern interpretations of probabilities. To resolve the problems of the objective/subjective distinction Hacking (2006) suggest to distinguish between epistemic and aleatory theories of probabilities. Like Gillies (2000: 20) I find this distinction very helpful, as it points to the underlying difference between the two probability conceptions, which is overlaid by the objective/subjective debate.

Under the epistemic interpretation, probability describes the degree of knowledge or ignorance a person holds about some hypothesis. It can also be interpreted as a degree of (rational or irrational) belief, which can be based on knowledge or intuition. It should become obvious that probability under the epistemic interpretation is an instrument to gain insight or make claims about things about which human knowledge is incomplete. Thereby it is irrelevant, whether the degree of belief, knowledge or ignorance is formed on purely subjective ground, like intuition or gut feeling, or whether it is formed on the basis of rational and fact-based reasoning, which can be objectified.

Aleatory interpretations of probability are those, which are based on the fundamental assumption of complete randomness. Under this view probabilities are interpreted as objects, fact or knowledge, which state some relation that holds independent of the observer. These types of probabilities are often used in the natural sciences.

There is a wide spectrum of different kinds of theories of probability in general (e. g. Todhunter 1865; Keynes 1921; Carnap 1950; Savage 1954; Salmon 1967; Hacking 2006(1975), 1990; Gillies 2000), but only few discussions of the probability foundations of economics (McCann 1994; Gilboa et al. 2008). From these discussions three types of probabilities, which are particularly important for economic theory and the economic measurement and management of uncertainty, can be derived. The denomination of different types of probabilities differ from author to author, nevertheless, all of them differentiate between objective and subjective theories of probability and classify the different theories in the same way, while labelling them in slightly different ways. This regularly causes confusion. Therefore, it is necessary in advance to clarify the meaning of the different types of probabilities relevant to economics before we can move on.

[1]Italic is in the original.

Here, I will use the differentiation schema of Savage (1954) and distinguish between frequency, logical or necessarian and personal probabilities. While frequency and logical probabilities belong to the category of objective probabilities, personal probability theory belongs to the subjective category (Lawson 1988: 40).[2]

5.1.1 Classical Theory of Probability

Under the classical theory, probability "[...] is definable as a single, unique value, being the ratio of actual (favourable) to possible types of occurrences in a sufficiently well-defined sequence of events [...]" (McCann 1994: 30). Classically, this theory gets applied to games of chance where the possibilities are known a priori.

The foundation of the classical theory of probability was laid already in the early days of probability reasoning in the eighteenth century by Pierre Simon Laplace. In his classical work "Philosophical Essay on Probabilities" Laplace (1820, initiated in 1795) developed the definitive statement of probability and the doctrine of necessity (McCann 1994: 31; FN 56). Laplace defines:

> The theory of chance consist in reducing all the events of the same kind to a certain number of cases equally possible, that is to say, to such as we may be equally undecided about in regard to their existence, and in determining the number of cases favourable to the event whose probability is sought. The ratio of this number to that of all the cases possible in the measurement of this probability, which is thus simply a fraction whose numerator is the number of favourable cases and whose denominator is the number of all the cases possible. (Laplace 1820: 6–7)

His definition can be formalized in the following way, if there are n equally possible cases and m of them are favourable outcomes: Prob (A) = m/n.

This is the classical definition of probability based on equally possible cases. It assumes that the world is close and perfectly determined, so that at least the natural realm is reducible to general and stable deterministic laws. Consequently, these laws are generally discoverable by anyone and therefore objective. However, men do possess limited knowledge and brain capacities, so that they cannot obtain these laws directly. Only through probabilistic inquiry men discover the laws that govern reality. These laws are absolute and stable.

Beside defining probabilities, Laplace (1820) gives one of the most famous definitions of complete determinism in his essay, which is today known as the Laplace's demon (Gillies 2000: 14) or the Laplace's Dream (Mirowski 2002). Laplace (1820: 4) writes:

> We ought then to regard the present state of the universe as the effect of its anterior state and as the case of the one which is to follow. Given for one instant an intelligence which could comprehend all the forces by which nature is animated and the respective situation of the

[2]For a more detailed discussion of the various conceptualisations of the different theories and types of probabilities, please see McCann (1994).

> beings who compose it—an intelligence sufficiently vast to submit these data to analysis—it would embrace in the same formula the movements of the greatest bodies of the universe and those of the lighted atom; for it, nothing would be uncertain and the future, as the past would be present to its eyes.

Laplace applied the concept of Newtonian mechanics, which can be used to calculate the future paths of planets and comets to the natural realm in general. It follows that the laws governing the macrostructure, like the motion of planets, also govern the micro-particles of which they are composed (Gillies 2000: 16). This presupposes that the entire course of the universe can be calculated in general. He assumes perfect determinism. The only limiting factor is the human nature. Laplace argues that if humans were facing no epistemological problems, they could foresee any event. Yet, Laplace acknowledges that human capacities are limited and therefore imperfect:

> The human mind offers, in the perfection in which it has been able to give to astronomy, a feeble idea of its intelligence. Its discoveries in mechanics and geometry, added to that of universal gravity, have enabled it to comprehend in the same analytical expressions the past and future states of the system of the world. (Laplace 1820: 4)

Due to these imperfections, humans are dependent on probabilistic reasoning, when they aim to make a claim about some future event. Gillies (2000: 18) therefore concludes that classical probability can be viewed as a measure of human ignorance.[3] Later applying the law of large numbers, which was first stated by Jakob Bernoulli in 1689 to probability calculus, enlarged the scope of the theory (Hacking 2006). It made classical probability theory applicable to empirical problems and social phenomena. The law assumes that any single event occurs on a purely random basis. If this is the case any probability, being the ratio between actual and possible types of occurrences, calculated on the basis of an empirical sample is almost as certain as a probability determined on the basis of a hypothetical game of chance situation. The larger the number of events in the sample gets, the more certain gets the probability ratio. In this way frequency type probabilities, can be used to identify regularities in empirical samples over a certain period of time. The theory allows to identify and construct orders in a random reality and thereby reveals regularities, which are often referred to as natural laws.[4]

For almost a century, Laplace's classical definition was not questioned. And even today its central assumption of complete randomness of any event is underlying most stochastic models in economics, insurance and financial risk management.

---

[3]Laplace (1820: 6) writes: "The curve described by a single molecule of air or vapor is regulated in a manner just as certain as the planetary orbits; the only difference between them is that which comes from our ignorance. Probability is relative, in part to this ignorance, in part to our knowledge. We know that of three or a greater number of events a single one ought to occur: but nothing induces us to believe that one of them will occur rather than the other. In this state of indecision, it is impossible for us to announce their occurrence with certainty."

[4]Later, in his "Logic of Chance" (1888) John Venn developed a frequentialist theory.

5.1.2 *Frequency Theory of Probability*

For the matter of completeness, I will also shortly introduce the frequency theory of probability. Yet, I will not discuss it in detail, as it is not particularly relevant to the topic of this book.

In the middle of the nineteenth century the frequentialist theory of probability was developed in Cambridge by Ellis and John Venn (1866). Gillies (2000: 87) argues that it was developed as a 'British empiricist reaction against the 'Continental rationalism' of Laplace and others. Later the Vienna circle and particularly Richard von Mises influenced the development of the theory. Von Mises paper "Grundlagen der Wahrscheinlichkeitsrechnung" (1919) as well as his 1928 book *Probability, Statistics and Truth* and his posthumous book *Mathematical Theory of Probability and Statistics* (1964) build the foundations of the frequency theory of probability. In these publications, von Mises set out to develop probability theory as a mathematical theory. He said:

> The essentially new idea which appeared about 1919 [...] was considered the theory of probability as a science of the same order as geometry or theoretical mechanics. (1950; quoted in Gillies 2000: 88)

This mathematical theory of probability was designed to deal with mass phenomena and repetitive events. Von Mises claimed that his mathematical theory of probability treats "problems in which either the same event repeats itself again and again, or a great number of uniform elements are involved at the same time" (1950: vii; quoted in Gillies 2000: 89). Examples for such events, which are thought of as observer independent and therefore as objective as the phenomena under study in physics, are (1) games of chance, which can be repeated endlessly, (2) life statistics, in which a large number of cases of a similar kind can be compared and (3) natural phenomena, like the considerations of molecules of a particular sample of gas (Gillies 2000: 89). In each of these mass phenomena there is a set of attributes which are regarded as a priori possible. Von Mises calls this the attribute space. Today, it is commonly called the sample space Ω. Now, von Mises defined probabilities of events only in relation to its sample space. According to his theory no single event can have a probability measure. A probability of an event can only be determined in relation to the sample space the event is part off. The probability then is an objective category as it follows from the axioms of this mathematical approach to probabilities. In this way statistical laws can be derived from empirical observations, which can be used for the prediction and explanation of empirical phenomena.

5.1.3 *Logical Theory of Probability*

The concept of logical probabilities emerged in the 1920s in Great Britain. The concept was mainly developed in Cambridge by Johnson (1921) and his student

Keynes (1921).[5] But also Keynes' fellow student Jeffreys (1939) contributed to the development of the concept. However, later the idea became popular among the opponents of the Vienna circle. Particularly, Carnap (1950) and Popper (1957) discussed the problem of logical probabilities.

In presenting the concept of logical probabilities, I will mainly focus on Keynes contributions, as they are particularly important to economics. I will first shortly present some background information to the development of the concept. Afterwards I will discuss the logical theory of probability as Keynes has proposed it. Hereby, I will show, that Keynes had a pragmatic view on probability. To him probabilistic reasoning was an instrument of rational thought, in situations in which knowledge is less than perfect. Instead of constructing a coherent mathematical theory of numerical probabilities, Keynes suggested using probabilities as a basis for rational argument. To him a probability (numerical or not) describes the rational degree of belief one can hold in situations of less than certainty in some hypothesis, given some evidence. One can therefore, interpret Keynes' logical theory of probability as a pragmatic theory of argument based on evidence, which can be used to make rational decisions in the face of imperfect knowledge.

5.1.3.1 Ethics and Probability

Skidelsky (2003: 152), who is one of the most important experts on Keynes and his biographer, argued that Keynes (1921: 309) first started to reason about probabilities due to ethical considerations. Gillies (2000: 28) rephrases Keynes:

> We should act in order to bring about the greatest amount of goodness, but we can only calculate the probable effects of our actions in the 'immediate future'. We really know nothing about their long-term consequences. Moreover, the long-term consequences may be such as to reverse the balance of good produced by our actions in the short term. Moor used these sceptical doubts to argue that we can do no better in most cases than to follow the existing rules of morality. Keynes disliked this conclusion, since he believed that a rational member of the Aposteles could judge with confidence that some actions contravening conventional morality were nonetheless good.

Keynes was a member of the Aposteles, which was an intellectual secret society at Cambridge University. Among the members were the mathematician and philosopher Alfred North Whitehead and the philosopher Ludwig Wittgenstein as well as Keynes' mentor George Edward Moore. Keynes' developed his view on probabilities by distancing oneself from Moore's ideas about moral action, which he had developed in his "Principia Ethica" (1903). In this essay, Moor shows how people ought to behave in the face of uncertainty. He suggested, that one should draw back on custom, when knowledge is incomplete. Keynes turned against this position and argued for the use of reason instead of custom in the face of

[5] *The Treaties on probability* was Keynes' dissertation, which had been set and proofed in 1913. However, it had only been published in 1921.

uncertainty. Central to his argument is what Keynes called 'the weight of argument' (Runde 1990). If men should make a choice in the face of uncertainty, they should not draw back on customs, morals or mere belief. Instead they should look for evidence that could help to develop an idea of how things might develop. The decision-maker then can compare the evidence for different options and thereby form a rational probability belief. The more confidant the decision maker is in the evidence for one option the higher is the probability for that option. Generally, the better the evidence is or the more facts or knowledge we have the more confident we are that our beliefs are justified and rational. Thus, Keynes suggests forming rational belief about possible options and evaluates them based on the 'weight of the argument' one can make in favour of one option. This however, still leaves the decision maker with the problem, that (s)he still has no basis to prefer one option over another. In order to solve this problem Keynes introduces the principle of 'moral risk'. According to that principle the decision maker should aim for a smaller good, which is more probable, instead of aiming for an unlikely larger good. In this way, Keynes suggests a risk averse strategy to moral questions, according to which the decision-maker should minimize the 'moral risk'.

The moral roots of Keynes considerations on probabilities, show that probabilities are a tool for action that help the decision-maker to make rational or, expressed differently, reasonable choices in the face of uncertainty. Later Keynes, applied this tool, which was originally developed for moral questions, to economic problems of choice, as they often must be taken in similarly uncertain situations. While moral questions in the face of uncertainty should be solved in order to reach the greatest amount of good, economic questions have to be solved in order to reach the greatest amount of profit. Economic and moral problems are thus similar in the way that they are problems of optimization in the face of uncertainty. Thus, probabilistic reasoning can be used as a tool for action in both cases.

Keynes view on probability is thus rather close to the original view of probability, which had emerged during the enlightenment (which had been presented earlier in this book). In a way one could argue that, Keynes was the one who theorised the folk view on probability. After, the trust in the clerical authority had decreased significantly during the enlightenment, people started to use probabilities as a guide to action in uncertain situations. Intuitively people formed probability belief based on the information available to them. Keynes gave a theoretical account of how people build these probability beliefs, and argued that it is rational to act based on them, as they are formed based on reason.

5.1.3.2 Knowledge and Probability

In the second chapter of his Treaties, Keynes (1921) discusses the relation of probability and the theory of knowledge. Here he defines knowledge as certain rational belief. By rational belief, Keynes means justified belief. Thus, the difference between rational and mere belief is, that in the former case we can make explicit the reasons that make us believe something, while in the latter case we just believe it, without being able to say why. To Keynes it was important to note that the difference lays not in the truth or falsity of a belief. Rational belief can thus be either true or false. The same holds for mere belief. Yet, he acknowledges, that we have more confidence in one rational belief than in another. The concept of probability now can be used to express the level of confidence in a rational belief. If we are certain of some rational belief in some proposition or hypothesis, which is in fact true, it can be said that we know that the proposition or hypothesis is true and therefore it can be defined as knowledge.[6] If this is the case the probability assigned to the rational belief is one and therefore certainty. Now, there are other cases in which we are less confident about our rational belief in some hypothesis. The graduations between these levels of confidence can be expressed in terms of probabilities. The less confident we are the less probable is the rational degree of belief.

Now, the question is, what determines the level of confidence in a rational degree of belief? Keynes (1921: 3) argues:

> Part of our knowledge we obtain directly; and part by argument. The Theory of probability is concerned with that part which we obtain by argument, and it treats of the different degrees in which the results so obtained are inclusive or inconclusive.

Thus, the degree of belief and therefore the probability for some proposition is dependent on the argument, by which we have come to the proposition. Keynes (1921: 3–4) summarises this point as follows:

> The terms *certain* and *probable* describe the various degrees of rational belief about a proposition which different amounts of knowledge authorise us to entertain. All propositions are true or false, but the knowledge we have of them depends on our circumstances; and while it is often convenient to speak of propositions as certain or probable, this expresses strictly a relationship in which the stand to a *corpus* of knowledge, actual or hypothetical, and not a characteristic of the propositions in themselves.

To Keynes probabilities are thus an instrument to distinguish between different levels of confidence in rational belief. Probabilities can thus be used to describe stages of knowledge, which lay between certain or full knowledge and ignorance.

5.1.3.3 Logic and Probability

Under Keynes' approach, probability theory is seen as a branch of logic, which extends deductive logic to the inductive case (Gillies 2000: 87). With his theory, Keynes turns against the frequentialist view on probability and particularly criticises Venn (McCann 1994: 34). He (1921: 103) argues that the frequentialists mistake 'probailities' for 'statistical frequencies'. Under the frequentialist definition, the calculation of probability relies solely on experience, sense data and empirical

[6] E. g.: Keynes (1921: 11): "[K]nowledge of a proposition always corresponds to certainty of rational belief in it and at the same time to actual truth in the proposition itself. We cannot know a proposition unless it is in fact true."

phenomena. It therefore is a posteriori concept that measures past statistical frequencies.

Probability, on the contrary is an a priori concept, which is used to find guidance, when knowledge is incomplete. Keynes, argued that one should link the concept of probabilities to beliefs rather than to empirical regularities. It was Keynes' confession that one should turn to reason instead of observation as a source of knowledge in the face of uncertainty (Skidelsky 2003: 283). McCann (1994: 34f) puts it this way:

> While acknowledging the valuable role played by experience, Keynes felt it insufficient by itself to serve anything but a supporting function; experience could not form the foundation of a probability theory. A theory of probability, because it represents a method by which one intuits a conclusion based on incomplete knowledge, cannot rely on calculations arising from a reference class which is itself imperfect; a probability theory must be founded upon a firmer, more precise foundation.

Keynes therefore, suggests to take probability calculus as a part of logic. To him probability is a relational calculus, which states the degree of certainty one has in some hypothesis. If one is certain, the probability measure is *one* and one can speak of knowledge. Any probability below *one*, describes the degree of belief in a certain hypothesis, while a probability of *zero* implies ignorance. Thus probability measures describe the degree of belief in some hypothesis that is between certainty or complete knowledge and ignorance. Furthermore, all probability judgements are relative to the knowledge one possesses about the hypothesis. Consider his own words:

> We are claiming, in fact, to cognise correctly a logical connection between one set of propositions which we call our evidence and which we suppose ourselves to know, and another set which we call our conclusion, and to which we attach more or less weight according to the ground supplied by the first [...] . It is not straining the use of words to speak of this as the relation of probability. (Keynes 1921: 5–6)

The idea of partial entailment is the starting point of Keynes logical theory of probability. Gillies (2000: 29) summarises Keynes' idea as follows:

> In the case of deductive logic a conclusion is entailed by the premises, and it is certain given those premises. ... But now let us consider an inductive, [...], case. Suppose the evidence (e say) that several thousand ravens have been observed, and they were all black. Suppose further that we are considering the hypothesis (h say) that all ravens are black, or the prediction (d say) that the next observed raven will be black. Hume argued, and this is in agreement with modern logic, that neither h nor d follows logically from e. Yet even though e does not entail either h or d, could we not say that e *partially entails* h and d, since e surely gives some support for these conclusions?

And he (p. 30) continues:

> This line of thought suggests that there might be a logical theory of partial entailment which generalises the ordinary theory of full entailment which is found in deductive logic.

In the case of deductive logic the conclusion follows from the premises. While in the case of induction the premises indicate some degree of support for the conclusion but does not entail it. Thus the conclusion does not follow necessarily from the premises. Keynes, however argued, that the probability for a conclusion is the degree to which the premises partially entails the conclusion. Consequently, Keynes advocated the view, that even in cases of an inductive argument, one can say that the conclusion is partially entailed in the premises and therefore necessarily follows from it. And the probability relation gives the degree of partial entailment. Wherefrom follows, that even in situations of uncertainty, in which only inductive arguments are possible, the conclusion follows necessarily (to a certain degree) from the premises. Keynes (1921: 4) clarifies this point by arguing:

> Let our premises consist of any set of proposition h, and our conclusion consists of any set of propositions a, then, if a knowledge of h justifies a rational belief in a of degree α, we say that there is a *probability-relation* of degree α between a and h.[7]

And Gillies (2000: 31) highlights this point by saying:

> Here Keynes makes the assumption that if h partially entails a to degree α, then given h it is rational to believe a to degree α. To put it less formally, he identifies 'degrees of partial entailment' and 'degrees of rational belief'.[8]

We can therefore conclude that a probability relation is the degree of partial entailment and the degree of rational belief (Gillies 2000: 30). The probability relation of a hypothesis follows (partially) from the evidence put forward in support of a hypothesis.[9] With his concept of partial entailment, Keynes transfers entailment as a key characteristic of deductive arguments to inductive ones. Thereby he strengthens inductive arguments. Based on evidence probability relations can be deduced logically and therefore they become objective and intersubjective (Gillies 2000). Thus, any two individuals must come to the same conclusions confronted with the same evidence. Furthermore, it is according to Keynes (1921) rational to believe in the conclusion to the degree of its probability. Keynes had been criticised for his violations of the laws of logic by Popper (1957) and also by Ramsey (1926, 1927, 1929). However, one could also conclude that Keynes, had a rather pragmatic account of rationality and objectivity. He, was well aware, that two persons confronted with the same evidence, will only come to the same conclusions in an ideal situation. Nevertheless, it is more rational, to base one's conclusion on evidence, than not to do it. This view, does not stand a critical academic review, yet, it proves itself in practice, as Keynes did it himself.

5.1.3.4 Ramsey's Critique

Even though, Keynes' Treaties on Probability had been praised as a modern and extraordinary piece of critical thought, Keynes ideas on probability did not prevail.

[7]Italic is in the original.

[8]Italic is in the original.

[9]Keynes (1921: 7) puts it this way: "No proposition is in itself either probable or improbable, just as no place can be intrinsically distant; and the probability of the same statement varies with the evidence presented, which is, as it were, its origin of reference."

One reason for this lack of interest in Keynes' theory of probability, were the criticism raised against it by Frank Ramsey. Ramsey was a highly talented philosopher and mathematician, who began studying at Cambridge in 1920 at the age of seventeen. Like Keynes, Ramsay became an Apostle and was elected a fellow of King's College in 1924 (Skidelsky 2003: 291). Ramsey put forward his criticisms in two essays. One was published in the Cambridge Magazine in October 1921 and the other was a contribution to the Cambridge Moral Science Club in 1925, published under the name "Truth and Logic". Skidelsky (2003: 291) writes of the presentation of this paper: "After an hour of so beautiful demolition work little of the baroque edifice of the *Treaties* was left standing."[10]

Speaking in broad terms Ramsey accused Keynes for muddling up the objective or existence and subjective or perception side of probability relations. Ramsey argued that statistical frequencies describe proportions or relations, which can be observed in nature. He then turns against Keynes idea, that probability statements like the utterance: "that is probably true" are similarly natural and objective. Keynes had argued that we conclude "that is probably true" by perception. Or expressed differently, given the evidence *i*, hypothesis *h* is probably true. Keynes had argued that, any rational men confronted with the evidence *i*, will also come to the conclusion that hypothesis *h* is probably true. Therefore, the probability statement "That is probably true" is similarly objective as the chance for rowing a six on a fair dice is *1/6*. Consequently, Keynes was convinced that we can proceed from full belief in the evidence to partial belief in the conclusion, which necessarily or objectively follows. However, Ramsey turns against this view, when he (1990: 59) argues:

> He supposes that, at any rate in certain cases, they can be perceived; but speaking of myself I feel confident that this is not true. I do not perceive them, and if I am to be persuaded that they exist it must be by argument; moreover I shrewdly suspect that others do not perceive them either, because they are able to come to so very little agreement as to which of them relates any two given propositions.

Skidelsky (2003: 291) sums up Ramsey's criticism as follows:

> The Emperor had no clothes. All Keynes had established was that we make judgements of probabilities, not that there were objective probabilities corresponding to them.

It is legitimate to infer a factual conclusion from a factual premise, yet we cannot say that the conclusion is logically necessary. Therefore, it is logically valid to reject the conclusion, while accepting the premises. Consequently, probabilities cannot follow deductively from factual evidence. This would be an unsound deductive argument, which violates the laws of thought.

Ramsey thus, accused Keynes for mixing up deductive and inductive elements of probabilistic reasoning. Instead he suggested separating them strictly. To Ramsey the statement "This is probably true" expresses a subjective degree of belief, and no matter how hard one tries it is impossible to proof it true. Yet, similar to Keynes,

[10]Italic is in the original.

Ramsey believed in the rationality of this subjective degree of belief. Ramsey assumes that agents act according to their desires and needs and therefore it is legitimate to assume that they are equipped with a consistent set of preferences. Agents then, derive from these preferences, strategies which, given the situation best serve their interests. The rationality of these strategies is to be judged according to Ramsey on the basis of their success. The more successful the actions of the agents are, the more rational their strategies have been. Strategies are built on the basis of probabilities. Ramsey assumes that agents attach subjective degree of belief probabilities to possible outcomes, and then choose or bet on the strategy that best satisfies their preferences. Beyond that, Ramsey assumes that agent's strategies are both coherent and consistent. If this is the case, numerical probabilities can be derived from the actual choices of the agents. Thus, instead of deriving probabilities from evidence, Ramsey, suggested to derive them from observed human behaviour. In this way, Ramsey's counter proposal differs fundamentally, from Keynes' initial conception of probabilities. Skidelsky (2003: 292) sums up the differences as follows:

> In Keynes' world, notions of objective goodness and probability form the foundation stones of ethical and practical reason. Without such foundations thought is 'adrift'. Ramsey's world was made up of preferences and bets. It is a world in which the subjective and pragmatic character of thought is accepted. We use techniques which work. Keynes' people are thinkers, and he equips them with the tool of thought: logic. Ramsey's people are actors, and he equips them with the tool of action: calculating power.

5.1.4 Subjective Theory of Probability

The theory of subjective probability attempts to provide quantitative probabilities in the face of uncertainty. It is a decision-oriented approach that allows choosing based on rational calculus, when knowledge is incomplete. The theory adopts classical interpretations of probability, as they have been provided by Bayes (1763), Laplace (1820), Koopman (1940) and Good (1950) and is based on the quantitative probability axioms proposed by Kolmogorov (1933). Borel (1909), Ramsey (1926), de Finetti (1929, 1937) and particularly Savage (1954) have developed subjective probability theory as an account of probabilistic reasoning for situations in which neither classical nor frequency probability theories can be applied. These are situations in which the reference class, or class of possible events, cannot be defined, as the decision-maker has no knowledge about it. This lack of knowledge about the possibilities one action or event may release is characteristic for situations of uncertainty and makes them fundamentally different to situations in which it is impossible to know what is going to happen, while knowing what could happen. In the same way, subjective probabilities are fundamentally different from objective probabilities. Borel makes this point clear, when he argues:

> For any modification in the system of knowledge in relation to which probability is defined has a consequence the modification of this probability. It is no longer a question of making more perfect or precise this probability, but of substituting for another probability which is entirely different. (Borel 1909: 51)

Subjective probability calculus allows us to assign numerical probabilities, similar to classical or frequency probabilities. And yet, they express something fundamentally different. Classical and frequency probabilities give an objective ratio of favourable events relative to possible events, which cannot be doubted by any other person, who had agreed on the mathematical axioms underlying the theories.

The probability ratio calculated on the basis of subjective probability theory, on the contrary, express consistent subjective beliefs of one individual. Subjective probabilities reveal the beliefs of one person and express them in terms of numerical probabilities. Subjective probabilities are therefore never right nor wrong. According to Ramsey (1931: 170) the degree of belief is a causal property of a probability ratio, which can be vaguely expressed " [...] as the extent to which we are prepared to act on it." This view is rather similar to that of Savage (1954: 3), who holds that the probability measure expresses " [...] the confidence that a particular individual has in the truth of a particular proposition." And de Finetti (1937, in Kyburg and Smokler 1964: 101) describes a subjective probability as the degree of belief in the happening of an event that the individual would reveal if forced to bet on the event. Koopman (1940: 269) even admits that probability rather derives directly from intuition rather than from objective experience. We can see that subjective probabilities are thought of as an instrument to quantify subjective degrees of belief and intuitions, which individuals confronted with alternative opportunities build. Subjective probability theory, therefore presupposed a situation of choice and a decision maker. Subjective probabilities thus do not exist independent of an individual and they can only be discovered in actual situations of choice. Choice therefore is a necessary condition for subjective probability theory and the formation of subjective probabilities should be understood as a subjective comparative process, which is always directed towards a particular situation and highly dependent on the person making the judgement. Keynes (1921) therefore points out that subjective probabilities have "different values for different individuals".[11]

[11]According to Fishburn (1986): "[T]he axioms of subjective probability refer to assumed properties of a binary relation *is more probable than*, or its nonstrict companion *is at least as probable as*, on a set of propositions or events. This relation often referred to as a qualitative or *comparative probability* relation, can be taken either as an undefined primitive (intuitive view) or as a relation derived from a preference relation (decision-oriented approach). In the latter case, to say that you regard *rain* as more probable tomorrow than *shine*, or that you believe the pound sterling is more likely to *fall* than *rise* against the dollar next year means roughly that you would rather bet on the first-named event for a valuable prize that you will receive if your chosen event obtains."

The axioms are thought of as criteria of consistency and coherence for choice in situations of uncertainty. Subjective probabilities therefore are always the result of human considerations and can therefore never exist independent of an individual. Subjective probabilities are the results of human action; therefore they cannot exist independently, and thus they are neither facts nor naturally existing. Their emergence is dependent on the individual, its experience and expectations and thus subjective probabilities presuppose personal engagement. They cannot be separated from the individual that has brought the ratio about and therefore treating subjective probabilities as though they were objectively given facts is illegitimate and ignores the nature of subjective probability theory.

Subjective probability theory does not aim to be realistic. It is no theory about how people actually choose nor is it meant to be a normative theory that describes how people should choose. It rather is the case that subjective probability theory is an axiomatic concept that characterises the partial beliefs of a rational, idealized individual (Fishburn 1986: 335).

As indicated above, subjective probability was developed in the 1920s by Borel (1924) and Ramsey (1926). They developed their theories as an alternative and criticism to Keynes (1921) logical theory of probability (McCann 1994: 45). It was their aim to develop a quantitative theory of subjective judgements. It was Borel (1924: 57) who had suggested that subjective judgements could be quantified through the use of betting:

> I can offer a choice between two bets procuring the same advantages in the case of gain [...]. The same method can be applied to all verifiable judgments; it allows a numerical evaluation of probabilities with a precision quite comparable to that with which one evaluates prices.

Ramsey (1926) incorporated the idea of Borel and argued for using behaviouralistic experiments for measuring subjective degrees of belief. He was convinced that belief could only be measured by examining actual human behaviour. It became his aim to develop "a purely psychological method of measuring belief" (1926: 62). Similar to Savage decades later, Ramsey used the concept of utility as departure point of his theory. He argued that actions are the result of people's attempts to maximize their individual utility. Utility includes all desires of men, conscious and unconscious, and goes beyond the Benthamian concept of pleasure (McCann 1994: 47).

If people aim to maximize their utility by making a choice, then the choice reviles the degree of belief the person holds in the occurrence of a certain event, given the utility the person attaches to the event. This choice and therefore the degree of belief are assumed to be rational, if the choices made are consistent. The only quality criterion for subjective probability measures is therefore constancy of choices.

This basic idea of measuring subjective degrees of belief, by observing actual decisions, builds the foundation of the subjective theory of probability. Savage (1954) formalised this basic idea, which had been developed by Borel, de Finetti and Ramsey. In his "Foundations of Statistics" Savage (1954) presents his formal account of subjective probability theory. Taking up Ramsey's idea of maximizing utility, Savage draws back on von Neumann and Morgenstern's theory of expected utilities (1947). Neumann and Morgenstern have argued, that people with complete knowledge possess a completely ordered set of preferences for any two events or possible events or imagined events, which reflect their expected utilities of the consequences of these events (p. 17). Savage then extended this theory to situations in which people do not possess complete knowledge by combining preferences with probabilities.

The departure point of Savages consideration is the choice between two alternatives. A decision maker has the choice to either choose alternative *A* or alternative *B*. Each of the alternatives is a bet and it is assumed that the decision maker maximises subjective expected utility. It follows that the choice taken reveal, both the utility function of the decision maker as well as his or her subjective probabilities. It is thus assumed that each state of the world has a probability (Binmore 2009: 95), which is said to be subjective.[12] This is the case because there need not be any objective reasons for the probability that decision maker *x* assigns to an event and it is also not necessary that decision maker *y* assigns the same probability to the same event. Subjective probabilities are therefore not necessarily based on reason or fact but must be based on subjective belief. Therefore a subjective probability is also often called subjective degree of belief. This description points to the constructive and subjective human nature of this measure.

Nevertheless, to get a numerical subjective probability Savage had to base his theory on five mathematical axioms, of which three are particularly important. He assumes that for any two bets, the decision-maker can always identify, which of the two bets (s)he prefers or which bet is as good as another. In this way, the decision-maker's preferences are assumed to be always complete.[13] The second axiom of transitivity requires that if a decision maker prefers bet A over bet B and bet B over bet C, then (s)he also must prefer alternative A over alternative C. And finally, people's preferences are assumed to be stable. Thus, if people's choice were consistent and preferences were complete, transitive and stable, subjective probabilities, would be measures of rational degrees of belief of one individual decision maker.

The lack of objectivity and knowledge also questions the scientificness of the theory. Even though scientific methods are applied in the case of subjective probability theory, the theory falls short of any scientific standard. Experiments are subjective, non-repeatable and the theory is unfalsifiable. Furthermore, it is sensible to Savage's subjective probability theory to always be consistent in choice

[12]See also Binmore (2009: 116): "It characterizes [...] choice behaviour in terms of both a Von Neumann and Morgenstern utility function *u* defined on her set *C* of consequences and a subjective probability measure *p* defined on [...] set *B* of states of the world. It is shown that she chooses from any feasible set *A* as though maximizing the expected value of her utility function *u* computed with respect to her subjective probability measure *p*." Italic is in the original.

[13]This assumption has been taken from consumer theory (Gilboa et al. 2008) and it is also part of Neumann and Morgenstern's (1947) Utility Theory.

behaviour. Otherwise it would become impossible to deduce the utility function and the subjective probability distribution from the choice behaviour of a decision maker. However Savage (1954) was aware that this requirement in most real world situations will not be met. In the real world, knowledge alters and therefore expectations, preferences and utility functions are in fluctuation. Furthermore, decision makers often do not decide according to the axioms outlined above. Thus real decision makers are often not consistent and therefore not rational in the way defined in subjective probability theory.

Savage (1954: 16) points out that as decision makers in the real world or in large worlds as he calls it, are not rational. His theory is therefore restricted to small worlds in which it makes sense to insist on consistency and the validity of the axioms of subjective probability theory. He rejects using subjective probability theory in any situation that does not apply to the axioms and calls any attempt of applying it to large world situations as "utterly ridiculous" and "preposterous".[14]

Consequently, subjective probability theory only applies to small worlds, which are according to Savage worlds in which it is always possible to "look before you leap". This implies, according to Binmore (2009: 117) that,

> [the decision maker] can then take account *in advance* of the impact that all conceivable future pieces of information might have and the underlying model that determine(s) [...] subjective beliefs. Any mistakes built into her original model that might be revealed in the future will then *already* have been corrected, so that no possibility remains of any unpleasant surprises.[15]

Savage himself was critical of the practical applicability of his theory. Binmore (2009: 117) therefore concludes:

> Although he is often cited as though he was the father of Bayesianism, Savage therefore disavowed this creed before it was even born. He didn't believe that Bayesian decision theory is the appropriate tool for all decision problems. He didn't think that Bayes' rule is the solution to the problem of scientific induction. And we shall see [...] that he didn't believe that rationality somehow endows us with prior probability measures with which to start off the process of Bayesian updating.

The first who was interested in defining a probability under ambiguous circumstances, was Thomas Bayes. His fundamental question was, how we determine the probability of an event occurring, when it could either occur or not (Bernstein 1998: 132). The departure point is, that "Given that the number of times in which an unknown event has happened and failed: Required the chance that the probability of its happening in a single trial lies somewhere between any two degrees of probability that can be named." (Bayes 1763)

Bayes suggests that any probability can be determined, yet it is not necessary that this probability will still be correct, when new information becomes available.

---

[14]Binmore (2009), however argues, that for the most part economists ignore Savages' warnings and apply subjective probability theory to large world problems, without even noting that it might be problematic.

[15]Italic is in the original.

He therefore argues that there is no strict regularity between past and future. Because something had happened in the past it is not necessary that it will hold in the future. Instead he proposed a dynamic point of view, according to which things change over time. This implies that there is no single probability that needs to be assigned to one event. Bayes, therefore, suggests, that probabilities need to be updated. Bernstein (1998: 132) describes the logic of his theory of probability as follows. "The primary application of the Bayesian system is in the use of new information to revise probabilities based on old information, or, in the language of statisticians, to compare posterior probability with the priors."[16] This approach implies the idea that reality unfolds over time and that probabilities are an instrument to deal with a particular reality. This implies that probabilities are no absolute guide to action, but a temporal assessment about reality, formed based on rational beliefs. Bayes' concept implies that probabilistic reasoning is a rational learning process, which turns against the view that there is only one true answer or probability (Smith 1984). This view opened a new perspective for both science and knowledge. Even scientific knowledge is not universally true; instead it is a temporal truth which we have good reason to believe in, for that moment. What classifies this knowledge as temporally true is, that it was reached on the basis of generally accepted epistemological standards.

The theory of probability in its many stages of development, initially, was a verbal concept and later as a mathematical theory, served as epistemological standard in a contingent reality. It provided a widely-accepted basis for making initially reasonable and later rational inference, when absolute knowledge and universal truth got out of reach. Naturally, the conclusions of their probabilistic inferences are dependent on the underlying assumptions. Particularly, subjective probability theory is rather limited. It is by definition not objective and only a formalization of individual belief under rather narrow conditions. Nevertheless, subjective probability theory became the synonym for uncertainty in modern mainstream economics.

5.2 The Neoclassical Uncertainty Paradigm

Uncertainty as we commonly conceive it today in economics, developed in the 1950s and 1960s. The way in which uncertainty became defined in economics was essentially dualistic. On the one hand there was risk, which is quantifiable on the basis of objective probability calculus and on the other hand there was uncertainty, which cannot be quantified on the basis of objective probabilities, but on the basis of subjective probabilities (Hodgson 2011).

[16]For a more detailed description of Bayes approach please see Stigler (1986: 124–130) and Bernstein (1998: 132).

If knowledge is imperfect, how can valid (economic) inferences be made? This fundamental question provoked a series of debates in the first half of the twentieth century both in philosophy (Ramsey 1926; Keynes 1921; de Finetti 1929, 1937) and economics (Knight 1921; Schumpeter 1934; Keynes 1936, 1937; Hayek 1945, 1968; Friedman and Savage 1952; Savage 1954; Shackle 1955, 1968, 1979, 1988; Neumann and Morgenstern 1947). Among the economists there was disagreement between those who believed that probability concepts are sufficient measures of ignorance that allow the integrated uncertainty of knowledge into the deductive economic research approach (Savage 1954; Anscombe and Aumann 1963) and those, who argued that probability measures are insufficient in situations of uncertainty (Knight 1921; Keynes 1936, 1937; Shackle 1955, 1968, 1979, 1988).

In the 1950s Knightian and Keynesian Uncertainty became highly problematic in their fundamental forms, because they do not allow for mathematical modelling and prediction, which gained importance in economic research by that time. By then economists had to make a choice between integrating uncertainty or predictive power of theories. Neoclassical economics went for predictive power and developed a theory of uncertainty that allowed for prediction. The Neoclassical Uncertainty Paradigm meets the spirit of that period. It was never meant to reflect the epistemological and ontological brisance of the problem of uncertainty in economics. As such, the Neoclassical Uncertainty Paradigm must be interpreted as a methodological artefact, rather than a general theory of uncertainty in economics (Hausman 1992).

By 1940 it was clear that there is no absolute knowledge in economics, but rather degrees of knowledge. Knight (1921) and Keynes (1936, 1937) had convincingly argued that uncertainty is both an epistemological and an ontological problem for the economy, but also for economic theory. Furthermore, uncertainty compromises prediction as the aim of economics. At the same time economics set out to become acknowledged as a science, similar to physics (Mirowski 1992, 2002, 2005). It was argued that the laws of statistical or empirical economics do not possess the same scientific status as the stochastic laws of physics. This fired the desire in economics for stochastic rather than statistic laws, and provided the breeding ground for the emergence and development of econometrics (Louca 2007). The emergence of econometrics however was not a unified development but rather a multifaceted reaction to the crisis in the economic research and explanation agenda.

During the 1930s it was impossible to foresee that econometrics would arise from this debate. And yet, the becoming of scientific econometrics was important for the legitimization of a more stochastic economics. Mirowski (1989: 228) therefore writes: "Only in retrospect can be observed that the problems of determinism vs. indeterminism, abstract theory vs. empiricism, static vs. dynamic and subjective vs. objective, and individualism vs. macroscopic laws were all bound up together as problems created by the original physics metaphor which prompted neoclassical theory in the 1970s, and therefore it was neoclassical theorists who were most concerned to find a potential solution under the rubric of "econometrics"." Similarly, it was the underlying aim to save and expand the scientific status of economics.[17]

In the 1940s economics saw an explosion of mathematical publications. Stigler et al. (1995) analysed the growing impact of mathematics in four leading journals. They showed that before 1920 verbal expositions dominated the published articles, while already in the 1940s the number of verbal articles decreased. In the 1960s only 1/3 of the articles were of a more verbal nature and by 1990 more than 90% of leading economics publications were mathematical in nature. This transition is often referred to as the "formalist revolution" (Blaug 1992, 2003; Weintraub 2002; Backhouse 2002, 2010). The transition of economics from a verbal science to a mathematical science was also accompanied with more extensive training in formal methods at the graduate, but also at the undergraduate level (Fourcade and Khurana 2011). Mathematical precision and prediction became the new primary aims of economics.

Milton Friedman's essay (1953) played an important role in the becoming of formal economics. Friedman argued in his essay that an economic theory or hypothesis must not be judged on the basis of the correctness of their assumptions, but on the basis of its simplicity and its fruitfulness. By simplicity Friedman means that the theory is able to predict at least as much as an alternate theory, while requiring less information. Fruitfulness refers to the precision and scope of the predictions derived based on a simple theory and implies that the more precise the predictions are, the more fruitful the theory is, no matter how incorrect their assumptions are. Friedman (1953: 14) argues: "Truly important and significant

[17]However there were also sceptics. Moore (1914: 84–86) for example summarizes the state of the art in economics at the turn of the century as follows: "In the closing quarter of the last century great hopes were entertained by economists with regard to the capacity of economics to be made an 'exact science'. According to the view of the foremost theorists, the development of the doctrines of utility and value had laid the foundations of scientific economics in exact concept, and it would be possible to erect upon the new foundation a firm structure of interrelated parts which, in definiteness and cogency, would be suggestive and of the severe beauty of the mathematico- physical sciences. But this expectation has not been realized [...]. The explanation is found in the prejudiced point of view from which economists regarded the possibilities of science and in the radically wrong method, which they pursued. It was assumed gratuitously that economics was to be modelled on the simpler mathematical, physical sciences, and this assumption created a prejudice at the outset both in selecting the data to be investigated and in conceiving the types of laws that were to be the object of research. Economics was to be a 'calculus of pleasure and pain', a 'mechanics of utility, a 'social mechanics', a '*physique sociale*' [...]. The biased point of view implied in these descriptions led to an undue stressing of those aspects of the sciences which seemed to bear out the pretentious metaphors. One would naturally suppose from this manner of conceiving the science that the economic theorists would have at once entered upon their task with the methods that had proved themselves useful in the physical sciences. But this they did not do. They seemed to identify the method of the physical sciences with experimentation, and since, as they had, scientific experimentation is impossible in social life, a special method has to be devised. This invention was a disguised form of the classical ceteris paribus, the method of the static state."

hypotheses will be found to have 'assumptions' that are wildly inaccurate descriptive representations of reality, and, in general, the more significant the theory, the more unrealistic the assumptions (in this sense)."

This passage can be read as a legitimation for the unrealistic, but in terms of predictability[18] highly successful Neoclassical Uncertainty Paradigm. Weintraub (2002), even argued that the essay marks a new formal era in economics in which predictability on the basis of precise and value-free mathematical models became the primary aim of scientific economics. Therefore, it is no surprise that the Neoclassical Uncertainty Paradigm emerged during this period as an analytic artefact that integrated uncertainty and predictability. The interpretations of uncertainty, which was used as a basis for the prediction of uncertain future events or values, however, was highly unrealistic, as it expurgated all elements of uncertainty from the theory. We will analyse the different stages of development of the Neoclassical Uncertainty Paradigm in what follows in order to understand the limitations of the theory.

5.2.1 Expected Utility and Subjectivity

The idea of utility—maximizing behaviour was formalised by Daniel Bernoulli in his "Expositions on the new theory on the measurement of risk" (1738). Here Bernoulli argued that decision makers confronted with the famous St. Petersburg paradox[19] should pay the price for the lottery ticket, which is justified by its expected utility. In the St. Petersberg paradox the probabilities are taken for granted in the sense of relative frequencies. The player wins 2k amounts of money with a probability of ½*k* (Binmore 2009: 37) as a fair coin is tossed until it shows heads for the first time and the player gets two units of money for every time the coin showed tail. The question in the St. Petersberg paradox then is, how much is the lottery ticket worth? Bernoulli argued that it is worth an infinite amount of money as its expected utility is infinite (½k × 2k). This appears paradoxical, as no real decision maker would pay an infinite amount of money for the lottery ticket, because the probability of gaining an infinite amount of money is very low. Nevertheless, Bernoulli's line of thought expresses the key idea of expected utility maximisation, which was formalised by von Neumann and Morgenstern's (1947). They combined the ideas of expected utility maximization (Bernoulli 1738) and rational choice (Jevons 1871).

[18]Unlike the Fundamental Uncertainty Paradigm the Neoclassical Uncertainty Paradigm allows for apparently precise predictions of future values. This does not imply that these values are correct, however based on Friedman's argument apparently precise but wrong predictions are better than no predictions.

[19]The St. Petersburg Paradox goes back to Bernoulli's cousin Nicolaus Bernoulli, who had proposed it in 1713 (Menger 1934; Arrow 1974; Aumann 1977; Samuelson 1977).

According to von Neumann and Morgenstern, agents choose rationally if they choose, confronted with risky alternatives (outcomes of a game attached with probabilities) the alternative with the highest expected utility, given their preferences, which are assumed to be complete, transitive, independent and continuous.[20] As they were investigating the behaviour of people in strategic games, they assumed that the probability distributions were logically given by the particular rules of the game and therefore objective to any player. However, in real world decision-situations probabilities are often not given. These situations are classified as uncertain, while those of von Neumann and Morgenstern's theory are risky.

Based on Ramsey's and de Finetti's subjective account of probability, Savage formalized the concept of choice-based subjective probability. Savage (1954) extended the von Neumann and Morgenstern rational expected utility maximizing concept to situations of uncertainty. In this way, Savage (1954) synthesized the ideas of de Finetti, Ramsey and von Neumann and Morgenstern. Savage (1954) formulated a formal model of decision-making where optimal decisions are made to maximise expected utility, and probability distributions are given by subjective evaluations instead of objective probability distributions. This formal model of rational choice under conditions of uncertainty builds the basis for any Neoclassical Theory under conditions of uncertainty.

Probability and utility are defined in terms of a person's beliefs about the future and their individual preferences under the so-called personal or subjective or Bayesian concept of probability (Anscombe and Aumann 1963: 199).[21] Under this concept, probabilities are therefore derived from subjective estimates or degrees of belief, as well as personal taste, which conjointly form people's preferences. Subjective preferences build the foundation of subjective probability theory. It is assumed that subjective probabilities and utilities can be derived from observed preferences. These preferences need to satisfy some consistency assumptions in order to calculate numerical probabilities.

In this way, subjective probabilities are calculated based on a fundamentally different basis than logical or empirical probabilities. Yet, the external appearance of any of these probabilities is not distinguishable. Based on either of these theories a probability is a standardised number between zero and one (Gilboa et al. 2008: 173).

The consequence of integrating subjective probability calculus into economics is that the technical difference between risk and uncertainty disappeared. Economists assume that situations of risk and uncertainty can be modelled equally, the only difference being that the underlying probability distribution is either objective (in the case of risk) or subjective (in the case of uncertainty). The duality of risk and uncertainty disappeared. Situations of uncertainty were no longer characterised

[20]For a more detailed discussion of the von Neumann and Morgenstern Expected Utility axioms, please see Neumann and Morgenstern (1947), Nash (1950: 155), Fishburn (1970) and Kreps (1988: Chaps. 2 and 5).

[21]For matters of simplicity I will hence force only write of subjective probability theory.

by a lack of probability distributions and therefore the classical distinction between risk and uncertainty became meaningless. Consequently, risk and uncertainty became used as synonyms for any kind of situation in which probability distributions (either objective ore subjective) are used to assess the future.

In modern economics (Frydman and Goldberg 2008; Colander et al. 2009; Kirman 2011a, b, 2014), imperfect information is dealt with in the way that it can be assumed, that agents act as if they had perfect knowledge about the past, present and future and consequently the rational actor model as well as the ideal of the perfect and complete market maintains. Finally, Knight's original distinction between risk and uncertainty was rejected. Hirshleifer and Riley (1979: 1378) argue: "Frank Knight attempted to distinguish between "risk" and "uncertainty," depending upon whether probability estimates are or are not calculable on the basis of an objective classification of instances. At times, he suggested that the probability concept is inapplicable under true uncertainty, for example, to such questions as whether or not a cure of cancer will be discovered in the next decades. It will not be possible to review the philosophical and operational underpinnings of the probability concept; for our purpose, it is sufficient that the "subjective" or "degree of belief" interpretation has proved fruitful even for Knightian uncertainty situations."

A similar view, had been put forward by Milton Friedman (1976: 282):

> In his seminal work, Frank Knight drew a sharp distinction between risk, as referring to events subject to a known or knowable probability distribution, and uncertainty, as referring to events for which it was not possible to specify numerical probabilities. I have not referred to this distinction because I do not believe it is valid. I follow L. J. Savage in his view of personal probability, which denies any valid distinctions along these lines. We may treat people as if they assigned numerical probabilities to every conceivable event.

These criticisms were like a stab in the back of Knight's distinction. No young economist that aimed to become acknowledged as a leading and modern economic thinker could have argued for Knight's position by that time. Such an argument would have declassified anyone as a backward-looking idealist.

5.2.2 Rational Expectations and Efficient Markets

Savages' integration of rational expected utilities and subjective probability thus caused an apparent identity of risk and uncertainty in neoclassical economics.[22] The only difference between the two that remained was that risk is a case of objective

[22]Hirshleifer and Riley (1979: 1378) used the concept as follows: "We will assume that each individual is able to represent his beliefs as to the likelihood of different states of the world by a "subjective" probability distribution. That is, an assignment to each state of a number between zero and one whose sum equals unity. Subjective *certainty* would be represented by attaching the full probabilistic weight of unity to only one of the outcomes. The degree of subjective *uncertainty* is reflected in the dispersion of probability weights over possible states." They continue (p. 1379): "The connection between the utility ordering of acts and the preference scaling of consequences is provided by the Neumann–Morgenstern "expected-utility rule". That is, the utility of each act is the

probabilities, while uncertainty is a case of subjective probabilities. Less than one decade later these differences disappeared as well. Taking up the thoughts of Koopman (1940), Good (1950), Savage (1954), Davidson et al. (1955), Kraft et al. (1959), Anscombet and Aumann (1963) presented a definition of subjective probability that allowed interpreting subjective probabilities in the same way as objective probabilities, or as they called it chances. They argued (p. 199): "Within the two main categories of logical probability (probability proper) and physical probability (chances), especially in the former, various lesser differences of meaning can be distinguished. In this paper, we are concerned with the personal or subjective concept of probability, as considered by Ramsey (1931) and Savage (1954). Probabilities and utilities are defined in terms of a person's preferences, in so far as these preferences satisfy certain consistency assumptions. The definition is constructive; that is, the probabilities and utilities can be calculated from observed preferences."

They described the aim of their essay as follows (pp. 199–200): "The purpose of this note is to define the person's probabilities in terms of chances, by an extension of the von Neumann-Morgenstern theory. The addition of only two plausible assumptions to those of utility theory permits a simple and natural definition of probabilities having the appropriate properties."

Their approach is based on combinations of "horse lotteries", for which probabilities are not specified, and "roulette lotteries, for which they are. They define six axioms, of which four are rather similar to those of Neumann and Morgenstern (1947) and Savage (1954), which allow to treat horse lotteries similar to roulette lotteries.[23] Consequently, situations of risk and uncertainty are treated entirely identical in Neoclassical Economics from this time on.

Almost at the same time, Muth 1961 developed the rational expectations hypothesis (Kantor 1979). He (p. 316) claims: "The hypothesis can be rephrased a little more precisely as follows: that expectations of firms (or, more generally, the subjective probability distribution of outcomes) tend to be distributed, for the same information set, about the prediction of the theory (or the "objective" probability distributions of outcomes)."

In 1995 George E. Lucas won the Nobel Prize in the economic sciences for his Rational Expectations Hypothesis. He took up the ideas of John F. Muth and integrated rational expectations in a general equilibrium macroeconomic model, which is according to his own words, an "abstract framework" (Lucas 1972: 103). In this abstract framework "all prices are market clearing, all agents behave optimally in light of their objectives and expectations, and expectations are formed optimally" (p. 103). According to his hypothesis expectations are not subject to

mathematical expectation or probability-weighted average of the utilities of the associated consequences." Italic is in the original, and mathematical formulas were omitted.

[23]For a detailed discussion of the axioms please see Anscombet and Aumann (1963) or Fishburn (1970).

systematic errors[24]. Lucas did not believe that economic actors actually form rational expectations, instead he highlights the analytical power of this conceptualisation of economic decisions in abstract mathematical macroeconomic models. He writes: "While rational expectations is often thought of as a school of economic thought, it is better regarded as a ubiquitous modelling technique used widely throughout economics." (Quoted in Sargent 1986: 76).[25] According to the Hypothesis, agents form expectations about future prices and quantities based on the available information, they form expectations about future prices and quantities. These expectations are assumed to be correct, if agents do not systematically violate the axioms of subjective probability theory. Choice then is the logical consequence of the agent's expectations and their rational interest to maximize their expected utility.

The Rational Expectation Hypothesis builds the foundation of New Classical Macroeconomics, most of New Keynesian Macroeconomics and particularly of Modern Financial Economics. In Modern Financial Economics the efficient markets theory of asset prices has become one of the most striking applications of the concept of rational expectations. Eugene Fama (1970) postulated that asset prices follow a random walk. Accordingly, the current price of an asset allows for the best possible prediction of future values. Asset prices cannot be too low or too high, as they adjust rapidly to new information, so that the price always reflects all information. Consequently, prices are equal to their fundamental value and they are assumed to behave randomly. In 1965 Fama defined efficient markets[26] by assuming that stock market prices follow a random walk. In the same year Samulason (1965) provided a mathematical proof that in well-informed and perfectly competitive markets prices will behave randomly. Thus the very definition of efficient markets excludes uncertainty as it assumes almost perfect information and perfect competition. Needless to say, that so far it was impossible to prove this theory empirically, as almost any real-world market environment does not meet these criteria.[27] Nevertheless, the efficient market hypothesis was extended from stock markets to any kind of market. In theory, thus any market is efficient in the way the efficient market hypothesis defined efficiency.

It is almost ironic, that uncertainty modelled via rational expectations got in the end transformed into the Efficient Market Hypothesis, which excludes in its pure form any kind of uncertainty. One could therefore argue, that the Neoclassical Uncertainty Paradigm states that there is no such thing as uncertainty in economic theory (Hodgson 2011). And as Economics is highly theory and methodology driven, the Paradigm implies that there could not be any uncertainty in economic reality. However, if there should be any such thing as uncertainty, it is legitimate to

---

[24]See also Muth (1961), Lucas and Sargent (1982), Sargent (1986) and Lucas (1987).

[25]See also Sargent (1986).

[26]This definition is based on his 1965 dissertation on random stock price movements. Cf. Fama (1965a, b).

[27]E. g.: Mandelbrot (1960, 1961, 1962, 1963a, b, 2008).

ignore it for methodological reasons. Thus, the application of subjective probability theory in economics and rational expectations help to cover the fundamental inability of modern economics to analyse economic phenomena, which are fundamentally subject to uncertainty.

5.2.3 *Rational Expectations Models in Modern Economics*

The incorporation of rational expectations into economic models and theories was widely recognized as one of the most significant advances in economic theory during the last century (Meltzer 1982; Mascaro and Meltzer 1983). Rational Expectations is a methodological improvement that had been used to improve macroeconomic models (Taylor 1979) and to develop Modern Financial Economics (Fox 2009; Colander et al. 2009). Today, Rational Expectations and the Efficient Market Hypothesis are still among the most widely used modelling techniques in Positive Economics. Particularly, economic models that indicate to operate under conditions of uncertainty still rely on these theories (McCallum 1980; Sugden 1986). Actually, these theories were accused of ignoring uncertainty, when they were released (Meltzer 1982: 18). Here I will briefly present some rational expectations based macro and financial economic models. The analysis shows that the theories are highly elegant and coherent, yet they are still not sufficient for modelling uncertainty. I begin my analysis with macroeconomic dynamic stochastic general equilibrium models (DSGE—models). Then, I turn to modern financial economics.

5.2.3.1 Rational Expectation Models in Macroeconomics

The Efficient Market Hypothesis is the cornerstone of modern macroeconomics. Almost all subsequent macroeconomic models build on the assumptions that expectations are rational and the market prices reflect all available information. There are various macroeconomic models today, which more or less ideally draw back on the assumption of rational expectations.

In the 1960s the well-established orthodoxy of Keynesian macroeconomics was facing an empirical crisis, which brought about a scientific counterrevolution. The first fundamental critique of the Keynesian approach was put forward by Milton Friedman and Anna J. Schwarz in 1963. They denied the effectiveness of monetary policy in depression periods based on empirical evidence. Therefore, the search for a new macroeconomic paradigm began (Woodford 1999: 16). By 1976, Lucas published his critique on contemporary macroeconomics, which is the starting point of New Classical Economics as the dominant school of macroeconomics. He

(p. 41) rejected policy conclusions drawn from by that time dominant large-scale econometric macroeconometric models. Because the parameters of those models were not structural and not dynamic:

> Given that the structure of an econometric model consists of optimal decision rules of economic agents, and that optimal decision rules vary systematically with changes in the structure of series relevant to the decision maker, it follows that any change in policy will systematically alter the structure of econometric models.

Instead of doing empirical economic analysis, he suggests purely analytical models based on behavioural microfoundations. These new models can account for observable or testable empirical regularities and predict individual behaviour. In a second step, changes in policy can be introduced to the model and on the basis of the stable microfoundations, individual behaviour under the new policy rule can be predicted. On the aggregate individual behaviour brings about macroeconomic effects of the policy change, which can be analysed based on the new model.

Only a few years later, Kydland and Prescott published the article "Rules rather than Discretion: The Inconsistency of Optimal Plans" (1977). This paper marks the beginning of purely positive and micro-founded macroeconomics, which use DSGE models as the dominant methodology for giving policy advice.[28]

These new DSGE models integrated the rational expectations hypothesis (Muth 1961; Samuelson 1965; Lucas 1972; Sargent and Wallace 1975) and the concept of equilibrium (Radner 1972) in macroeconomics.[29] Hence, the microfoundations of any DSGE model assumes that any new policy or change in the economy will sooner or later converge to equilibrium due to the rational expectations and the more or less rational behaviour of the individuals. Consequently, DSGE models can only account for economic crisis in the short run. Furthermore, uncertainty gets interpreted as a form of calculable risk and is therefore neglected. It is no surprise when leading economic thinkers argue that macroeconomics is blind for economic problems and helpless, as their dominant methodologies (like DSGE-models) blank out economic reality (Colander et al. 2009).

5.2.3.2 Rational Expectations and Financial Economics

Modern Financial Economics, similar to the positivistic foundation of economics in general, is the result of a professionalization of the management science in the USA after World War II and the formalisation and mathematisation of the science of economics (Fourcade and Khurana 2011). The core theories of modern financial economics emerged between 1950 and 1970 and they are still the building blocks of twenty-first century financial economics (Caldentey and Vernengo 2010: 69). Portfolio Theory, the Capital Asset Pricing Model (CAPM), the Modigliani-Miller

[28] See also Kydland and Prescott (1982).

[29] New Classical macroeconomics was most aggressively advanced by Lucas and Sargent in their pamphlet "After Keynesian Macroeconomics" (1979).

theorem and the Black-Scholes-Merton approach to option prices are all grounded on the Neoclassical Uncertainty Paradigm. Similar to modern macroeconomics the Efficient Market Hypothesis is the basis for the theories at the core of modern financial economics. Only Portfolio Theory was developed prior to the Efficient Market Hypothesis, yet it is also grounded on the idea, that uncertainty can be measured on the basis of subjective probabilities. At the same time portfolio theory established the relation between risk and return. According to Markowitz (1952), a higher expected risk must be accompanied by a higher expected return. The mean and variance of returns is the focus point of the investor. The theory assumes that investors chose portfolios to minimize the variance of returns, which is assumed to be the measure for risk, for a given expected return to maximize expected returns for a given risk (Fama and French 2003; Caldentey and Vernengo 2010: 71). Expected variance of return and the expected returns, are derived from past variances and rational expectations. In this way, this chief theory of modern financial theory is rooted in the same conviction underlying the Neoclassical Uncertainty Paradigm. Markowitz gives reference to Louis Bachelier's first account of the random walk hypothesis (1900). Bachelier's dissertation is the basis of all financial mathematics. Fifty years ahead of economic theory, he established the random foundations of financial economics.

The CAPM is an extension of Portfolio Theory. It analyses the relationship between risk and return under conditions of market equilibrium. It assumes in accordance with Efficient Market Hypothesis that equilibrium market prices reflect all information and therefore incorporate risk and uncertainty correctly. Beta was introduced to measure the elasticity of the rate of return of an asset in relation to that of the market. The more elastic the asset's return is in relation to the market the higher is the assumed systemic risk of the asset. Yet, it is assumed that the risk is fully reflected in the asset price.

The third core theory of modern financial economics is the Modigiani-Miller theorem. It states that the way firms finance its real activities does not affect the costs of capital and it has no impact on the firm's market value. Furthermore, it is assumed that investment decisions are independent, so that they do not affect production or consumption of other market participants. Underlying this theory is the assumption that financial markets work perfectly, in the way that prices incorporate all potential hazards.

Finally, the Efficient Market Hypothesis influenced the Black-Scholes-Merton formula for option pricing, which is fundamental to the modern financial industry. An option is a contract between buyer and seller that gives the buyer the right but not the obligation to buy or sell an underlying asset in a particular period of time at a pre-specified price. The underlying asset might be for example a common stock, property or a particular commodity. The formula derives the price of a particular option based on, for example, the current market price of the underlying asset, the exercise price of the option, the maturity date of the option or other estimates. The general formula already existed prior to Black-Scholes-Merton, yet they incorporated it into a general efficient market equilibrium framework (Taleb 2007: 278–279). Based on the Black-Scholes-Merton it is due to the assumed market efficiency possible to construct a risk-free portfolio via dynamic hedging. According to their theory, changes in the value of the option would be offset by equal changes in the value of the underlying stock and cash (Caldentey and Vernengo 2010: 72).

These fundamental theories of modern financial economics are unrealistic on a different dimension (Fox 2009). For the purpose of this book, however, it is important to note that though all these theories state to be about economic conditions of risk or uncertainty, they ignore the very existence of it.

5.3 Conclusion

Probabilistic reasoning and probability calculus are used as an instrument to deal with the limits of human knowledge, caused by the contingency of reality. Probability theory is an epistemic concept. It is a theory that describes how valid inference can be reached. The application of this theory is, depending on, which kind of theory of probability is used, limited to particular circumstances. The axioms underlying any kind of theory of probability are producing internal rationality, which is used as a legitimisation for the conclusions of the theory. The conclusions of any type of probability theory, however, are neither false nor true and they do not allow for any claim about the nature of reality. The only thing that we can get from probability theory is internal validity. It allows us, given the limitations of the theory, to say, what is reasonable to believe about reality and future states of reality. Depending on which type of probability theory gets used, inference proceeds either inductively in classical or frequency (statistical) probability theory or deductively in logical or subjective probability theory.

Under the logical theory, probability is seen as a branch of logic. It is an extension of the deductive logic to the inductive case. The subjective approach defined probabilities as subjective degrees of belief of particular individuals. The classical theory defines probabilities as relations of favourable cases to possible cases. And the frequentialist theory sees probability theory as a mathematical science that allows deriving general laws from empirical mass observations.

The latest developments in the theory of probability were crucial for the creation of the Neoclassical Uncertainty Paradigm. Only due to the advancements in the subjective theory of probability, the development from rational choice to rational expectations was possible in economics. Though, economics has incorporated the idea of subjective probability calculus in the face of uncertainty, economists ignored almost all philosophical debates associated with the problem of probability and truth. Therefore, economics adapted a rather pragmatic and methodology driven ideal of uncertainty, which reinterprets situations of uncertainty as situations of risk. Consequently, the original dualism between risk and uncertainty has been suspended.

References

Anscombe FJ, Aumann RJ (1963) A definition of subjective probability. Ann Math Stat 34 (1):199–205

Arrow KJ (1974) The use of unbounded utility functions in expected-utility maximization: Response. Q J Econ 88(1):136–138

Aumann RJ (1977) The St. Petersburg paradox: a discussion of some recent comments. J Econ Theor 14(2):443–445

Bachelier L (1900) Théorie de la spéculation. Ann Sci École Norm S 3(17):21–86

Backhouse RE (2002) The Penguin history of economics. Penguin, London

Backhouse RE (2010) The puzzle of modern economics: science or ideology? Cambridge University Press, Cambridge

Bayes T (1763) An essay towards solving a problem in the doctrine of chance. Philos Trans R Soc Lond 53:370–418

Bernoulli D (1738) Expositions on the new theory on the measurement of risk

Bernstein PL (1998) Against the gods: the remarkable story of risk. Wiley, New York

Binmore K (2009) Rational decisions. Princeton University Press, Princeton

Blaug M (1992) The methodology of economics: or how economists explain. Cambridge University Press, Cambridge

Blaug M (2003) The formalist revolution of the 1950s. J Hist Econ Thought 25(2):145–156

Borel E (1924) A propos d'un traité de probabilités. Rev Philos 98:321–336

Borel É (1909) Éléments de la théorie des probabilités. Hermann, Paris

Caldentey EP, Vernengo M (2010) Modern finance, methodology and the global crisis. Real-world Econ Rev 52: 69–81

Carnap R (1950) Logical foundations of probability. Chicago University Press, Chicago

Colander D, Föllmer H, Haas A, Goldberg M, Juselius K, Kirman A, Lux T et al (2009) The financial crisis and the systemic failure of academic economics. Institute for the World Economy, Kiel

Cournot AA (1843) Exposition de la théorie des chances et des probabilitiés. Hachette, Paris

Daston L (1988) Classical probability in the enlightenment. Princeton University Press, Princeton

Davidson D, McKinsey JCC, Suppes P (1955) Outlines of a formal theory of value. Philos Scie 22 (2):140–160

de Finetti B (1929) L'invenzione della verità. R. Cortina

de Finetti B (1937) La prévision: see lois logiques, ses sourcessubjectives. Annales de l'Henri Poincaré 7:1–68

Fama EF (1965a) The behaviour of stock-market prices. J Bus 38(1):34–105

Fama EF (1965b) Random walks in stock market prices. Selected Papers Graduate School of Business at Chicago University, 16

Fama EF (1970) Efficient capital markets: a review of theory and empirical work. J Fin 25 (2):383–417

Fama EF, French K (2003) The capital asset pricing model: theory and evidence. Working Paper No.550. Center for Research in Security Prices

Fishburn PC (1970) Utility theory for decision making. Huntington, New York

Fishburn PC (1986) The axioms of subjective probability. Stat Sci 1(3):335–358

Fourcade M, Khurana R (2011) From social control to financial economics: the linked ecologies of economics and business in twentieth century America. Harvard Business School, Boston

Fox J (2009) The myth of the rational market: a history of risk, reward, and delusion on Wall Street. Harper Business, New York

Friedman M (1953) The methodology of positive economics. In: Friedman M (ed) In positive economics. Chicago University Press, Chicago

Friedman M (1976) Nobel memorial lecture, December 13. The University of Chicago

Friedman M, Savage L (1952) The expected-utility hypothesis and the measurability of utility. J Polit Econ 60:463–474

Friedman M, Schwarz AJ (1963) A monetary history of the United States. Princeton University Press, Princeton
Frydman R, Goldberg M (2008) Macroeconomic theory for a world of imperfect knowledge. Capital Soc 3(3):1–76
Gilboa I, Postlewaite AW, Schmeidler D (2008) Probability and uncertainty in economic modelling. J Econ Perspect 22(3):173–187
Gillies D (2000) Philosophical theories of probability. Routledge, London
Good IJ (1950) Probability and the Weighing of Evidence. Charles Griffin, London
Hacking I (1990) The taming of chance. Cambridge University Press, Cambridge
Hacking I (2006) The emergence of probability: a philosophical study of early ideas about probability, induction and statistical inference. Cambridge University Press, Cambridge
Hausman DM (1992) The inexact and separate science of economics. Cambridge University Press, Cambridge
Hayek FA (1945) The use of knowledge in society. University of Chicago Press, Chicago
Hayek FA (1968) Competition as a discovery procedure. Quart J Aust Econ 5(3):9–23
Hirshleifer J, Riley JG (1979) The analytics of uncertainty and information—an expository survey. J Econ Lit XVII:1375–1421
Hodgson GM (2011) On the limits of rational choice theory. World Econ J 17:1–16
Jeffreys H (1939) The theory of probability. Oxford University Press, Oxford
Jevons WS (1871) The theory of political economy. Palgrave Macmillan, London
Johnson WE (1921) Logic. Cambridge University Press, Cambridge
Kantor B (1979) Rational expectations and economic thought. J Econ Lit 17:1422–1441
Keynes JM (1921) A treatise on probability. Rough Draft Printers, New York
Keynes JM (1936) The general theory of employment, interest and money. Palgrave Macmillan, London
Keynes JM (1937) The general theory of employment. Quart J Econ 52(3):209–223
Kirman A (2011a) The crisis in economic theory. Rivista Italiana degli Economisti, SIE—Societa' Italiana degli Economisti 16(1):9–36
Kirman A (2011b) Complex economics: individual and collective rationality. Routledge, London
Kirman A (2014) Is it rational to have rational expectations? Mind and Society 13(1):29–48
Knight FH (1921) Risk, uncertainty and profit. Nabu Press, Charleston
Kolmogorov A (1933) Foundations of the theory of probability. Chelsea Publishing Company, New York
Koopman BO (1940) The axioms and algebra of intuitive probability. Ann Math 41:269–292
Kraft CH, Pratt JW, Seidenberg A (1959) Intuitive probability on finite sets. Ann Math 30:408–419
Kreps DM (1988) Notes on the theory of choice. Westview Press, Boulder
Kyburg HE, Smokler HE (1964) Studies in subjective probability. Wiley, New York
Kydland FE, Prescott EC (1977) Rules rather than discretion: the inconsistency of optimal plans. J Polit Econ 85(3):473–492
Kydland, FE, & Prescott, EC (1982) Time to build and aggregate fluctuations. Econometrica 50, 1345–1370
Laplace PS (1820) Philosophical essay on probabilities. Wiley, New York
Lawson T (1988) Probability and uncertainty in economic analysis. J Post Keynesian Econ 11 (1):38–65
Louca F (2007) The years of high econometrics: a short history of the generation that reinvented economics. Routledge, London
Lucas RE (1972) Expectations and the neutrality of money. J Econ Theor 4:103–124
Lucas RE (1987) Models of business cycles. Basil Blackwell, Oxford
Lucas RE, Sargent TJ (1979) After Keynesian macroeconomics. Federal Reserve Bank of Minneapolis Quart Rev 3(2):1–16
Lucas RE, Sargent TJ (1982) Rational expectations and econometric practice. University of Minnesota Press, Minneapolis, MN

Mandelbrot B (1960) The Pareto-Lévy law and the distribution of income. Int Econ Rev 1(2):79–106
Mandelbrot B (1961) Stable paretian random functions and the multiplicative variation of income. Econometrica 29(4):517–543
Mandelbrot B (1962) Paretian distributions and income maximization. Q J Econ 75(1):57–85
Mandelbrot B (1963a) The variation of certain speculative prices. J Bus 36(4):394–419
Mandelbrot B (1963b) The stable paretian income distribution when the apparent exponent is near two. Int Econ Rev 4(1):111–115
Mandelbrot B (2008) The (mis)behaviour of markets: a fractal view of risk, ruin, and reward. Profile, London
Markowitz H (1952) Portfolio selection. J Financ 7(1):77–91
Mascaro A, Meltzer AH (1983) Long- and short-term interest rates in a risky world. J Monet Econ 12(4):485–518
McCallum BT (1980) Rational expectations and macroeconomics stabilization policy: an overview. J Money Credit Bank 12:716–756
McCann C (1994) Probability foundations of economic theory. Routledge, New York
Meltzer AH (1982) Rational expectations, risk, uncertainty, and market reactions. In Wachtel P (ed) Crisis in economic and financial structure. Lexington, Lexington, pp 3–22
Menger C (1934) Das Unsicherheitsmoment in der Wertlehre Betrachtungen im Anschluss an das sogenannte Petersburger Spiel. Zeitschrift für Nationalökonomie 5(4):459–485
Mirowski P (1989) The probabilistic counter-revolution, or how stochastic concepts came to neoclassical economic theory. Oxf Econ Pap 41:217–235
Mirowski P (1992) More heat than light: economics as social physics, physics as nature's economics. Cambridge University Press, Cambridge
Mirowski P (2002) Machine dreams: economics becomes a cyborg science. Cambridge University Press, Cambridge
Mirowski P (2005) The contract research organization and the commercialization of scientific research. Soc Stud Sci 35(4):503–548
Moore GE (1903) Principia Ethica, Stuttgart (Reclam)
Moore HL (1914) Economic cycles: their law and cause. Macmillan, New York
Muth JF (1961) Rational expectations and the theory of price movements. Econometrica 29 (3):315–335
Nash JF (1950) The bargaining problem. Econometrica 18(2):155–162
Popper KR (1934) The logic of scientific discovery. Taylor & Francis, New York
Popper KR (1957) The propensity interpretation of the calculus of probability and of the quantum theory. In Korner S, Price MHL (eds) Observation and Interpretation. Buttersworth Scientific, London, pp 65–70
Radner R (1972) Existence of equilibrium of plans, prices, and price expectations in a sequence of markets. Econometrica 40(2):289–303
Ramsey FP (1926) Truth and probability. Ramsey (1931) The foundations of mathematics and other logical essays. Harcourt, Brace, New York, pp 156–198
Ramsey FP (1927) Facts and propositions. Harcourt, Brace, New York
Ramsey FP (1929) On a problem in formal logic. Harcourt, Brace, New York
Ramsey FP (1931) In: Braithwaite RB (ed) Mathematics and other logical essays. Harcourt, Brace, New York
Ramsey FP (1990) F. P. Ramsey: philosophical papers. Cambridge University Press, Cambridge
Runde J (1990) Keynesian uncertainty and the weight of arguments. Econ Philos 6(2):275–292
Salmon W (1967) Foundations of statistic inference. University of Pittsburgh Press, Pittsburgh
Samuelson PA (1965) Proof that properly anticipated prices fluctuate randomly. Ind Manage Rev 6:41–49
Samuelson PA (1977) St. Petersburg Paradoxes: defanged, dissected, and historically described. J Econ Lit 15(1):24–55
Sargent TJ (1986) Rational expectations and inflation. Harper and Row, New York

Sargent TJ, Wallace N (1975) "Rational" expectations, the optimal monetary instrument, and the optimal money supply rule. J Polit Econ 83(2):241–254
Savage L (1954) The foundations of statistics. Dover Publications, New York
Schumpeter JA (1934) The theory of economic development: an inquiry into profits, capital, credit, interest, and the business cycle (social science classics series). Transaction, New Brunswick
Shackle GLS (1955) Uncertainty in economics and other reflections. Cambridge University Press, Cambridge
Shackle GLS (1968) Expectations, investment and income. Oxford University Press, Oxford
Shackle GLS (1979) Imagination and the nature of choice. Columbia University Press, New York
Shackle GLS (1988) Business, time and thought: selected papers. Palgrave Macmillan, London
Skidelsky R (2003) John Maynard Keynes. MacMillan, New York
Smith V (1984) Experimental tests of an allocation mechanism for private, public or externality goods. Scand J Econ 86(4):468–484
Stigler SM (1986) The history of statistics: the measurement of uncertainty before 1900. Belknap Press of Harvard University Press, Cambridge
Stigler GJ, Stigler SM, Friedland C (1995) The journals of economics. J Polit Econ 103:331–359
Sugden R (1986) New developments in the theory of choice under uncertainty. Bull Econ Res 38:1–24
Taleb N (2007) Fooled by randomness: the hidden role of chance in life and in the markets. Penguin, London
Taylor JB (1979) Estimation and control of a macroeconomic model with rational expectations. Econometrica 47:1267–1286
Todhunter I (1865) A history of the mathematical theory of probability from the time of Pascal to that of Laplace. Macmillan, London
Venn J (1866) The logic of chance. McMillan, London
von Mises R (1919) Grundlagen der Wahrscheinlichkeitsrechnung. Mathematische Zeitschrift 5 (1–2):52–99
von Mises L (1950) Human action: a treatise on economics. Liberty Fund, Indianapolis
von Mises R (1964) Mathematical theory of probability and statistics. Academic, New York
von Neumann J, Morgenstern O (1947) Theory of games and economic behaviour. Princeton University Press, Princeton
Weintraub ER (2002) How economics became a mathematical science. Duke University Press, Durham
Woodford M (1999) Revolution and evolution in twentieth-century macroeconomics. Working Paper Princeton University, pp 1–32

Part II
Philosophies of Uncertainty

The Neoclassical Uncertainty Paradigm developed during the 1950s and dispelled the Fundamental Uncertainty view held by David Hume, Adam Smith and also Carl Menger. Even though the Neoclassical Uncertainty Paradigm became the dominate theory of uncertainty in economics in the following years, there still were lively, but rather elitist discussions of alternative conceptions of uncertainty in economics, which were much more in line with the uncertainty fundamentalists. Hereby I mean those economic thinkers,[1] who have argued that uncertainty is a fundamental source of economic problems. Their legacies were kept up by a, then, rather unknown group of young intellectuals,[2] who became some of the most famous economists of the twentieth century. Their fame, however, came in large parts from other lines of thought, then, those on uncertainty. Still, uncertainty, comparatively little discussed, is central to their legacies.

In this Part I unfold different philosophies of uncertainty in economics. The analysis shows, that uncertainty is both an ontological and an epistemological challenge to economics. Furthermore, the discussed approaches suggest, that the probabilistic modelling of uncertainty a la Neoclassical Uncertainty Paradigm, is both illegitimate and insufficient. Yet, the opponents of the Neoclassical Uncertainty Paradigm failed to establish a unified Fundamental Uncertainty Paradigm. The theoretical landscape is highly fragmented; therefore it is impossible to identify one particular Fundamental Uncertainty Paradigm and to discuss all Fundamental Uncertainty Approaches. I have selected the most significant approaches and decided to leave out those, which are kindred to the selected ones. Although they distinguish themselves from the selected approaches in facets the main findings and conclusions are rather similar and would not add anything to the argument put forward here (Rizzo 1979; O'Driscoll and Rizzo 1985). Also, I do not discuss

[1]E. g.: Hume (1738), Smith (1776) and Menger (1871).

[2]Most prominently Frank H. Knight, J. M. Keynes, Friedrich A. von Hayek and G. L. S. Shackle suggested alternative approaches.

particular techniques of modelling uncertainty or advancements of the Neoclassical Uncertainty Paradigm as they all fall short on the similar criticisms as the Fundamental Uncertainty Paradigm. The competing Fundamental Uncertainty Approaches share their fundamental rejection of subjective probability modelling of uncertainty and suggest that uncertainty is the fundamental source of all economic phenomena. Without uncertainty, they argue, there would not be any need for the science of economics as there would not be any economic progress, innovation or even markets and profit. Consequently, they share the conviction that uncertainty needs to become one of the prime assumptions of all economic thought.

Beside classical Fundamental Uncertainty Approaches, such as those of Frank H. Knight, J. M. Keynes, Friedrich A. von Hayek and G. L. S. Shackle, I also discuss modern theories of uncertainty economics. I focus on the Critical Realists Critique on the Neoclassical Uncertainty Paradigm and discuss sociological approaches to the problem.

References

Hume D (1738) A treatise of human nature. Biblio Bazaar, Charleston
Menger C (1871) Grundsätze der Volkswirtschaftslehre. Mohr Siebeck, Tübingen
O'Driscoll GP, Rizzo MJ (1985) The economics of time and ignorance. Blackwell, Oxford
Rizzo MJ (1979) Time, uncertainty, and disequilibrium. Lexington Books, Lexington
Smith A (1776) Wealth of nations: an inquiary into the nature and causes of the wealth of nations. Prometheus Books, New York

Chapter 6
The Origin of Profit

Once again, the concepts of uncertainty and risk underlying modern economic theory have their origins in Frank H. Knight's classical book *Risk, Uncertainty and Profit* (1921).[1] Knight was the first to clearly distinguish between risk and uncertainty as two distinct types of imperfect knowledge about the future, which have different implications for the functioning of the market mechanism. Yet, in economics it is commonly revered to Knight as the one who distinguishes between measurable risk and immeasurable uncertainty in terms of probabilities.[2] The classical quote given to verify this claim is the following:

> To preserve the distinction [. . .] between the measurable uncertainty and an unmeasurable one we may use the term "risk" to designate the former and the term "uncertainty" for the latter. (Knight 1921: 233)

This representation of Knight's concepts leaves out important aspects of Knight's thoughts about risk and uncertainty. I do not want to remove the distinction between the two concepts, yet, I want to show that the difference goes far beyond the availability of numerical probabilities. Furthermore, Knight's theory of uncertainty questions the economic theory of the individual and gives much more freedom to the individual, than neoclassical economic theory would allow before. It is therefore the aim of this chapter to show that the classical interpretation of Knight's distinction between risk and uncertainty is too narrow.

---

[1]The book was published based on Knight's dissertation from 1916.

[2]Consider for example the following quote by Friedman (1976: 282): "In his seminal work, Frank Knight drew a sharp distinction between risk, as referring to events subject to a known or knowable probability distribution, and uncertainty, as referring to events for which it was not possible to specify numerical probabilities." Also other prominent economists claim that the difference between risk and uncertainty is in the availability of numerical probabilities, E.g.: Hirshleifer (1970: 215).

J. Köhn, *Uncertainty in Economics*, Contributions to Economics,
DOI 10.1007/978-3-319-55351-1_6

I will argue that the distinction is not about the availability of probabilities but about the limits of human knowledge.

Knight shows that profit arises because competition is not perfect. The reason is that knowledge is imperfect or put differently, that there is uncertainty. While some individual knowledge imperfections may be overcome, those, which characterise situations of risk, other, those which characterise situations of uncertainty, cannot be overcome. Different types of probabilities may be used in situations characterised by risk to deal with the bounds of knowledge by creating an apparent calculability of the uncertain. Yet, they are not able to overcome the bounds of human knowledge. Furthermore, Knight does not deny the availability of subjective probabilities in the face of uncertainty, yet he regrets that it would help to overcome the actual problem of uncertainty, namely that we cannot know the future.[3] This has consequences for the way men do decide in situations of uncertainty. Not rational calculus but intelligible, wise, creative and entrepreneurial decisions are the guide to action in situations of uncertainty. Knight, understands uncertainty as a fundamental condition for economic problems and argues that both profits and losses are the necessary consequence of this Fundamental Uncertainty. These hypothesises will be substantiated in the remainder of the chapter.

This chapter will help to place the distinction between risk and profit in the right context. Secondly, I will investigate the sources of risk and uncertainty, namely the limits of human knowledge, which classifies uncertainty as an epistemological problem. Thirdly, Knight's trigonomical theory of probability, which distinguishes between a priori probabilities, statistical probabilities and estimates, will be presented and linked to Knight's theory of limited knowledge. It will be shown that a subjective theory of probability is applicable in Knight's framework, yet it is useless to overcome the bounds of human knowledge, as Knight doubts the key assumption of complete randomness. Furthermore, Knight underlines the creative aspect of economic action and argues that therefore, even if the epistemological challenges could be solved, economic actions would still be surrounded by uncertainty, because uncertainty is part of the economic ontology and cannot be overcome.

---

[3]A similar argument had been put forward by LeRoy and Singell (1987: 396). They show that the subjective approach to probabilities as it had been argued for by Savage (1954) and others is unifiable with Knight's concepts of risk and uncertainty, however misses the central thesis of Knight's book. They argue (p. 396): "Rather, Knight designated by risk situations in which insurance markets do exist an by uncertainty situations in which they do not. His discussion of uncertainty provides a striking anticipation of the modern treatment of market failure." Though I do not share their interpretation that the difference between risk and uncertainty is in the availability of insurance markets, their conclusion is right, that the book is neither about the existence or possibility for subjective probability, nor would Knight except subjective probabilities as means to overcome the very problem of uncertainty.

6.1 Uncertainty and Profit

The purpose of Knight's book was to explain profit, and not to define risk and uncertainty. His PhD supervisor Alvin S. Johnson expected his student to clear away the disagreement that surrounded the contemporary economic theory of profit. Knight was supposed to develop a theoretical basis of the excising view on profit and to integrate it with marginal productivity theory (Emmett 2009: 31). Johnson (1952: 227) trusted in the brilliant analytical and theoretical skills of his student Knight, while being aware that he offered him an ambitious project. The persisting debate about Knight's dissertation still today suggests that Johnson was correct. Yet, it has to be admitted that there is disagreement and dispute about what Knight actually wanted to say in his book, as well as about the quality of his analysis. Emmett (2009: 47) therefore concludes: "A confused book? Perhaps. A paradoxical book? Certainly. But these paradoxes lie its therapeutic strength. [...] Though Knight's thoughts are not always well developed and put forward in a rigorous and clear style, his core thesis is still relevant."

It is the aim of this section to present Knight's core thesis. I will argue that Knight's account of risk and uncertainty is a sidestep on his way to explain profit. While "Risk, Uncertainty and Profit" is today mainly quoted with reference to the stochastic distinction between risk and uncertainty, Knight's original insight was about the relationship between the limits of human knowledge and the potential for profit. In order to substantiate my theses, let me now shortly summarise the argument Knight puts foreword in his book. Knight starts out by presenting the theory of perfect competition, which is, according to him, the dominant view by the time he was writing his dissertation (p. 51 ff.). According to the theory of perfect competition, there is no profit because the value of a good or price equals its costs (p. 91). He dedicated the whole second part of his dissertation to explicating the assumptions underlying the theory of perfect competition and discussing the economic as well as political consequences of them (Cf. Knight 1921: Chaps. III; IV; V; VI) and (p. 19) concludes that the theory is fundamentally flawed because it is unable to explain profit as one important phenomenon of real economic activity and states: "The problem of profit *is* in fact this very problem of the divergence of actual business conditions from the theoretical assumptions of perfect competition."[4]

The central assumption of the theory of perfect competition is, according to him, that of perfect knowledge (p. 199).[5] It is this assumption, which explains the difference between theoretical competition and real competition, namely the

[4]Italic is in the original.

[5]E. g.: "If we are to understand the workings of the economic system we must examine the meaning and significance of uncertainty; and to this end some inquiry into the nature and function of knowledge itself is necessary." (Knight 1921: 199)

existence of profit (Knight 1921: 51).[6] In real economies human knowledge is limited and therefore imperfect, which leads to the effect, that the conditions of competition are not certain, but uncertain. This uncertainty is the cause and ground of profit in Knight's theory (Cf. Emmett 2009: 41–43). The central thesis of "Risk, Uncertainty and Profit" can therefore be summarised as follows:

> The general nature of the conclusion may be stated at the [outset]. [. . .] It is that perfect competition depends on perfect knowledge. All the essential elements of current industrial society may be present without destroying the ideal no-profit resultant of competitive forces. The one fatal element is *uncertainty*, the imperfection of the knowledge upon which economic conduct is based.[7] (Knight 1916: 9, quotes in Emmett 2009: 42)

Perfect knowledge and perfect competition are contrasted with imperfect knowledge and imperfect competition. And it is imperfect knowledge that leads to imperfect competition, which again opens the possibility for profit.[8] Human knowledge is assumed to be imperfect in the way that the future will be different than the past, but it is unknown in the present how it will differ. However, this does not imply that Knight assumes complete ignorance about the future (p. 198f.):

> Even though the business man could not know in advance the results of individual ventures, he could operate and base his competitive offers upon accurate foreknowledge of the future if quantitative knowledge of the probability of every possible outcome can be had.

Knight, at the same time denies the availability of perfectly correct probabilistic knowledge of the future. To him this could be the only explanation for the imperfection of market clearing. If probabilistic knowledge about the future would be perfect, any profit or loss would be impossible. The degree in which the expectations about the future converge with the actual realisation of the future, determine the levels of profit or loss. This suggests that Knight had a differentiated concept of knowledge in mind, with perfect knowledge on the one side of the spectrum and uncertainty on the other side of the spectrum.

Based on the assumptions of imperfect knowledge and competition Knight concludes that profit is the reward the entrepreneur gains for bearing uncertainty:

---

[6]See also Knight (1921: 19): "Hence, the study of profit [...] and of the forces and conditions which give rise to it, is the study of the contrast between the ideal situation presupposed in economic theory on the one hand and real economic life on the other."

[7]Italic is in the original.

[8]The following quote summarizes Knight's line of argument (p. 197f.): "For profit arises from the fact that entrepreneurs contract for productive services in advance at fixed rates, and realize upon their use by the sale of the product in the market after it is made. Thus, the competition for productive services is based upon anticipation. The price of the productive services being the costs of production, changes in conditions give rise to profit by upsetting anticipations and producing a divergence between costs and selling price, which would otherwise be equalized by competition. If all changes were to be taken place in accordance with invariable and universally known laws, they could be foreseen for an indefinite period in advance of their occurrence, and would not upset the perfect apportionment of product values among the contributing agencies, and profit (or loss) would not arise. Hence it is our imperfect knowledge of the future, a consequence of change, not change as such, which is crucial for the understanding of our problem."

"It is this true uncertainty which [...] given the characteristics from of 'enterprise' to economic organizations as a whole and accounts for particular income of the entrepreneur." (p. 232) This is the case because 'true uncertainty' is defined as a state in which potential hazards cannot be insured against, because expectations are not reliable enough to find anybody to provide insurance.

Furthermore, there are cases in with the potential for potential hazards are unknown, so that there is not even a chance to protect against. Entrepreneurs are constantly in the situation that they have to take decisions in the face of true uncertainty. For example, if an entrepreneur develops a new product, (s)he cannot know whether the customers are going to buy it or not. Furthermore, (s)he would not find anybody who would offer an insurance at an attainable price against the possibility that the new product is going to be a flop. Nevertheless, the entrepreneur believes that developing the new product is a valuable decision. If the conviction holds and the product becomes a bestseller, the entrepreneur is going to make profit. If it is a flop the entrepreneur will suffer losses. While risk is a form of limited knowledge that causes hazards, businesses can protect themselves against by buying insurance on the insurance market, businesses cannot protect themselves against the hazards following from true uncertainty, which is also characterised by limited knowledge.[9]

How come those businesses are assumed to be able to protect themselves against risks, but not against true uncertainty? Under conditions of risk, knowledge is limited, yet there are functioning insurance markets, which provide guarantees that allow the businesses to hedge against the hazard for a certain price. Uncertainty is turned into certainty for the buyer of the insurance, which can be a security bond or a fire insurance, while the uncertainty is turned over to the insurer. This instrument shifts the uncertainty, yet it does not eliminate it in the end. This mechanism allows translating the consequences of the imperfect knowledge into the cost structure of the company (Esposito 2007). Consequently, the company is able to identify the costs correctly and thus take the decisions, which allow the market mechanism to work smoothly. In the case of true uncertainty, however, no insurance market exists, so that the above-described mechanism does not work and consequentially businesses cannot account for the costs. This breaks the market mechanism and allows for profits and losses.

6.2 Uncertainty, Knowledge and Probability

It is our next task to investigate the difference between situations of risk and uncertainty. One difference is that there are insurance markets in the face of risk, while there are none in the face of uncertainty. The reason for this difference seems

[9]LeRoy and Singell (1987) make the same point. According to them the existence or nonexistence of insurance markets make the difference between risk and uncertainty.

to have its origin the character of the limited knowledge. In order to identify the difference between the limited knowledge underlying risk and the limited knowledge underlying uncertainty, we have to examine Knight's theory of knowledge and the associated concepts of probability more closely.

Central to Knight's concepts of risk and uncertainty is the concept of limited knowledge. Under both conditions of risk and of uncertainty human knowledge is limited. Knight assumes that this limitation of knowledge hiders rational behaviour in situations of uncertainty, while it does not in situations of risk. In order to set light on this rather fuzzy theory, we have to have a closer look at the relationship between knowledge and decision making.

Knight (1916: 175; quoted in Emmett 2009: 42) argues that people can only behave rationally if they possess perfect knowledge:

> For perfect rational behaviour it is necessary for each individual to know that he does possess perfect knowledge and that all other individuals are similarly equipped.

This implies that a rational decision is based on perfect knowledge and on expectations about the behaviour of other individuals, which also possess perfect knowledge. Under these conditions people take rational decisions, which lead to efficient resource allocations. In situations of risk and uncertainty, knowledge is not perfect and so are the expectations about the choices of other individuals, which also possess limited knowledge. In such situations, choices may still be reasonable, yet they are not rational to Knight, because they lead by definition to inefficient allocations. This shows that the quality of knowledge available to the decision maker is significant for the efficiency of the recourse allocation, yet it does not explain the difference between risk and uncertainty emphasised by Knight.

Emmett (2009: 42) suggests that the difference lies in the quality of the limited knowledge. Under conditions of risk individual knowledge is limited, the market however provides additional knowledge, which had been discovered over the years by the public. This public knowledge seems to be something like the collective experiences of all men. Insurance companies use this knowledge to develop insurances that can be brought by the not perfectly informed individual. Then, public knowledge becomes incorporated into the individual's decisions via the price mechanism, as descried above. Furthermore, the decision-making individual expects, that the other individuals also possess this knowledge and take it into account, when making their decisions.

Consequently, the individual decision maker only possesses limited knowledge, yet (s)he has access to additional public knowledge and can form rational expectations about the choices of other individuals. This does not render the individual knowledge perfect, but allows for rational decisions under conditions of limited individual knowledge, which lead to almost efficient allocations.

In situations of uncertainty, in contrast, individual knowledge is limited and in addition to that there is no publicly available knowledge that may fill the knowledge gap. Consequentially, the individual has to decide based on his/her limited knowledge and the anything but perfect expectations. Knight points out that though the decisions are not rational and market allocations are not perfectly efficient under these conditions, decisions under conditions of uncertainty are not arbitrary. When knowledge is limited, the knowledge available just as the experiences and expectations has to be considered carefully, in order to make an intelligent decision. At this point, not economic calculus, but moral judgement and entrepreneurial spirit guide human action. By highlighting the importance of uncertainty for economic processes, Knight underlined the importance of creative and moral judgements by individuals. Emmett (2009: 43), therefore concludes: "True uncertainty does not leave the individual impotent; rather, it provides the occasion for the individual to draw upon their experience in a creative fashion in order to form the best and wisest judgement they can."

Knight turns against rational choice theory in situations of uncertainty, not because there are no probabilities available in situations of uncertainty, but because there is simply no rational basis for taking a decision because the future is unknown.

Technically, Knight distinguishes between the different qualities of knowledge by the availability or unavailability of certain types of chances. To complete Knight epistemological concept, we shall now shortly examine Knight's theory of probability and its interconnection with his theory of knowledge.[10]

From the above analysis, we know that knowledge is either perfect, and therefore certain, or imperfect and therefore either risky or uncertain. If knowledge is imperfect probability calculus, past experiences and general knowledge is applied as a strategy to handle the lack of knowledge, of which he wrote (p. 202):

> We do not perceive the present as it is and in its totality, nor do we infer the future from the present with any high degree of dependability, nor yet do we accurately know the consequences of our own actions.

Thus, even though probability calculus is considered to be a valuable technique to handle the consequences of our limited knowledge it is not able to overcome the limits of knowledge, neither in the case of risk nor in the case of uncertainty. The actual consequences of our actions remain unknown a priori. Nevertheless, it is according to Knight possible to form expectations about the consequences of our actions in the face of risk based on probabilities. There are two categories of probabilities that apply to situations of risk: a priori probabilities and statistical probabilities. In the case of a priori probabilities the chances can be computed based on general principles, while the future is still uncertain (p. 224):

> Absolutely homogeneous classification of instances completely identical except for really indeterminate factors. This judgement of probability is on the same logical plan as the propositions of mathematics (which also may be viewed, and are viewed by the writer, as 'ultimately' inductions from experience).[11]

---

[10]By the time Knight was writing about probabilities, the economists profession did not used this concept. Only 20 years later economists used probabilistic calculus into their theories and reasoning. A second economist, who was already concerned with the theory of probability, was J. M. Keynes in his Treaties on Probability (1921).

[11]Knight's view is similar to that put forward by the opponents of Classical Probability Theory. See also Sect. 5.1.1.

In the case of statistical probabilities on the other hand chances are calculated based on "[e]mpirical evaluations of the frequency of association between predicates [...]" (p. 225). These kinds of probabilities rely on the classification of instances. It is assumed that if instance *x* has happened in the past with a chance of *p*, *x* it will happen in the future with a chance of *p*. The only difference between the two types of probabilities thus is that classification in the case of a priori probabilities is really identical except for indeterminate factors, whereas the intermediateness of instances is limited in the case of statistical frequencies as it rests on empirical rather than on mathematical classifications of instances. The logic of computing probabilities, however, is similar according to Knight.[12] Both types of proximities compute the chances of an event *x* based on the reference class *B*. In the case of a priori probabilities a logical relation between *B* and *x* holds. A classic example is rolling a dice. The a priori chance to get a one is, if the dice is thrown once, is *1/6*. This relationship holds independent of the circumstances, as the reverence class is stable no matter what. It is more ambiguous to compute the chance of an empirical type probability. In the case of empirical probabilities, the reference class is not given logically. Instead it has to be defined. The chance of 'rain on Christmas Eve', for example, can be computed on the basis of the weather statistics on the 24th of December 20 years hence or since whether is casted. Depending on which reference class is taken the change will be slightly different. However, according to the law of large numbers this difference is negligible, as long as the sample is large enough. Nevertheless, the calculated probability does not tell us, if it is actually going to rain. It only helps us to assess how the weather could be. Knight objects to the argument that the two types of probabilities are similar on the basis of the law of large numbers, which implies the intermediateness of instances, if the number of empirical observations is large enough. In fact, it is impossible according to Knight to eliminate all factors not really indeterminate. Chances either based on a priori or statistical probabilities do not cover all unknown outcomes. He notes (p. 225):

> We act upon estimated rather than inferences, upon 'judgement' or 'intuition,' not reasoning, for the most part. Now an estimate or intuitive judgment is somewhat like a probability judgement, but very different from either of the types of probability judgement already described [a priori and statistical probability].

In the case of estimates, he continues, "[...] there is *no valid basis of any kind* for classifying instances".[13] Though, subjective quantitative probabilities can be assigned in these cases they are still subject to uncertainty, as the existence of a probability, does not eliminate the fact that human knowledge about the future is limited. It is a valid strategy to handle the bounds of knowledge with the help of probability calculus. The existence of a rational basis to deal with the lack of knowledge does not eliminate it. In addition to that Knight admits that estimates or subjective probabilities or judgements as he also calls them "are 'liable' to err" (p. 225).

[12]This second category of probability measures is comparable to the frequentialist interpretation of probability. See also Sect. 5.1.2.

[13]Italic is in the original.

Hence it is clear that Knight distinguishes between three categories of unknown outcomes: a priori probabilities, statistical probabilities and estimates. Whereas the first two can be expressed in objective numerical chances, the last lacks any basis for objective calculation due to the lack of classification of instances. However, subjective probability calculus may be applied. Still, in all three cases, the outcome of a decision is unknown or uncertain and therefore ontological in nature. This influences human life in general and especially business decisions as this example given by Knight (p. 226) shows:

> A manufacturer is considering the advisability of making a large commitment in increasing the capacity of his works. He 'figures' more or less on the proposition, taking account as well as possible of the various factors more or less susceptible of measurement, but the final result is an 'estimate' of the probable outcome of any proposed course of action. What is the 'probability' of error (strictly, of any assigned degree of error) in the judgement? It is manifestly meaningless to speak of either calculating such a probability a priori or of determining it empirically by studying a large number of instances. The essential and outstanding fact is that the 'instance' in question is so entirely unique that there are no other or no sufficient number to make it possible to tabulate enough like it to form a basis for any inference of value about any real probability in the case we are interested in. The same obviously applies to the most of conduct and not to business decisions alone.

Probabilities may be a guide to action if outcomes are uncertain, however, probabilities, at least all types of probabilities that are not a priori probabilities, are still only estimates and never probabilities never create certainty.[14] Furthermore, the existence of any type of probabilities does not affect the bounds of human knowledge, which are the fundamental problem of uncertainty and not the lack of objective probabilities (Cf. Jeffreys 1961; Shapiro 1983; Daston 1987, 1988; Krüger 1989). This conclusion, similar to some other conclusions of the above analysis are in opposition to what is commonly subsumed under Knight's distinction between risk and uncertainty.

6.3 Uncertainty, Change and Instability

Now, I want to draw attention to the impact of uncertainty, change, creativity and innovation that shapes the epistemological agenda underlying Knight's theory. Ahead of his time, Knight doubted the deterministic worldview underlying neoclassical economics. Instead he thought of the economy as an open and complex system which changes constantly in a way we cannot predict.

[14]Only insurance instruments possess the power to turn uncertainty into certainty for the insurance taker, yet the limitedness of human knowledge still exists. In this way uncertainty gets commoditised and the market mechanism is used to find the price for this commodity. Sometimes the price is correct, than there are no profits and sometime the price is incorrect, which causes profits or losses.

Unlike most economists of his time, Knight assumes that the world and particularly the business world is subject to unpredictable change. This assumption fundamentally questions the deterministic worldview, according to which it would be possible to take rational decisions, if only human knowledge were not limited. Knight opposed to that and assumed that the world of tomorrow is created by our actions today in a way we do not know and therefore the future it is by definition today unknowable (Knight 1921: Chap. XI). I refer to this view as ontological uncertainty, because Knight assumes that uncertainty is embedded in the very nature or structure of our economic reality and not solely a result of the cognitive limitations of human actors in the economy, which represents the epistemological side of uncertainty.

To Knight, uncertainty is both epistemological and ontological in nature. While theories of probability and hedging can be used to overcome, or limit the problem of epistemological uncertainty, any probabilistic instruments are insufficient for meeting the challenges of ontological uncertainty. The subjective theory of probability is an epistemological instrument, which assumes that situations of ontological uncertainty can be handled similar to or "*as if*" they were situations of epistemological uncertainty. Knight warns us, that this strategy is insufficient, as probabilities in general and particularly subjective probabilities are "liable to err". Consequently, the Neoclassical Uncertainty Paradigm as a general theory of uncertainty must be rejected on the basis of Knight. The neoclassical theory of uncertainty is a partial one, which only accounts for situations of epistemological uncertainty. Furthermore, following Knight's thoughts we must expect that even though it allows for a probabilistic treatment of uncertainty, the future may realise itself in a different way the probabilities, which are in most cases degrees of belief calculated on the basis of some rationality axioms, may suggest. To Keynes, the source of uncertainty lays in the nature of the real—nonergodic—world. It had to do, not only—or primarily—with the epistemological fact of us not knowing the things that today are unknown, but rather with the much deeper and far-reaching ontological fact that there often is no firm basis on which we can form quantifiable probabilities and expectations.[15]

6.4 Conclusion

Frank H. Knight is often referred to as the originator of the risk and uncertainty dichotomy in economics. Beyond that, many economics textbooks define uncertainty as subjective probability with reference to him (e.g. Mankiw 2001; Samuelson and Nordhaus 2009; Acemoglu et al. 2014). The analysis of his original text, however suggests, a different reading, which is in strong opposition to the mainstream interpretation. Knight, did not rejected the possibility of subjective

[15]E. g.: "The historic problem of thought is this of *real* change. The point for us here is that change according to known law (whether or not we call it change) does not give rise to uncertainty." (Knight 1921: 313) Italic is in the original.

probability calculus in the face of uncertainty. Instead, he suggested that it would be meaningless, because it is not able to overcome the limits of human knowledge and the uncertainty brought about by the creative nature of economic action. To Knight, uncertainty, is both a fundamental epistemological challenge as well as inherent to economic ontology. Furthermore, uncertainty is the explanation for fundamental economic phenomena and the source of economic progress. No type of probability that had been discussed in the first part of this book, is to him, sufficient to overcome the knowledge problem nor to express the consequences of uncertainty in any economic theory, as it distorts its nature. Albeit, he does not neglect that probabilistic information might be successfully used in day to day business, yet, this is no legitimation for subjective probability theory to become the fundament of most modern economic theories.

References

Acemoglu D, Laibson D, List J (2014) Economics. Pearson, Upper Saddle River, NJ
Daston L (1987) The probabilistic revolution. MIT Press, Cambridge
Daston L (1988) Classical probability in the enlightenment. Princeton University Press, Princeton
Emmett R (2009) Frank Knight and the Chicago school in American economics. Routledge, London
Esposito E (2007) Die Fiktion der wahrscheinlichen Realität. Suhrkamp, Berlin
Friedman M (1976) Nobel memorial lecture, December 13. The University of Chicago
Hirshleifer J (1970) Investment, interest, and capital. Prentice Hall, Englewood Cliffs
Jeffreys H (1961) The theory of probability. Oxford University Press, Oxford
Johnson AS (1952) Piokneer's progress: an autobiography. Viking Press, New York
Knight FH (1921) Risk, uncertainty and profit. Nabu Press, Charleston
Krüger L (1989) The probabilistic revolution. MIT Press, Cambridge
LeRoy S, Singell L (1987) Knight on risk and uncertainty. J Polit Econ 95:394–406
Mankiw GN (2001) Principles of economics. Harourt, New York
Samuelson A, Nordhaus (2009) Economics, McGraw-Hill International Editions. Mcgraw-Hill Higher Education
Savage L (1954) The foundations of statistics. Dover Publications, New York
Shapiro B (1983) Probability and certainty in seventeenth-century England: a study of the relationships between natural science, religion, history, law and in literature. Princeton University Press, Princeton

Chapter 7
Uncertainty and Economic Instability

Uncertainty is a central topic in Keynes' "General Theory of Employment, Interests and Money" (1936), but also his dissertation "A Treaties on Probability" (1921) empathises the importance of uncertainty in social systems. Here he argued that social life is aleatory and yet not random. This implies that social systems (of which the economy is part) cannot in general yield certainty because they are open and organic (Chick 2003; Chick and Dow 2005). This means that structures and interrelations evolve in such a way that the past is a very limited guide to the future (Lawson 1988; Dow 2002, 2003). Therefore, Keynes doubts that rational probability calculations are particularly helpful in the social realm. Keynes' early rather philosophical thoughts on uncertainty strongly influenced his economics and became central to his legacy. Some, among them Skidelsky (2010: 83), have claimed that: "Uncertainty pervades Keynes' picture of economic life. It explains why people hold savings in liquid forms, why investment is volatile, and why the rate of interest doesn't adjust savings and investment. It also explains why economic progress throughout history has been so slow and fitful. All the actors in his (Keynes') drama are motivated to a greater or less extent by uncertainty about the future, and regard the possession of money, or liquidity, as an important way of coping with it. Uncertainty breaks the tight link between supply and demand assumed by Say's Law.[1]"

Following this line of thinking, uncertainty seems to be central to Keynes' analytical framework to economics (Weintraub 1975). The roots of uncertainty lay in Keynes' philosophy and his early years in Cambridge. It has been argued that Keynes had devoted all his spare time between 1906 and 1911 to the development of his theory of probability (Harrod 1990: 133; Skidelsky 2003: 283). His thoughts

[1]Say (1880: 138) had argued that demand necessarily equals supply: "A product is no sooner created, than it, from that instant, affords a market for other products to the full extent of its own value." And continues: "As each of us can only purchase the productions of others with his own productions—as the value we can buy is equal to the value we can produce, the more men can produce, the more they will purchase."

J. Köhn, *Uncertainty in Economics*, Contributions to Economics,
DOI 10.1007/978-3-319-55351-1_7

of that time were later published under the name "A Treaties on Probability" (1921). Herein he developed his concept of uncertainty.[2] He used this concept in his "General Theory" (1936), and prominently in his article, "A General Theory of Employment" (1937).[3]

Uncertainty is omnipresent in Keynes' legacy. Here I focus on three fundamental aspects. Firstly, I discuss his theory of knowledge, which is interwoven with his already presented thoughts on probability (Sect. 5.1.3). Secondly, I focus on his account of reasonable choice under conditions of uncertainty. Thirdly, I present his rejection of general theory in the face of uncertainty. The analysis shows that Keynes rejects an abstract and probability based positive science of economics for epistemological and ontological reasons. He suggests a model of reasonable choice in the face of uncertainty that integrates conventional knowledge, psychological aspects (like what he calls animal spirits) and logical reasoning as a basis for economic action in the face of uncertainty.

7.1 Knowledge and Ignorance

Neoclassical microeconomic theory usually assumes that the world surrounding economic decisions is certain. Agents have full knowledge about this world or at least about the part of the world relevant to their decisions. Furthermore, agents know their preferences and decide according to the axioms of rational choice theory and maximize their utility. Keynes' understanding of the world surrounding economic decisions deviates from this sketch of the neoclassical world, fundamentally. He assumes that the world is uncertain rather than certain, which means that agents facing economic decisions do not necessarily possess knowledge about the facts relevant to their decisions, which would allow for a rational decision in the sense of neoclassical rational choice theory. However, the assumption that the world is uncertain also does not lead Keynes to the conclusion that every situation is uncertain. Rather, he distinguishes between different stages of certainty. In other words, one could also say that Keynes distinguishes between different degrees of uncertainty. Dequech (1999, 2000, 2001, 2003a, b, 2008) has argued that Keynes' accounts for four stages of the world. First of all, there is certainty, which implies that people have direct knowledge of the world. Secondly, the world is risky, which implies that people have probabilistic knowledge about the world. Additionally,

[2]By the time, Keynes was working on his first drafts of his "A Treaties on Probability", the topic of uncertainty also preoccupied Frank Knight and Friedrich A. von Hayek (Hutchison 2009).

[3]There seems to be an inconsistency between Keynes' theory of probability in "A Treaties on Probability" and his later economic writings. Some have argued, among them Bateman (1987, 1996), Davis (1994, 2003) and Gillies (2003), that Keynes changed his theory of probability later on in his life. In his "Treaties on Probability," he initially stated with a logical account, but later, he would adopt Ramsey's subjective account of probability. In what follows, I will initially focus on the logical concept of probability, which Keynes developed in his 1921 book.

Keynes distinguishes between two types of uncertainty; thirdly, epistemological and fourthly, Fundamental Uncertainty.[4] Epistemological uncertainty implies that all relevant facts are part of the world, only men are due to their limited cognitive abilities or due to their limited resonating power are not able to possess the relevant knowledge and therefore have to act on the basis of uncertainty. Fourthly, fundamental uncertainty implies that the relevant facts are not or not yet part of the world and therefore cannot be known.

While knowledge can be assessed directly, risk, epistemological uncertainty and Fundamental Uncertainty can only be obtained by arguments.[5] This is the basis for Keynes logical theory of knowledge, which interprets probability calculations as different forms of arguments, which can be used to gain indirect knowledge in a risky or uncertain environment.

By direct knowledge, Keynes refers to the knowledge people have "complete confidence" about, which refers to people's belief that the knowledge they possess is correct, regardless of whether the belief is true or false. In Keynes' framework (p. 9), people possess knowledge if they believe rationally:

> The highest degree of rational belief, which is termed certain rational belief corresponds to knowledge. We may be said to know a thing when we have a certain rational belief in it, and vice versa. [. . .] it is preferable to regard knowledge as fundamental and to define rational belief by reference to it.

Knowledge is thus defined as rational belief, and is therefore a property of human reasoning and subject to the individual. Certain or direct knowledge, however, is characterised by complete confidence in the rational belief. Therefore, when we speak of direct knowledge, we speak of a claim about reality which we believe to be certain and true. According to the concept of direct knowledge, knowledge is by definition true and obtainable by men. Keynes (1921: 12) describes the process of gaining knowledge as follows:

> We start from things, of various classes, with which we have, what I choose to call without reference to other uses of the term, direct acquaintance. Acquaintance with such things does not in itself constitute knowledge, although knowledge arises out of acquaintance with them. The most important classes of things with which we have direct acquaintance are our sensations, which we may be said to experience, the ideas or meanings about which we have thoughts and which we may be said to understand, and facts or characteristics or relations of sense-data or meanings, which we may be said to perceive;—experience, understanding and perception being three forms of direct acquaintance.

This indicates that knowledge evolves through conscious or unconscious reasoning based on facts. Thus, it is a subjective category linked to the objective world. Keynesian knowledge is based on evidence, though it is still a subjective property. Keynes (p. 12) gave the following example for direct knowledge:

[4]Fundamental uncertainty is identical to ontological uncertainty. Keynes and Knight thus identified similar stages of knowledge.

[5]E. g.: Keynes (1921: 1). "Part of our knowledge we obtain direct; and part by argument."

> From acquaintance with a sensation of yellow I can pass directly to a knowledge of the proposition 'I have a sensation of yellow'. From acquaintance with a sensation of yellow and with the meaning of 'yellow,' 'colour,' 'existence' I may be able to pass to a direct knowledge of the propositions 'I understand the meaning of yellow,' 'my sensation of yellow exists,' 'yellow is a colour' Thus, by some mental process of which it is difficult to give an account, we are able to pass from direct acquaintance with things to knowledge of propositions about the things of which we have sensations or understand the meaning.

Thus, direct or certain knowledge is the result of being acquainted with its content. Knowledge is the result of "individual experience," and one cannot speak of it absolutely. It is the property of a particular person (p. 17).

Although people possess direct knowledge in Keynes' concept of human knowledge, indirect knowledge dominates humans' body of knowledge. This is the part of knowledge "[. . .] we obtain by argument, and it treats of the different degrees in which the results so obtained are conclusive or inconclusive." (p. 3) An argument, or a probability relation, is a logical relation between two sets of propositions, where one cannot directly argue from one to the other (p. 9). Therefore, it is not possible to conclude from the existence of h that conclusion a will follow directly. Moreover, *a* and *h* are connected via a probability relation in which a is related to *a* given premises *h* via a probability relation or an argument. This is written: a|h = P· *A* being the conclusion, *h* the premises, and *P* denotes the probability in proposition or conclusion *a* gave the evidence or premises *h* (Lawson 1985a, b: 911f.). Indirect knowledge is thus the kind of knowledge we do not know directly, but by argument and only in probability. Though indirect knowledge is not certain, it is still rational and has some importance (Keynes 1921: 3). The probability expresses the degree of rational belief one has in the correctness of the relation. The weight of the argument is thus determined by the rational degree of belief one holds in its correctness. Therefore, the probability in *a*, given *h*, is "objective or fixed and corresponds to the degree of belief it is rational for a person to hold in the hypothesis given the information available" (Lawson 1985a, b: 911). Gillies (2003) points to the fact that the distinction Keynes made between "degree of belief" and "rational degree of belief" is crucial. While "degree of belief" is an entirely subjective concept that expresses the personal belief of one person in some conclusion, "rational degree of belief" implies that the degree is based on evidence and furthermore it is rationalizable by others. Keynes' logical theory of probability has thus to be distinguished from a purely subjective theory.

The discovery of new premises, h_1, leads to a new probability, P_1, and it does not cause the previous argument to be wrong. This shows that probability is not a feature of the world, but a property of how we think about the world. In this way, it is subjective to the extent that probability under this definition is a degree of belief that varies from person to person and time to time. However, it is not arbitrary, as preposition *a* and evidence *h* are observable directly.

Thus, Keynes distinguishes between direct knowledge and indirect knowledge. While direct knowledge is certain, indirect knowledge is only possessed probabilistically. Probability, under the logical theory of probability applied by Keynes, is degree of belief based on direct observable facts. The more one believes that certain knowledge is true, given the evidence, the higher the probability is in it.

Along the same lines, it has been indicated that Keynes assumed that both forms of knowledge (direct and indirect) lead to rational behaviour. Underlying this claim is the assumption that any kind of behaviour based on reason is rational. Reasoning, however, depends on the existence of knowledge. Even if uncertainty is assumed, knowledge under Keynes' subjective framework of knowledge exists. Therefore, it is possible to behave rationally according to Keynes' concept of rationality even if uncertainty is assumed. This concept of rationality deviates fundamentally from standard microeconomic theories of rationality.

7.2 Uncertainty and Reason

According to what has been said, one can speak of certain knowledge if P equals one. Still, every kind of probabilistic knowledge entails some kind of direct knowledge about the preposition and/or the premises, which is certain by definition. Keynes pointed out (1921: 11):

> [K]knowledge of a proposition always corresponds to certainty of rational belief in it and at the same time to actual truth in the proposition itself. We cannot know a proposition unless it is in fact true. A probable degree of rational belief in a proposition, on the other hand, arises out of knowledge of some corresponding secondary proposition.

Uncertainty is a lack of certainty, which makes it impossible to make a probabilistic claim about some proposition a based on the evidence h. In the face of uncertainty, P is unknown. Keynes distinguished between the two different cases. The probability in the first case is "unknown to us through our lack of skill in arguing from given evidence. The reasoning power prevents our knowing what the degree is." (p. 34) In this case, the probability could be known if one could discover the relevant evidence. Keynes distinguished this case of epistemological uncertainty from a second type of uncertainty, which is in line with Dequech's idea of Fundamental Uncertainty (1999, 2000). His idea is that people are creative and change the world by their decisions. This constant change leads to the fact that some things cannot be known a priori as they will be the result of future actions, not yet knowable.

In the case of Fundamental Uncertainty, probabilities do not exist for two different reasons. Keynes claimed, "either in some cases there is no probability at all; or probabilities do not belong to a single set of magnitudes measurable in terms of common unit." (p. 35) In the cases of Fundamental Uncertainty, probabilities are thus either immeasurable or indeterminate.

It has been claimed above that people facing uncertainty and lacking probabilistic knowledge, are not ignorant and they also do not behave irrationally. In order to set light on this prima facie paradoxical claim, I will show how uncertainty does not lead to ignorance and that uncertainty does not abolish reason in Keynes' framework.

Keynes starts from the assumption that people's capacity to reason or to build arguments is not limited by the existence of uncertainty. Rather, the limits of human knowledge show their threshold in the face of uncertainty. If a situation is too complex for human reasoning power, people can no longer build an argument, but they are still able to reason as best as they personally can. The result of people's limited reasoning in complex situations is an indeterminable probability, and therefore it is similar to Keynes' concept of epistemological uncertainty.

The case of Fundamental Uncertainty deviates from this in the way that the relevant evidence cannot be found. Though people are neither ignorant nor foolish, they are incapable of formulating an argument because the relevant evidence is hidden by complexity, or it is only apparent in the future and therefore necessarily unknown in the present. The reason for Fundamental Uncertainty lies in the fact that "the future is yet to be created" (Dequech 2000), and not in people's limited reasoning power or knowledge. The distinction between epistemological uncertainty and Fundamental Uncertainty points to the fact that the inability of men to form an argument in situations of uncertainty, is not solely a problem of the human being, but a feature of the world. Thus, even if men would possess complete knowledge, as stated by rational choice theory, uncertainty would still be a problem as there are things, which are relevant, that cannot be known.

Thus, people facing epistemological uncertainty or Fundamental Uncertainty possess knowledge in general, and therefore, they are able to reason. Only their own lack of reasoning power or lack of evidence prevents them from forming an argument about a particular proposition. Similar to Lawson (1985a, b, 1988), I conclude that uncertainty does not imply ignorance, but limited knowledge. The limits of knowledge, however, strike one particular argument, hence not human knowledge in general. Beside this, Keynes did not assume uncertainty to be omnipresent, but an infrequent yet relevant part of reality, which is relevant in the present but can only be known in the future (Hutchison 1978; Meeks 1978; O'Donnell 1982, 1989, 1990; Machina 1987). After having established that people possess knowledge in a general form even if uncertainty is assumed, we can now turn to the question of how people do decide in the face of uncertainty under the Keynesian framework. Keynes suggests drawing back on *conventions* or *animal spirits*, when lacking knowledge and arguments about the particular decision in question.

7.2.1 Conventional Knowledge

Lawson (1985a, b: 917) shows that even though people cannot form an argument due to either epistemological or Fundamental Uncertainty, they still "have extensive knowledge of social practices of the society in which they find themselves, and that an important way (although not the only way) in which such knowledge is obtained (or at least modified) is through 'direct acquaintance' or, equivalently, through their own participation." People facing situations of uncertainty draw back on this conventional knowledge and use it as a basis for decisions as the following quote shows:

> [. . .] knowing that our own individual judgment is worthless, we endeavour to fall back on the judgment of the rest of the world which is perhaps better informed. That is, we endeavour to conform with the behaviour of the majority or the average. (Keynes 1937: 114)

According to Lawson (1985a, b, 1983), falling back on conventional knowledge can be interpreted as rational behaviour. Conventional knowledge has developed over time. The knowledge of mankind is aggregated in conventions, rules or norms. It is therefore rational to believe that this knowledge may be helpful if one does not possess direct knowledge about a situation, and it is also rational to act upon it (Levi 1986). Conventional knowledge is a kind of social knowledge, though men can only acquire it directly through social experiences. Conventional knowledge may also be described as joint expectations. Instead of drawing on once own subjective beliefs about a certain situation, people imitate each other's expectations. What follows is a shared subjective degree of belief of a group of people. The consensus about the shared degree of belief is reached by social interaction. Gillies (2003) argued that this kind of shared subjective degree of belief involves the notion of intersubjective probability. An intersubjective probability is a subjective probability, which is believed to be true not only by one individual but by a group of people. One could therefore argue that intersubjective probabilities are more reliable, as they are based on the knowledge and expectations of many, rather than pure subjective beliefs. On these grounds, it is legitimate to argue that following conventional knowledge, if personal knowledge is absent, is rather rational.

7.2.2 Animal Spirits

> Most, probably, of our decisions to do something positive, the full consequences of which will be drawn out over many days to come, can only be taken as the result of animal spirits—a spontaneous urge to action rather than inaction, and not as the outcome of a weighted average of quantitative benefits multiplied by quantitative probabilities. (Keynes 1936: 161)

The quote clearly shows that economic agents facing uncertainty are not able to make a decision based on rational choice theory. Instead, they make their decisions based on what Keynes called animal spirits. Animal spirits are according to Matthews (1984: 209), "[. . .] conceived by Keynes as a feature of human nature that serves to give a pervasive, positive impulse to investment." Furthermore, they allow humans to act in situations of uncertainty and make humans more than just neoclassical calculating machines. Since it is not sufficiently clear what these animal spirits are and how they allow humans to overcome the problem of uncertainty, considering the concept of animal spirits is necessary.

Keynes took the notion from Descartes and Hume (Matthews 1984: 211f.). Descartes used the term animal spirits to describe the forces that cause the movement of the human body by penetrating the nerves and muscles. Human willpower directs only the movement. Keynes commented in his notes on this explanation as "unconscious mental action".

According to Keynes (1936: 162), entrepreneurs have more likely than other individual intuitions they are acting upon. These intuitions help them to design flourishing businesses in the face of uncertainty. Also Dow and Dow (1985: 52) follow this interpretation. They described animal spirits as "business intuitions". To use these intuitions is, according to them, wholly rational. I share this characterization, due to the evolutionary character of animal spirits. The animal spirits are the product of evolution and therefore have been objectively tested by its relative helpfulness for the individual to survive in the process of natural selection. But the use of animal spirits is an unconscious mental action according to Keynes. This suggests that animal spirits are, contrary to Koppel's (1991: 205) interpretation, not irrational forces, but non-rational forces. Koppel is correct that people facing uncertainty are using intuitions rather than reason. Still, this does not imply that their actions are contrary to rationality and thereby irrational. I would rather argue that animal spirits fall out of the framework of reason and are therefore non-rational.

Thus, economic agents facing uncertainty cannot use rational choice theory, nor are they behaving irrationally. Based on this, there is no reason to argue that uncertainty leads to irrational behaviour. Instead, I would contend that in the face of Fundamental Uncertainty, people do behave non-rationally based on intuitions, feelings and instincts. In order to appraise Keynes' concept of behaviour against the criticisms of Lucas (1972) and Coddington (1976, 1982) the connection between rational behaviour, knowledge and different stages of uncertainty has to be inquired in more detail.

For economics, this implies that a theory of human behaviour under uncertainty is obligatory. The question now is whether the above-presented theory of uncertainty is compatible with economic rationality. Along these lines, it has been shown that Keynes assumed people to behave rationally, and even in the face of uncertainty, he rejected that people would behave irrationally. This leads to the presumption that his account of rationality deviates from the standard microeconomic models of rationality. The reason being that he claimed that people behave rationally even if choice according to rational choice theory is impossible. My impression, however, is that Keynes was not attacking the concept of rationality underlying economic thinking, but solely the numerical rational choice model underlying standard neoclassical microeconomics theory, as the following quote shows:

> Some cases, therefore, there certainly are in which no rational basis has been discovered for numerical comparison. It is not the case here that the model of calculation, prescribed by theory, is beyond our power or too laborious for actual application. No method of calculation, however impracticable, has been suggested. (Keynes 1921: 32)

His critique is two sided. On one hand, the model is restricted to certainty, which makes it unrealistic or even naive. And on the other hand, it is purely mathematical and therefore unable to account for situations without a numerical basis, namely Fundamental Uncertainty.[6]

Obviously, Keynes did not define rational behaviour as utility maximizing behaviour. For him, rational behaviour is behaviour according to reason. Reasoning is based on knowledge, which may be either certain, probabilistic, or uncertain. However, as long as people use the knowledge, even if it is limited and/or of a general kind, they behave rationally according to Keynes' account. This concept of rationality is highly subjective and Coddington (1982) was right in arguing that Keynes' model of human behaviour lacks an objective standard comparable to normative rational choice theory.

Even in situations involving uncertainty, people do possess knowledge in the form of conventional knowledge, thus behaviour does not become irrational under Keynes' concept of rationality. In addition to that, it has been argued that people acting on animal spirits behave non-rationally, as the reason for their behaviour lies outside the sphere of reason. Although, the neoclassical concept of rationality is logically consistent, it is no basis for the evaluation of human behaviour. I think the reason for this is that Keynes was not very interested in the rationality of human behaviour, but in the question of how people act on the basis of different kinds of knowledge (McKenna and Zannoni 2001: 335). Therefore, the merits of Keynes' account do not lie in the underlying concept of rationality, but in the fact that acknowledging uncertainty leads to different stages of knowledge. This, however, has an impact on human behaviour that goes beyond the analytical model of rational choice and leads to a model of human behaviour that integrates neoclassical models of human behaviour with institutional as well as behavioural and psychological accounts.

7.2.3 A Keynesian Model of Choice Under Conditions of Uncertainty

To Keynes, uncertainty was the central characteristic of the economy. Certainty, by contrast, as it was assumed by classical economics describes a special utopian case, which is not representative for economics. Instead he argues, that knowledge is limited to different degrees in the economy. This limits the potential for rational choice, in the way it is discussed in neoclassical economics. To Keynes both the

[6]Naturally, the second critique fails as soon as one introduces Subjective Bayesianism (or subjective probability theory). It assumes that individuals in circumstances of uncertainty have well-defined subjective probabilities. Thus, the numerical basis for rational choice theory is no longer missing. Decisions in the face of uncertainty become like choices involving risk. Decisions are based on a subjective rather than on an objective concept of probability. Consequently, modelling rational choice involving uncertainty did become unproblematic. Though the modelling issue seems to be solved today in the aftermath of expected utility theory (Savage 1954), the question remains whether people behave rationally.

classical and the neoclassical theory of choice are special cases, while the general case of choice, is choice under conditions of uncertainty.[7] This general case of choice is characterised by different degrees of knowledge, reaching from certainty to Fundamental Uncertainty. Different types of probabilities are of limited or no value to the decision maker and in most cases, they are indeterminable. Dow (2010: 6) argues: "It is therefore not possible to order all possibilities according to risk and uncertainty in a reliable way. Even if it were feasible to contemplate an identification of all future possibilities and complete orderings of these according to risk, the degree of uncertainty attached to these calculations is liable to discrete shifts according, not only to new information, but also how that information feeds back into the subjective knowledge system which generated the risk estimates."

Nevertheless, agents are also not assumed to be ignorant. Instead they possess individual knowledge, which includes facts and statistics. Furthermore, agents have access to a wide range of social knowledge, which includes customs, norms and rules of thumb. Now, in order to take a decision agents, form reasonable expectations based on these types of knowledge, in the way that they form a reasonable argument for a certain expectation, given the knowledge they have. The more reasonable the argument is, the more likely it is that the agent makes a decision based on this expectation. This procedure does not involve any form of probabilistic reasoning, instead agents form logically valid arguments, which is according to Keynes the only way to behave rationally if confronted with uncertainty. This argument building process is accompanied by what Keynes calls *animal spirits*. These animal spirits force the agent to act, even if knowledge is incomplete.

Dow (2010: 21–23) sums up Keynes ideas on reasonable choice as follows: "In considering rationality and the microfoundations issue in the light of Keynes' ideas, we have seen the centrality of uncertainty. For agents, uncertainty prevents a definitive complete ordering of assets (and possibilities more generally), such that decision-making must rely on additional input from social convention and from animal spirits. Since these are both liable to indeterminate discrete shifts, as well as mutual conflict, there is scope for market behaviour to be unstable in a way, which is very difficult to anticipate (as to timing, direction and degree). Such behaviour may well be reasonable [. . .]. At the same time, conventional understandings will reduce uncertainty and stabilise markets. But there may also be conflict with other social conventions prompting individual responses and a political response in the form of regulation. The knowledge base for individual decision-making is not homogeneous. The rationality implied for agents is more like something we could call 'reasonableness', avoiding the strict conditions for the mainstream notion of rationality which uncertainty precludes us from satisfying. This focus on the possibilities for knowledge for the individual has pointed us in the direction of

[7]E. g.: Dow (2010: 3): "By 'probability' Keynes meant logical probability, 'the various degrees of rational belief about a proposition which different amounts of knowledge authorize us to entertain'. Quantified probability based on frequency distributions was a special case; the general case was uncertainty, where even non-quantifiable (ordinal) probability may not be identifiable."

the social, in the form of social conventions. Uncertainty too is crucial for economists themselves in attempting to theorise about this non-homogeneous economic system, with its interplay between individuality and sociality. Given this subject matter, both deductive and inductive logic fall short, so that economists too must employ conventions as to how to proceed. While a dominant convention has been to seek one best, formal, general equilibrium model, this has created inconsistencies with actual behaviour, which is conditioned by uncertainty. The methodology which emerges from Keynes' theory of knowledge is instead a pluralist one, mirroring the multi-pronged approach he suggested we take to knowledge as agents."

Keynes was not thinking in terms of valid economic models or general theories of choice. Instead, he was doing economics from a practitioner's perspective. He introspected and speculated, how people and particularly entrepreneurs actually decide in uncertain economic situations. His answer is that they act based on, both, reason and intuition.

7.3 Uncertainty, Instability and Science

Finally, I will briefly focus on the consequences of uncertainty for the economy and economics. According to Keynes, uncertainty is a major force for economic phenomena, such as profit, unemployment, investment or saving. Furthermore, uncertainty can be used to explain economic slump. For economics uncertainty is highly problematic, as it questions the deterministic and mathematical methods as well as the potential for general laws in the sense of a positive science.

In the inter war period Keynes was a leading intellectual figure and a strong critic of the economic policy and theory of that time (Skidelsky 2003: 324). His General Theory was not only a theoretical economics book, instead he thought of it as the fundament for better economic policy (Backhouse 2010). During the time, Keynes was writing his magnum opus, the British economy was in deep recession and it appeared as if the British statesmen had no clue, how to explain this dilemma, nor had they effective political reforms in petto. Keynes made the attempt, both to explain the economic disaster and to offer political reforms, able to bring the economy back on track (Skidelsky 2010). Particularly, in his analysis of the economic downward spiral, uncertainty is a major source of explanation. According to Keynes, both the tendency towards hording money in a crisis as well as the sudden and excessive decline of effective demand, are caused or reinforced by uncertainty. Explaining the demand for money, Keynes writes: "The Precautionary—motive—To provide for contingencies requiring sudden expenditure and for unforeseen opportunities of advantageous purchases and also to hold an asset of which the value is fixed in terms of money to meet a subsequent liability fixed in terms of money, are further motives for holding cash." (Keynes 1936: 196)

This general motive for holding money extends during crisis, consequently the demand for money, as well as the rise in the interest rates. This leads to a further decline in investment and effective demand:

> Moreover, the dismay and uncertainty as to the future which accompanies a collapse in the marginal efficiency of capital naturally precipitates a sharp increase in liquidity-preferences- and hence a rise in the rate of interest. Thus, the fact that a collapse in the marginal efficiency of capital tends to be associated with a rise in the rate of interest may seriously aggravate in the decline in investment. (Keynes 1936: 316)

Once, these dynamic and self-reinforcing mechanisms got unleashed, political interventions become particularly difficult, because even if, politicians were able to fix the economic parameters like the interest rates, uncertainty still prevents the economy and its members from restarting economic activities like investment and consumption. The uncertainty concerning the future economic developments as well the feeling of insecurity evoked by the downturn, brings them in a state of inactivity and collective depression. Keynes (1936: 317), therefore, concludes:

> If a reduction in the rate of interest was capable of providing an effective remedy by itself, it might be possible to achieve a recovery without the elapse of any considerable interval of time and by means more or less directly under the control of the monetary authority. But, in fact, this is not usually the case; and it is not so easy to revive the marginal efficiency of capital, determined, as it is by the uncontrollable and disobedient psychology of the business world. It is the return of confidence, to speak in ordinary language, which is so insusceptible to control in an economy of individualistic capitalism.

In this way uncertainty is a central source and explanation for economic the slump and it plays a key role in the political framework of Keynes. Most political reforms, suggested by Keynes, means to fight the economic crisis aim, more or less directly, at the reduction of uncertainty, in order to restart effective demand. Yet, also in normal times, uncertainty plays a major role in Keynes theory of the economy. Most of his Chap. XII (The State of Long-term Expectations) on investment and entrepreneurial behaviour discusses the wise management of uncertainty.

Beyond these rather practical and theoretical insights, Keynes also discussed the role of uncertainty in the philosophy of the science of economics.[8] Already in his

---

[8]In a letter to Harrod, Keynes (1938) argued: "It seems to me that economics is a branch of logic, a way of thinking; and that you do not repel sufficiently firmly attempts a la Schultz to turn it into a pseudo-natural-science. One can make some quite worthwhile progress merely by using your axioms and maxims. But one cannot get very far except by devising new and improved models. This requires, as you say, "a vigilant observation of the actual working of our system". Progress in economics consists almost entirely in a progressive improvement in the choice of models. The grave fault of the later classical school, exemplified by Pigou, has been to overwork a too simple or out of date model, and in not seeing that progress lay in improving the model; whilst Marshall often confused his models, for the devising of which [b] he had great genius, by wanting to be realistic and by being unnecessarily ashamed of lean and abstract outlines. [. . .] Economics is a science of thinking in terms of models joined to the art of choosing models, which are relevant to the contemporary world. It is compelled to be this, because, unlike the typical natural science, the material to which it is applied is, in too many respects, not homogeneous through time. The object of a model is to segregate the semi-permanent or relatively constant factors from those which are

self-reflexive article "Am I a Liberal" Keynes (1925 [2011]: 311) discussed the scope of economics. Here he argued that it is the task of economics "[...] to combine three things: economic efficiency, social- justice and individual liberty. The first needs criticism, precaution, and technical knowledge; the second, an unselfish an enthusiastic spirit that loves the ordinary man; the third, tolerance, breadth, appreciation of the excellencies of variety and independence, which prefers, above everything, to give unhindered opportunity to the exceptional and to the aspiring."

Keynes, methodological point of view, was strongly influenced by his theory of uncertainty and a deep scepticism about the possibility for general laws in a dynamic social environment. In such a dynamic environment situations are hardly comparable and the auxiliary conditions change permanently and often in a way not observable, so that it is impossible to form comparable arguments, which are the logical precondition for an empirical science that aims at law-like generalizations (Skidelsky 2010: 84). The deductive alternative, on the other hand, is according to Keynes, analytically highly elegant, however, empirically irrelevant. To Keynes, similar to Knight and, as we shall see in the next chapter, Hayek, the classical or neoclassical economic theory was a special-case unattainable by the real economy and therefore irrelevant as a basis for political reform.

7.4 Conclusion

Keynes' early insights on uncertainty, from his Treaties on Probability, had influenced his economic theory, his philosophy of economic methodology as well as his policy recommendations, and therefore can be regarded as the key to Keynes' intellectual legacy. Skidelsky (2010: 83) sums Keynes' main conclusion up: "Under capitalism, uncertainty is generated by the system itself, because it is an engine for accumulating capital goods whose rewards come not now but later. The engine of wealth creation is at the same time a source of economic and social instability."

Following Keynes, we can therefore conclude that uncertainty is immanent to the economic system. Whereas the economic system subject to uncertainty and at the same time its source. Thereby uncertainty unleashes economic dynamics, which can have both positive and negative effects for the economy as well as the individual economic actor.

transitory or fluctuating so as to develop a logical way of thinking about the latter, and of understanding the time sequences to which they give rise in particular cases. Good economists are scarce because the gift for using "vigilant observation" to choose good models, although it does not require a highly specialised intellectual technique, appears to be a very rare one. In the second place, as against Robbins, economics is essentially a moral science and not a natural science. That is to say, it employs introspection and judgments of value". Harrod (1938) discusses Keynes concerns regarding the possibility of general laws in economics. For a complete reprint of the letter please, see http://economia.unipv.it/harrod/edition/editionstuff/rfh.346.htm (2014-07-03).

Furthermore, uncertainty renders any general economic theory impossible. There are no general laws that can be discovered by economists. Instead the economic system creates itself, its' norms and institutions and thereby constantly alters its conditions, in a way unknowable. This ontological uncertainty hinders not only predictability but also positive science. Instead Keynes suggests reasonable individual judgement on the theoretical level, in economic activities as well as in economic policy,[9] which is necessarily normative and non-rational. These judgements must alter, during the dynamic genesis of the economy and therefore presuppose reasonable and wise decision-makers[10] that adapt to new knowledge.

References

Backhouse RE (2010) The puzzle of modern economics: science or ideology? Cambridge University Press, Cambridge
Bateman BW (1987) Keynes' changing conception of probability. Econ Philos 3(1):97–119
Bateman BW (1996) Keynes' uncertain revolution. University of Michigan Press, Ann Arbor
Chick V (2003) Theory, method and mode of thought in Keynes' General Theory. J Econ Methodol 10(3):307–327
Chick V, Dow SC (2005) The meaning of open systems. J Econ Methodol 12(3):363–381
Coddington A (1976) Keynesian economics: the search for first principles. J Econ Lit 14 (4):1258–1273
Coddington A (1982) Deficient foresight: a troublesome theme in keynesian economics. Am Econ Rev 72(3):480–487
Davis J (1994) Keynes' philosophical development. Cambridge University Press, Cambridge
Davis JB (2003) The relationship between Keynes' early and later philosophical thinking. In: Runde J, Mizuhara S (eds) The philosophy of Keynes' economics: probability, uncertainty and convention. Routledge, London
Dequech D (1999) Expectations and confidence under uncertainty. J Post Keynesian Econ 21 (3):415–430
Dequech D (2000) Fundamental uncertainty and ambiguity. East Econ J 26(1):41–60
Dequech D (2001) Bounded rationality, institutions, and uncertainty. J Econ Issues 35(4):911–929
Dequech D (2003a) Conventional and unconventional behavior under uncertainty. J Post Keynesian Econ 26(1):145–168
Dequech D (2003b) Uncertainty and economic sociology: a preliminary discussion. Am J Econ Soc 62(3):509–532
Dequech D (2008) Neoclassical, mainstream, orthodox, and heterodox economics. J Post Keynesian Econ 30(2):279–302
Dow SC (2002) Economic methodology: an inquiry. Oxford University Press, Oxford
Dow SC (2003) Understanding the relationship between mathematics and economics. J Post Keynesian Econ 25(4):547–560
Dow SC (2010) Keynes on knowledge, expectations and rationality. In: Phelps ES, Frydman R (eds) Microfoundations for modern macroeconomics. Princeton University Press, Princeton, pp 1–28

[9]See also Minsky (2008: Chaps. VIII & IX).

[10]Priddat and Koehn (2014), suggest that Keynes as a dandy himself, imagines a well educated statesman as the ideal decision maker.

Dow SC, Dow A (1985) Animal spirits and rationality. In: Lawson T (ed) Keynes' economics: methodological issues. Croom Helm, London
Gillies D (2003) Probability and uncertainty in Keynes' the general theory. In: Runde J, Mizuhara S (eds) The philosophy of Keynes' economics: probability, uncertainty and convention. Routledge, London
Harrod RF (1938) Scope and method of economics. Econ J 48(191):383–412
Harrod RF (1990) The life of John Maynard Keynes. Easton, Norwalk
Hutchison TW (1978) On revolutions and progress in economic knowledge. Cambridge University Press, Cambridge
Hutchison TW (2009) A formative decade: methodological controversy in the 1930s. J Econ Methodol 16(3):297–314
Keynes JM (1921) A treatise on probability. Rough Draft Printers, New York
Keynes JM (1925) Am I a liberal? Essays in persuasion. W.W. Norton, New York
Keynes JM (1936) The general theory of employment, interest and money. Palgrave Macmillan, London
Keynes JM (1937) The general theory of employment. Quart J Econ 52(3):209–223
Koppl R (1991) Retrospectives: animal spirits. J Econ Perspect 5(3):203–210
Lawson T (1983) Different approaches to economic modelling [On Keynesian model building and the rational expectations critique]. Camb J Econ 7(1):77–84. Oxford University Press
Lawson T (1985a) Uncertainty and economic analysis. Econ J 95(380):909–927
Lawson T (1985b) Keynes' economics: methodological issues. Croom Helm, London
Lawson T (1988) Probability and uncertainty in economic analysis. J Post Keynesian Econ 11 (1):38–65
Levi I (1986) The paradoxes of Allais and Ellsberg. Econ Philos 2:23–53
Lucas RE (1972) Expectations and the neutrality of money. J Econ Theor 4:103–124
Machina M (1987) Choice under uncertainty: problems solved and unsolved. J Econ Perspect 1:121–154
Matthews RCO (1984) Animal spirits. Proc Br Acad 70:209–229
McKenna EJ, Zannoni DC (2001) Post-Keynesian economics and nihilism. J Post Keynesian Econ 23:331–347
Meeks JG (1978) Bray on Keynes on scientific method. J Econ Stud 5(2)
Minsky H (2008) John Maynard Keynes. McGraw-Hill, New York
O'Donnell RM (1982) Keynes: philosophy and economics, an approach to rationality and uncertainty. PhD Dissertation. University of Cambridge
O'Donnell RM (1989) Keynes: philosophy, economics and politics, the philosophical foundations of Keynes' thought and their influence on his economics and politics. MacMillan, London
O'Donnell RM (1990) The epistemology of J. M. Keynes. Br J Philos Sci 41:330–350
Priddat BP, Koehn J (2014) Keynes war ein Liberaler. In: Pies I, Leschke M (Hrsg) J. M. Keynes Gesellschaft. Mohr Siebeck, Tübingen
Savage L (1954) The foundations of statistics. Dover Publications, New York
Say JB (1880) A treatise on political economy or the production, distribution, and consumption of wealth. Batoche Books, Kitchener (This is an English translation of Say's Traité d'economie politique, first published in 1803)
Skidelsky R (2003) John Maynard Keynes. MacMillan, New York
Skidelsky R (2010) Keynes: the return of the master. Publicaffairs, New York
Weintraub RE (1975) 'Uncertainty' and the Keynesian revolution. Hist Polit Econ 7(4):530–548

Chapter 8
The Division of Knowledge and Unknowledge

Already in 1937 Friedrich A. von Hayek raised serious concerns about the economic perception of knowledge in his essay "Economics and Knowledge". In the following years (1942, 1943, 1944, 1945, 1968) he expressed himself in a series of articles about knowledge and the state of economic methodology and theory and even dedicated his 1974 Nobel speech "The Pretence of Knowledge" to this topic. The concept of knowledge is underlying his economic as well as his philosophical legacy. It is the glue that holds his thoughts about the economy, society and economic policy together. The criticisms he raised concerning the concept of knowledge underlying contemporary economic thinking were ahead of his time and precisely criticising different layers of economics. He split up the criticism in ontological and epistemological queries, discussions of economic methodology and theory as well as questions about economic policy. Additionally, he discussed the problem of knowledge with regards to statistics, creativity and rationality. His all-compassing treatment of uncertainty underlines the importance of the limits of knowledge in his legacy.

Hayek's student G. L. S. Shackle followed his mentor and emphasised the role of unknowledge in economics. Inspired both by Hayek and Keynes, Shackle developed a fundamental critic of probability-based uncertainty and suggested an alternative account. His non-numerical theory of uncertainty suggests looking for possibilities instead of calculating probabilities. The aim is to prevent surprises instead of making an optimal decision.

The chapter is organized in five sections. Initially, I focus on Hayek's theory of uncertainty. I discuss his concept of knowledge, which is constitutive for the nature of the economic problem, first. Then I turn to his theory of cognition and finally I present his account of the free market and the price mechanism as his solution to the knowledge problem underlying economics. In the following sections I concentrate on Shackle. First, I present his rejection of probability theory. Afterwards I discuss his non-numerical theory of uncertainty. The chapter shows, that there are alternatives to the probabilistic modelling of uncertainty in economics. Furthermore, it seems to be the case that the economy itself is an uncertainty solving mechanism

J. Köhn, *Uncertainty in Economics*, Contributions to Economics,
DOI 10.1007/978-3-319-55351-1_8

and that probability calculus is neither sufficient nor necessary to deal with the bound of knowledge in economics.

8.1 The Nature of the Economic Problem

To Hayek, the economic problem was essentially a problem of knowledge. Knowledge is according to Hayek always local or even personal. For one person, it is neither possible to know what another person desires or wishes, nor what the person expects. Furthermore, the knowledge about goods or services is also scattered. This implies that no single individual can know the price of a good before the person has entered in an information exchange with other individuals and found out about their ideas about the quality and desirability of the good or service. Here, we can deduce two fundamental assumptions Hayek makes. Firstly, he assumes that knowledge, which can be knowledge about goods, things, facts, feelings, expectations is never given fully to one single individual, even not if the knowledge only needs to be about a very particular subject. Secondly, he assumes that in order to serve ones needs and desires, people have to interact with each other and discover the knowledge needed to reach a desired end. Thereby knowledge is spread and yet not publicly available.

Hayek's concept of knowledge is highly situational and individual. He concludes that the origin of all economic allocation problems is the individual human limit of knowledge. Because people do not know and cannot know all relevant facts, even if they are particularly intelligent or ridiculously talented, it is necessary for human beings to interact with each other.[1] In this point Hayek goes back to Adam Smith famous demand, that economics needs to create mechanisms, which when used correctly, help everybody who uses them. Smith (1776) made an example about a butcher.[2] He said that in order to get a piece of meat, a person should not ask the butcher to give the meat for free, because then the butcher would be worse off. Instead the person should offer the butcher something in exchange that he desires and the person can do without. If this would be the case both the person and the butcher would be better off. Yet in order to find out what the butcher could desire, at least the two persons need to interact with each other and find out about their desires and the exchange relation suitable for both. Maybe they also

[1]Hayek (1968: 9) argues: "It would not be easy to defend macroeconomists against the charge that for 40 or 50 years they have investigated competition primarily under assumptions which, if they were actually true, would make competition completely useless and uninteresting. If anyone actually knew everything that economic theory designated as "data", competition would indeed be a highly wasteful method of securing adjustments to these facts."

[2]Smith (1774: I ii) writes: "It is not from the benevolence of the butcher, the brewer, or the baker that we expect our dinner, but from their regard to their own self-interest. We address ourselves not to their humanity but to their self-love, and never talk to them of our own necessities, but of their advantages."

have to ask other people what they think is a suitable price for the meet. The study of such phenomena is, following Hayek and Smith, the task of economics. In order to come to a valuable deal the person and the butcher need to exchange information about their needs and desires. Otherwise they would not be able to find a solution to their problem. The origin or nature of all economic problems is therefore for Hayek the general insurmountable incompleteness and imperfection of knowledge on the individual as well as on the social level.

> The peculiar character of the problem of a rational economic order is determined precisely by the fact that the knowledge of the circumstances of which we must make use never exists in concentrated or integrated form, but solely as the dispersed bits of incomplete and frequently contradictory knowledge which all the separate individuals possess. Hayek (1945: 519)

Earlier, Hayek (1937) discussed the role which assumptions and propositions about the knowledge given to the individual and society as a whole play in economic analysis. Already in this early publication, he argues against perfect knowledge about the present state and complete foresight about the future states of the world, while turning against the primacy of the mathematical method in economics and equilibrium analysis. In his view knowledge and foresight about present and future states may include information about relevant facts, which are objectively given as well as about expectations and desires of oneself and of other members of society, which are necessarily subjective. He argues that under equilibrium conditions, objective and subjective knowledge need to correspond in the way that individual or subjective perceptions of some fact or data need to equal objective facts (1968). Under this view the subjective perceptions of some data of one individual are part of the objective knowledge of other individuals. According to Hayek this is an illegitimate transition of subjective perceptions of data into objective facts. The equilibrium concept also implies that expectations and foresight need to be correct. These conditions have to hold on the large scale, yet also on the individual level. Hayek doubts the empirical correctness of this assumption.

However, his main point is the tautological structure of the concept. Hayek argues, that the assumptions of equilibrium economics already entail the conclusions, namely equilibrium conditions. This insurmountable logical fallacy renders equilibrium economics meaningless. Furthermore, equilibrium economics alienates economics from its original tasks because the situation in which equilibrium conditions are meet is of no interest for economists. Rather the opposite is the case. Economics needs to study situations of disequilibrium—situations in which, people's desires and expectations do not coincide.

For Hayek, the economic problem was essentially a problem of knowledge. Whereas equilibrium economics mainly focuses on the allocation problem and ignores the more fundamental knowledge problem. The knowledge problem however is more important and complex. Generally, one must distinguish between factual knowledge about the nature, which might be incomplete, wrong or meaningless and social knowledge. In the social realm, different to the natural realm knowledge is always ambiguous, while it might also be partial or meaningless.

Hayek's description of the economic realm and the economic problem implies that economics is always confronted with different types of information ambiguity and uncertainty. Wherefrom follows, that equilibrium is a very rare and meaningless state of the economy. Economics is the study of a permanent and mutable knowledge discovery procedure.[3]

8.2 Epistemology

Hayek not only turns against equilibrium economics, but also against an epistemological process in economics, which is similar to that of the natural sciences. He argues that the knowledge problem underlying economics is fundamentally social, so that the process of gaining knowledge about economic phenomena needs to be different than the process of gaining knowledge about natural phenomena. This difference also needs to be reflected in the applied methodology. Hayek therefore turns against abstract mathematical economic theories, which are according to him tautological.[4] The deductive method is inappropriate for solving economic problems, because the conclusion is always implicit in the assumptions, from which the conclusion is drawn. This would imply that the economic problem is a pure allocation problem, which can be solved by logical reasoning. Hayek does not deny the value of logical and reasonable thinking for solving economic problems.

[3]E.g.: Hayek (1937: 66): "Consider the preparations which will be going on at any moment for the production of houses. Brickmakers, plumbers and others will all be producing materials, which in each case will correspond to a certain quantity of houses for which just this quantity of the particular material will be required. Similarly we may conceive of prospective buyers as accumulating savings, which will enable them at certain dates to buy definite quantities of houses. If all these activities represent preparations for the production (and acquisition) of the same amount of houses we can say that there is equilibrium between them in the sense that all the people engaged in them may find that they can carry out their plans. This need not be so, because other circumstances which are not part of their plan of action may turn out to be different from what they expected. Part of the materials may be destroyed by an accident, weather conditions may make building impossible, or an invention may alter the proportions in which the different factors are wanted. This is what we call a change in the (objective) data, which disturbs the equilibrium, which has existed. But if the different plans were from the beginning incompatible, it is inevitable that somebody's plans will be upset and have to be altered, and that in consequence the whole complex of actions over the period will not show those characteristics which apply if all the actions of each individual can be understood as part of a single individual plan he has made at the beginning." He continues (p. 67): "There would of course be no reason why the subjective data of different people should ever correspond unless they were due to the experience of the same objective facts. But the point is that pure-equilibrium analysis is not concerned with the way in which this correspondence is brought about."

[4]Hayek (1945: 521): "It seems to me that many of the current disputes with regard to both economic theory and economic policy have their common origin in a misconception about the nature of the economic problem of society. This misconception in turn is due to an erroneous transfer to social phenomena of the habits of thought we have developed in dealing with the phenomena of nature."

Yet, he argues that pure logic cannot solve the economic problem, because it cannot account for moral judgements, learning and the limits of knowledge (Sprich 2009). The essential feature of the economic problem is that knowledge is incomplete and ambiguous and, therefore, rules out pure logical reasoning. Hayek (1945: 519) sums up:

> If we possess all the relevant information, if we can start out from a given system of preferences and if we command complete knowledge of available means, the problem which remains is purely one of logic. That is, the answer to the question of what is the best use of the available means is implicit in our assumptions.

Furthermore, deductive economic theory assumes that all the information relevant for a decision is given to the decision-maker. This assumption is in conflict with the nature of the economic problem, which is the incompleteness and ambiguity of knowledge. Hayek (1945: 519) argues: "The reason for this is that the "data" from which the economic calculus starts are never for the whole society "given" to a single mind, which could work out the implications, and can never be so given."

As an opponent of methodological individualism, Hayek takes the individual as the starting point of economic analysis. Yet, he does not strive for general laws of behaviour, nor does he claim that it is possible to derive the behaviour of a large crowd of people from the individual behaviour. His methodological individualism is rather different from that of equilibrium analysis. According to his view the economic problem is not static one, which can be observed directly, or examined in controlled experiments. The economic problem furthermore is not repeatable and it cannot be solved on the aggregate level.[5] The economic problem is a problem that can only be solved on the individual level. Only individuals can share information and find out about the motivations and desires of other market participants. Communication is always an individual process.[6] From this insight Hayek draws the conclusion that, if economics is a knowledge problem, it is an individual problem, which needs to be solved at the individual level. The main

---

[5]Hayek (1942: 289–290) gives the following example: "The physicist who wishes to understand the problems of the social sciences with the help of an analogy from his own field would have to imagine a world in which he knew by direct observation the inside of the atoms and had neither the possibility of making experiments with lumps of matter nor opportunity to observe more than the interactions of a comparatively few atoms during a limited period. From his knowledge of the different kinds of atoms he could build up models of all the various ways in which they could combine into larger units and make these models more and more closely reproduce all the features of the few instances in which he was able to observe more complex phenomena. But the laws of the macrocosm which he could derive from his knowledge of the microcosm would always remain "deductive"; they would, because of his limited knowledge of the data of the complex situation, scarcely ever enable him to predict the precise outcome of a particular situation; and he could never verify them by controlled experiment-although they might be disproved by the observation of events which according to his theory are impossible."

[6]It depends on the recipient of some information, how the massage is perceived. So even if we find ourselves in large social groups, it always depends on the individual, what he or she abstracts from a certain massage and how he or she uses this information.

task of economics therefore is to develop mechanisms, which allow people to communicate with each other, so that they are at least temporary and locally able to solve information problems and develop solutions to them. For Hayek, therefore highly sophisticated theories, which describe how people behave or should behave, are of little help. For him it is the task of the economist to provide the society with a knowledge transmission mechanism. Than the individuals will solve the economic problems themselves.

8.3 Uncertainty and the Price Mechanism

Hayek perceived the economy as a spontaneous order, which is neither chaotic nor totally deterministic or mechanistic, and which changes over time. Economic actors, therefore, necessarily possess limited knowledge, which is private, diverse and dispersed in society. These assumptions shape Hayek's convictions about the methods appropriate for the economic problem, which is to him the efficient allocation of recourses in society. In order to reach efficient recourse allocations, the scattered knowledge needs to be utilized. Hayek (1945) argues that only the price mechanism, which is central to Hayek's epistemological framework, is able to bring together local and dispersed knowledge in such a way that efficient allocations can be reached.

To Hayek the price mechanism is the most efficient information processing tool and his explanation for efficient market allocations (Streit 1993). To him the price mechanism and not individual rationality leads to efficient recourse allocations.[7] The problem that the price mechanism solves is not just a problem of allocation given recourses but how to use the recourses for some particular goals. The price mechanism discovers and creates new way of using the recourses and satisfying ends. It is not a pure logical or mechanical optimization machine but a creative institution.[8] For Hayek there is individual as well as social learning. Learning happens through trials over time. It is a dynamic and creative process as new and previously unthinkable and unknowable possibilities get discovered.

[7]Consider Hayek's (1945) thoughts in "The Use of Knowledge in Society": "The economic problem of society is not merely a problem of how to allocate 'given' resources [...] It is rather a problem of how to secure the best use of resources known to any members of society, for ends whose relative importance only the individuals know [...] it is a problem of the utilization of knowledge not given to anyone in its totality. The character of the fundamental problem has, I am afraid, been rather obscured than illuminated by many of the recent refinements of economic theory, particularly by many of the uses made of mathematics."

[8]E.g.: Hayek (1968: 9): "By contrast, it is useful to recall that *wherever* we make use of competition, this can only be justified by our *not* knowing the essential circumstances that determine the behaviour of the competitors."

Markets are often failing. This is part of the discovery procedure.[9] Market processes are not perfect, yet there are the best way to discover relevant information and find out what works ad what does not. One cannot expect from the market mechanism to provide stability and perfect allocations. The market mechanism is the best test society has for the application of certain tools, legal orders and institutions. One can learn from the market mechanism, concepts can proof themselves in competition and the market mechanism will show, if the concept is working well in the period, when it is tested.[10] This however does not imply that a certain concept, which had worked well in the past, will work well in the future. Some consequences of the application of a certain concept may even show up only later. This concept is open to change and neglects any kind of static knowledge.

8.4 Economics, Unknowledge and Surprise

The fundamental hypothesis of G. L. S. Shackle is that economic events are unique events. Based on this conviction he objected primarily frequency probabilities as a guide to action in situations of uncertainty. Frequency probabilities require a large number of trials under equal conditions. As conditions in economics are never sufficiently equal frequency probabilities are meaningless to economic events. Furthermore, he argued that this critique also holds for a priori probabilities, as economic decisions can by definition not be repeated indefinitely. Later he extended his critique on frequency and a priori probabilities also to subjective degree of belief type of probabilities. In what follows I will present his critique in detail and reconstruct his argument against a probabilistic concept of inference in situations of uncertainty. His first hypothesis is that a priori and frequency type probabilities are meaningless in economic situations. Secondly, he argues that probability concepts, either objective or subjective degree of belief type probabilities are not useful for economic arguments.

Shackle demands, that in order to use probability concepts either a priori or statistical a situation must be indefinitely repeatable. Therefore, the condition of the indefinite trial must be equal. Keynes required similar conditions (1921: 224). He argued that cases grouped together have to be similar. And Knight (1921: 224) in a similar manner demanded: “Absolutely homogeneous classification of instances, completely identical expect for really indeterminate factors.” In the case of a priori probabilities the indefinite repeatability and homogeneity of trials has to be hypothetically possible, like in case of throwing a dice, while it has to be a feature of the trials in the case of statistical probabilities. Real economic situations have to apply to the same criteria, if probabilities, either statistical or a priori, should not be

[9]Schumpeter (1934) had called this process creative disruption.

[10]Cf. Hayek (1968: 9): “Competition is a procedure for systematically “[...] discovering facts which, if the procedure did not exist, would remain unknown or at least would not be used.”

meaningless. According to Shackle (1955: 24) this condition is not meet in most economic decision-situations, as they are neither indefinitely repeatable (even not hypothetically) nor do they rest on various single trials that could be grouped together. This is the case because economic decisions are unique and unique experiments are non-divisible and non-seriable. Consider for example a typical economic decision like investing in a new technology. The adjective new already implies that the situation is not one in a row of similar or equal situations, but a different one, which by definition cannot belong to a homogeneous class of situation. Furthermore, the situation is not repeatable indefinitely. Repeating the situation is in fact impossible and even hypothetically it would not work. If one could imagine to invest in the new technology again and again, it would soon lose its most important feature, which is that it is a novelty. It is therefore comprehensible that Shackle argues that economic decision situations frequently or almost ever do not apply to the axioms of probability calculus.

Beyond that, there are unique and non-divisible events that can be turned into divisible experiments in the aggregate. Such events are seriable events, like house fire, a car accident or burglaries. Usually on can buy insurance against those individual misfortunes. Although there is no individual probability that one will suffer from one of these misfortunes, there are enough pooled results, from which a statistical probability can be derived. In most economic situations, there are not enough pooled results, so that there is no basis to infer a meaningful probability. Frank H. Knight had made the same argument the other way around, when he argued, that most economic decisions are subject to uncertainty because no serious insurance company would ever provide insurance against investment mistakes, even if it would be possible to give a probability ratio. The reason herefore is according to Shackle that the derived probabilities are irrelevant. Consider Shackle's (1955: 28f) own words:

> Suppose, for example, that a probability of 1/6 is assigned ex ante to some hypothesis concerning the outcome of a non-divisible experiment. Then if the hypothesis proves false, the decision—maker was plainly wrong not to assign it a probability of zero instead of 1/6 while if it proves true, he was plainly wrong not to assign it a probability of unity.

Thus probabilities (a priori or statistical) are irrelevant in any unique decision-situation, as they can by definition never be right or wrong. They are non-falsifiable in unique decision-situations and therefore not a reasonable guide to action. In other words, probability ratios are meaningless in any case in which it is impossible to set up a Bernoulli trial in order to attain log-term objective stability.

Again, similar to Knight and Keynes, Shackle argues that there are cases in which it is impossible to determine probabilities, because the event alters the conditions under which it takes place. A classic example of such an event or experiment as Shackle calls it is the game of chess. A chess move alters the conditions under which it was performed in the way that it can never be performed in the same way in the same game. The same is true for economic decisions. Once an entrepreneur has made a certain investment decision, the whole set up has changed in a way that it becomes impossible to take the same decision again. It is according to Shackle the very nature of economic decisions that they destroy the conditions under which they were performed. This dynamic of the economic realm makes it impossible to establish repeatable objective probabilities. Shackle calls this type of economic decisions, which alter the situation crucial experiments. In the case of crucial experiments repeated trials are impossible.

Similarly, it is in crucial experiment situations also impossible to determine all possible outcomes of the event. This makes the use of any kind of objective probability calculus impossible, as no exhaustive list of possible consequences can exist. The decision taken changes the decision situation in an away unknown or unknowable to the decision maker, so that it is impossible to know what are the possible consequences of the decision are, a priori. In other words, there is no reference class. In such situations, subjective probability calculus is frequently used as a guide to action. Shackle objects this strategy strongly.

Objective probability calculus assumes that all possible consequences of an event can be known a priori. Wherefrom follows that an exhaustive list of all hypothetical consequences exists. If this is not the case any form of objective probability calculus becomes technically impossible, as the reference class, based on which probabilities are calculated does not exist. Thus, if the list of hypothetical consequences is incomplete objective numerical probabilities are indeterminable.[11] As described above Shackle assumes, that most economic decisions fall into this category of events, objective probability calculus is not only meaningless in economic situations it is also for the most time inapplicable. The alternative to objective numerical probabilities is subjective degree of belief type probabilities, which may also be expressed in numerical terms.

In subjective probability calculus, it is assumed that individuals are guided by their expectations, which are assumed to be rational. As described in Sect. 5.1.4, rational is a terminus technicus, which implies that the individual expectations apply to the axioms of transitivity, completeness and independence. Consequently, subjective theory of probability similar to the objective theory of probability demands that a conclusive list of the hypothetical consequences of a decision exists, so that either rational expectations can be formed by the decision-making agent or objective probabilities may be calculated. Shackle, however, argues that situations of uncertainty possess a strong capacity for surprise. This implies that neither the consequences of an action can be anticipated, nor is it possible to build comprehensive expectations about a situation and its consequences. For Shackle this is reason enough to reject numerical subjective degree of belief theories of probability. Alternatively, he suggests a non-numerical theory of uncertainty in which surprise plays a major role.

[11]For a more detailed discussion of this problem please see also Svetlova and Fiedler (2011: 51).

8.5 Surprise and the Non-Numerical Theory of Uncertainty

Similar to Keynes (1921, 1936) argued that human expectations, which are assumed to be the guide to action in situations of uncertainty, are not rational under the technical definition. Whereas Keynes argues that individuals draw back on conventional knowledge and gut feeling in situations of uncertainty, Shackle emphasises the creativity of acting in situations of uncertainty. Consider the following quote (2012: 1):

> By expectations I mean the act of creating imaginary situations, of associating them with named future dates and of assigning to each of the hypotheses thus formed a place on a scale measuring the degree of belief that a specified course of action on our own part will make this hypothesis come true, such a hypothesis I call an expectation.

Based on this creative concept of expectation, Shackle (1955) developed his non-numerical theory of uncertainty, which somehow turns the conventional view upside down. Instead of asking, what is the probability that a certain event happens or how confidant am I that the event will come true, Shackle asks would I be surprised if the event happens? He (1952: 30f) gives the following example:

> By disbelief (or potential surprise) I do not now mean the absence of perfect certainty, but the positive recognition of some disabling circumstances. If I am shown a closed hat-box and asked to guess what kind of hat is within, I shall attach no disbelief, [. . .], to the idea that the hat may be a topper, a ten-gallon hat from Texas, or a mortar-board, but I shall attach a high degree of disbelief to the hypothesis that the hat is of the three-foot diameter kind, [. . .], because such a hat would not go in the box.

Thus, instead of assigning the probability of 1/3 to the hypotheses that the hat is a topper or a 10-gallon or a mortar-board and a zero probability that the hat is a three-foot diameter kind, Shackle demands that decision-maker asks oneself, whether (s) he would be surprised if the hypothesis would come true. The question now is, *what is possible and not what is actually going to happen.* According to Shackle this potential surprise framework of uncertainty escapes some of the fundamental problems numerical theories of uncertainty have to face in situations of uncertainty (Basili and Zappia 2005). Firstly, if the probability assigned to the hypothesis that the hat is a topper was 1/3 before the hatbox had been opened and it turned out that the hat was actually a topper, the hypothesis was true, while all other hypotheses were wrong. Still, the probability of 1/3 for a topper was wrong. It must have been unity. Shackles concept, thus is not about the truth or certainty of a hypothesis but about its possibility. Instead Shackle solely focuses on the absence of disbelief of a hypothesis, which allows him to escape the above-described problem of standard probability accounts of uncertainty, that if one hypothesis is true the others must be false and even worse that the probabilities attached to the hypothesises are in almost all cases false and meaningless.

Another advantage of Shackles concept that focuses on the state of mind that makes the individual decision-maker unsurprised to see a particular hypothesis come true, is that it is open for new alternatives. Consider Shackle's own words (1955: 34).

> If, on the other hand, I had begun by naming five kinds of hat and assigning to each kind a probability of 1/5, and there had then occurred to me two additional types, I should have had to reduce the 1/5 to 1/7. But what would have been the justification for doing this? The hypothesis that the hat-box contains a topper is not rendered less plausible by the occurrence of the idea that it might, instead, contain a blower.

This idea allows the decision maker to treat the hypotheses independently and furthermore to account for an uncertain future. Particularly in situations in which the consequences of a decision cannot be foreseen, because the decision influences the future in a way the decision-maker does not know, the concept is an alternative to numerical probabilities, which simply cannot be calculated in such situations. An entrepreneur, who is investing in a new technology, cannot know how the new technology will pay off, but (s)he might have a feeling that (s)he would be surprised if it would not pay off at all.

Now, let us turn back to the logical problem of numerical probabilities and investigate how Shackles theory is a solution to the problem. Expressing perfect confidence in one mutually exclusive hypothesis implies a belief in the falsity of all alternatives hypothesises. Assigning numerical probabilities, which are neither zero nor one, thus implies that all probabilities are false. On the other hand, this implies that a hypothesis is either true or false, which is not the case. The hypothesis might have been possible and therefore true; however it did not become reality, which does not imply that the hypothesis was wrong in the beginning. Yet, it was not certain. While a probability of one, implies perfect certainty, the absence of disbelief does not imply perfect certainty. Instead it implies potential surprise. So that if a hypothesis comes true, to which the decision maker had assigned an absence of disbelief to, (s)he would not be surprised, without rendering the hypothesis or its rivals true or false. The truth-value of a hypothesis is thus irrelevant under Shackle's concept. He (1955: 30) points out:

> Let me insists again on the distinction I wish to make between two entirely separate ideas: *certainty* that a particular hypothesis is true, and *absence of disbelief* in the hypothesis. By absence of disbelief I mean a state of mind such that, if the person concerned were suddenly to obtain knowledge of the matter and find that the hypothesis was in fact true, he would feel no mental discomfort or shock, he would not be in the least surprised. Now I think it will easily be agreed that while a person can only feel perfectly certain of the truth of one member of a set of mutually exclusive hypotheses at a time, he can, by contrast, feel a complete absence of disbelief in any number of mutually exclusive hypotheses simultaneously, in the sense in which I am using the word 'disbelief'.[12]

Furthermore, the absence of disbelief does not imply certainty. Yet, it implies zero potential surprise. The decision-maker must not be certain, that a certain hypothesis becomes true; still the decision-maker may attach zero potential surprise to the event that the hypothesis becomes true. Thus, if the hypothesis becomes true,

[12]Italic is in the original.

the decision-maker would not be surprised, without being certain in advance that this hypothesis will become true. This approach does not prevent the decision-maker from potential mistakes. Yet, it allows him to escape the logical fallacy described above, as potential surprise is a measure that, unlike probability ratios, which are necessarily wrong unless they are either one or zero, does not contain a faulty judgement. Furthermore, the potential surprise is assigned independently of the number of hypotheses considered. Consequently, the list of non-excludable hypotheses can be extended or updated without affecting the potential surprise attached to any individual hypothesis. Similar to probability ratios, the potential surprise framework is able to give degrees, which reflect the potential misjudgement.

Still, it is obvious that Shackle's concept is rather unusual. Shackle was well aware that sympathy will not be on his side, when he stated that "those accustomed to think in terms of the actuarial calculation of the result will find this hard to appreciate" (1955: 42f). Even to me his concept seems to be rather bulky and not practicable. Nevertheless, it points out three fundamentals, which are largely ignored in standard economics. Firstly, his analysis shows, that important economic situations are mostly, characterised by uncertainty in the way that either the consequences of an event are unknown a priori or that they are unknowable a priori, because they are to be crated in the future. Secondly, Shackle had shown that numerical probability calculus of any kind is not applicable, insufficient or meaningless in most important economic situations. And thirdly, it became apparent that economic situations are necessarily situations liked to surprise, which implies that creativity, rigorous reasoning and imagination and not mechanical probability ratios are the guide to action in important economic situations.

8.6 Conclusion

Uncertainty can neither be modelled nor handled with the means of probabilities. Economic phenomena are characterised by uncertainty and at the same time uncertainty diminishes via economic phenomena, like the price mechanism. Furthermore, uncertainty cannot be overcome, yet it can be mediated via the exchange of information among market participants. Managing uncertainty is according to Hayek a collective, social and endless endeavour that produces innovation while discovering and creating information and welfare.

Similar to Hayek, Shackle rejects the positivist account of uncertainty in economics. Probabilistic uncertainty is a logically invalid simplification of the problem and an insufficient analytical instrument. Instead of building a new theory of uncertainty, Shackle gives a pragmatic account of how to manage the ontological and epistemological bound of knowledge in economics. He suggests building coherent hypothesise of possible future states and verifying them in market's information discovery procedure. Thus, though Shackles account is much more concrete, it is similarly evolutional and social in character.

References

Basili M, Zappia C (2005) Ambiguity and uncertainty in Ellsberg and Shackle. Dipartmento di Economia Politica 460(Settembre):1–34
Hayek FA (1937) Economics and knowledge. University of Chicago Press, Chicago
Hayek FA (1942) Scientism and the study of society. Part I. Economica 9(35):267–291 [reprinted in (Hayek 2010)]
Hayek FA (1943) Scientism and the study of society. Part I
Hayek FA (1944) Scientism and the study of society. Part II
Hayek FA (1945) The use of knowledge in society. University of Chicago Press, Chicago
Keynes JM (1921) A treatise on probability. Rough Draft Printers, New York
Keynes JM (1936) The general theory of employment, interest and money. Palgrave Macmillan, London
Knight FH (1921) Risk, uncertainty and profit. Nabu Press, Charleston
Schumpeter JA (1934) The theory of economic development: an inquiry into profits, capital, credit, interest, and the business cycle (social science classics series). Transaction, New Brunswick
Shackle GLS (1952) On the meaning and measure of uncertainty: I. Metroeconomica 4:111–128
Shackle GLS (1955) Uncertainty in economics and other reflections. Cambridge University Press, Cambridge
Shackle GLS (2012) Expectation in economics. Cambridge University Press, Cambridge
Smith A (1974) The theory of moral sentiments [reprinted Penguin Classics (2010)]
Smith A (1776) Wealth of nations: an inquiary into the nature and causes of the wealth of nations. Prometheus Books, New York
Sprich C (2009) Der unbekannte Hayek: Der Erkenntnistheoretiker. Beitrag zum Workshop der Nachwuchswissenschaftler der Hayek-Tage, Jena
Streit ME (1993) Cognition, competition, and catallaxy. Constit Polit Econ 4(2):223–261
Svetlova E, Fiedler M (2011) Understanding crisis: on the meaning of uncertainty and probability, in the first great recession of the 21st century. Edward Elgar Publishing
Hayek FA (1968) Competition as a discovery procedure. Quart J Aust Econ 5(3):9–23

Chapter 9
The Nature of Economics

Unrealisticness is one of the key challenges to Neoclassical Uncertainty Paradigm. In this chapter I discuss the Critique Realist's approach to uncertainty. I begin by clarifying the meaning of critical Realism and argue that it is not about realisticness per se. Instead, Critical Realism aims at understanding the problem of phenomenon under study, by analysing its ontological structure. Based on these ontological analyses, methods appropriate to the problem need to be identified. Therefore, the Critical Realists Approach of uncertainty begins with an ontological analysis of the structure of economic reality. It is argued that the economy has to be understood as an open and complex system with emergent properties, which is structured and in which demi-regularities can be identified. Furthermore, economic reality is mutable, so that the degree of uncertainty, which originates from the ontological structure of economic reality, may be different in any two economic situations. From my point of view four stages of uncertainty, which vary in their degree of uncertainty, can be differentiated. Though Critical realism allows for this, compared to neoclassical economics rather detailed analysis of economic reality, it also gives no sufficient answer to the question, of how economic analysis should proceed in the face of Fundamental Uncertainty, which is according to Critical Realism the standard case in economics.

The sociologist Elena Esposito (2013) suggests, exploiting the uncertain nature of economic reality for explaining, understanding and prognosing economic phenomena. The non-random structure of economic reality and the performativity of economic action and economic theory conjointly allow for wise economic action by the means of critical reasoning. In this way, Esposito shares the convictions of Knight, Keynes, Hayek and Shackle concerning the handling of economy inherent uncertainty. Furthermore, she shares the view, that optimal choice is impossible in the economy, yet reasonable choice and local predictability are attainable. Particularly, the performative power of economic action and economic theory can be exploited for this purpose. Her account presupposes a responsible economic actor that is able to create the future and not just discovering a necessary deterministic reality.

J. Köhn, *Uncertainty in Economics*, Contributions to Economics,
DOI 10.1007/978-3-319-55351-1_9

The chapter is organized in three sections. First, I introduce recent accounts of realism and economic ontology. Then, I focus on the conceptualisation of economic reality as an open system with different degrees of uncertainty and demi-regularities. Finally, I present Esposito's account of non-random uncertainty and performative economics. The chapter shows, that uncertainty does not render economic theory and action meaningless. Rather the opposite is the case. If the economy and economics is subject to uncertainty, then reasonable economic action is inevitable.

9.1 Realism and Ontology

In most parts of economics, success is dependent on finding and using methods, theories and models, including modes of reasoning, which do not need to be appropriate to the nature of the phenomenon under study (Friedman 1953; Klamer 2007; Lawson 1995, 1997, 2003, 2004; Lawson et al. 1998; Mäki 1988, 1989, 1994, 2002, 2008, 2009; Mäki et al. 2004; Mäki and Dilworth 1992). In economics, it seems to be the case that the applied methodology is more important than the problem under study (Hausman 1992, 1998). The methodologies of the natural sciences and particularly that of physics and mathematics have been introduced to the science of economics, even though the phenomenon understudy in economics are not natural or neutral, but social and also normative. Critical realism[1] challenges this view on the philosophy of economics and suggests an ontological approach instead. Ontology does not imply realism per se and yet it demands for ontologically realistic theories, which represent significant ontological structures of the problem under study. For most economic problems uncertainty is a significant ontological variable and therefore critical realism demands that it has to be

[1]Realism has many different faces in economic and the many faces of realism are now emerging within the methodological literature Hands (2001: 53). Boylan and O'Gorman (1995: 89–93) list four stereotypes of scientific realism thought to be broadly acceptable to those who regard themselves as scientific realists: "(1) The minimum criterion is that the statements of a theory are (or may be) either true or false (contrary to instrumentalism). (2) Furthermore, the statements have to be true or false apart from ourselves that is that although a theorist creates such statements their truth or falsehood is independent of the mind that created them (contrary to relativism). (3) At the ontological level, this can be taken to mean the view that the world exists independently of us, that the world really is this way rather than that, and what we think or feel about it makes no difference (contrary to constructivism). (4) Moreover, it is possible to know what the independently existing objects and their properties in the world truly are (contrary to Kantian idealism). Thus in principle there is no impenetrable veil between such objects, even if they are not directly observable, and their access to the human mind. It is the task of science and the role of theory to discover more precisely what the objects and their essential properties are. The main differences between scientific realism and other philosophies of science concern the role of theories as regards description, prediction and explanation. A theory may do all three things but an empiricist's basic instinct is to describe, an instrumentalist's is to predict and the scientific realist's is to explain." E. g.: Mäki (1998, 2012) and Hands (2001).

introduced into economic theories in a way that reflects its impact on the phenomenon under study. Subjective Probability modelling of uncertainty a la Neoclassical Uncertainty Paradigm is insufficient for this task (Lawson 2009; Mirowski 2012).

From an ontological perspective, there is a fundamental difference between the natural and social realm and it is puzzling, that economics, which belongs to the social realm is defining itself not with regards to the social realm and the social economic problems and phenomena, but with regards to methodology, which is particularly successful in explaining and predicting phenomena of the natural realm. The science of economics therefore is not a science that studies economic problems, but a bunch of methodologies, with which a whole bunch of problems can be studied, which need not be economic (Hausman 1992). This, however, is opposed to what ontologist's belief is good or successful science. Success in science is or should be dependent on identifying problems, phenomena or puzzles, describing their nature and finding methods appropriate to study these phenomena. Under this definition science is about understanding, describing and rethinking phenomena, in order to get enlightened. The fundamental aim of science from an ontological perspective is understanding. Prediction and policy or business advisory by economists is only a secondary goal of the economic science (from a realist's perspective) and can only be reached on the basis of a profound understanding of the economic problems and phenomena. Any method appropriate to reach these aims that simultaneously fits the phenomenon under study is thought of worthy considering. Thus, the process of science should be, problem first and method second and not the other way around, as it is in most of modern economics. Consequently, the starting point of any realist theory is an ontological study of the phenomena. For our purpose the question would be. What is the nature of uncertainty in the economic realm?".

9.2 Open and Closed Systems

Critical realism suggests, that economic ontology needs to be perceived as a complex and open system. Chick and Dow (2005: 365) define: "A system is a unit that consists of parts, which are in relationship. The parts may act independent of one another and may be systems (subsystems). Any system shows emergent properties and capacities, which are brought about by the relationship of the parts of the system and distinguish it from other systems."

This definition implies that the economy is a complex relationship structure, which can be distinguished from other systems, such as nature or society. It has emergent properties and capacities, which are brought about by the internal structure of the system. In critical realism, it is assumed that the structure of the economic system is characterised by openness, dynamics, complexity and yet still it has emergent properties or patterns (p. 366). Furthermore, it is argued that the economics is a social system, with is connected and influenced by the natural system (nature). Only open systems can combine these properties. However, most

Table 9.1 Conditions for closed theoretical systems (Chick and Dow 2005: 363)

1. All relevant variables can be identified
2. The boundaries of the system are definite and immutable; it follows that it is clear which variables are exogenous and which are endogenous; these categories are fixed
3. Only the specified exogenous variables affect the system, and they do this in a known way
4. Relations between the included variables are either knowable or random
5. Economic agents (whether individuals or aggregates) are treated atomistically
6. The nature of economic agents is treated as if constant
7. The structure of the relationships between the components (variables, subsystems, agents) is treated as if it is either knowable or random

of economic theory operates at the level of closed systems.[2] It is therefore, crucial to clarify the difference between open and closed systems in the following.

Closed systems, such as most neoclassical economic theories, are characterised by only endogenous variables. Table 9.1 lists all conditions for closed systems. In a closed system event regularity and determinism is assumed.[3] This implies, that if x necessarily or probably y follows. Chick and Dow (2005) argue, that this relation only holds if a system meets the following eight necessary conditions.

Critical realists argue that these necessary conditions are never conjointly fulfilled in real economic situations and therefore the mathematical methodology of orthodox economics, which presupposed the closure of economic reality are insufficient to tackle economic problems or phenomena.[4] They do not deny that some of the conditions may sometimes be met in economic reality. Yet, close system methods can only be applied if all conditions are conjointly fulfilled. Thus, even though, orthodox methodology may be useless from a Critical Realist perspective, economic reality need not be chaotic. It rather is open in various degrees,

[2]E.g.: Dow (2012: 14): "Faced with uncertainty, however, economists have developed conventions as to how best to reduce it. The dominant convention, which has gained force over the last 50 years, is to build theory within a formal deductivist framework. This framework builds up formal deductivist models on the basis of axioms about optimising behaviour on the part of individual agents, where knowledge is held with certainty (or certainty equivalence) although specific knowledge may be concealed (asymmetric information). The theoretical system is closed in the sense that variables are classified as endogenous or exogenous. Endogenous variables interact in a predetermined way within a given structure, while exogenous variables are known to be random. There is no place for uncertainty in the form of unquantifiable risk. If addressed at all, uncertainty is understood as an impediment to rational choice."

[3]For Lawson (1997, 2003, 2004), a closed system is fully identified by the occurrence of event regularities. Conversely, openness is equated with an absence of event regularities. The latter, he argues, corresponds to reality as we know it.

[4]In practice the endogeneity of variables is not always obvious. Van der Lecq argued (2000: 161), "[c]onfusingly, in [mainstream] economics the terms closed and open are applied to formal models. A model which consists of only endogenous variables is called a closed model, whereas a model in which exogenous variables are included in order to solve it, is called an open model. The term open model reflects the idea that the model would be indeterminate without information from outside [. . .] In the terminology [of systems], both closed and open models are examples of a closed system approach."

Table 9.2 Conditions for open systems (Chick and Dow 2005: 365)

1. The system is not atomistic; therefore at least one of the following holds:
a. Outcomes of actions cannot be inferred from individual actions (because of interactions)
b. Agents and their interactions may change (for example agents may learn)
2. Structure and agency are interdependent
3. Boundaries around and within the social or economic system are mutable; for at least one of the following reasons:
a. Social structures may evolve
b. Connections between structures may change
c. The structure-agent relation may change
4. Identifiable social structures are embedded in larger structures; these may mutually interact, for the boundaries of a social system are in general partial or semi-permeable
Implications for theoretical systems
1. There may be important omitted variables or relations and/or their effects on the system may be uncertain
2. The classification into exogenous and endogenous variables may be neither fixed nor exhaustive
3. Connections and/or boundaries between structures may be imperfectly known and/or may change

yet never closed entirely. If we are to define openness in a negative way, then a system is open, if one or more of the eight necessary conditions for a closed system are not meet by economic reality. Chick and Dow (2005: 365) define an open system, such as economic reality in a positive way. Table 9.2 shows all their conditions for open systems.

It has to be noted, that these conditions need not be fulfilled conjointly. Chick and Dow (2005), therefore, argued that there is no duality between open and closed systems or between chaos and structure. Instead they argued that open and closed systems constitute a spectrum (Mearman 2014). On the one side of the spectrum there is a theoretical system that fulfils criteria 1–8 of Table 9.1, while on the other side of the spectrum a perfectly open system meets criteria 1–4 of Table 9.2. In between there is a wide range of types and degrees of openness.

9.2.1 Critical Realism, Systems and Explanation

In critical realism, it is argued that the ontology of economics needs to be addressed as an open system. The basic assumption underlying this demand is that the nature of economic reality can best be described as a system. Yet, the term system is used in many ways in ordinary language as well as in other sciences. Defining it sharply is therefore indispensable, if we are going to use the term for describing economic reality.

Two constituting characteristics of systems in general can be identified. On the one hand a system is *externally limited* and on the other hand it is *internally structured.* A system is externally limited in the way that it is an object, which can be distinguished from other objects. Even though, often no sharp lines can be drawn and systems are overlapping, one system can be distinguished from another system. The second constituting characteristic is that a system is internally structured. This criterion implies that a system is composed of parts. Furthermore, it is assumed that there are relationships between these parts. The parts are connected to each other in many ways. These connections form a structure, which is characteristic for a system. Thus, there might be two systems, which are composed of the same parts, the relationship between the parts however will always be different, so that there are no two systems, with the same internal structure. The relationships between the parts of a system determine the properties of a system, which allows us to determine the external limits of a system as well as the capacities of a system. Thus, a system is internally structures and externally limited. It has emergent properties and capacities, which can be distinguished from that of other systems.

This view on systems is very much in line with Chick and Dow (2005). They (p. 364) argued that the defining characteristic of a system (as it is used in Critical Realism) is the interconnection within a collection of things or ideas that can be regarded as having a recognizable coherence or unity. Furthermore, they argue that, it is constitutive for a system that all elements of which it consists are somehow interrelated and bring about the overall structure or system.[5] Thereby the relationships between the parts of one system distinguishes it from other systems (Chick 2004: 5).[6]

9.2.2 *Structure and Dialectic*

Somewhat like the modern accounts of explanation in the social sciences, Lawson (1997, 2003) suggests in account of explanation in economics via non-strict regularities. In this way, his approach does not fundamentally depart from the scientific endeavour to identify relations, structures and mechanisms. At the same time he acknowledges that it is very unlikely that regularities concerning social phenomena, such as economic phenomena, will hold strictly or uniformly. This is the case because social and therefore economic reality is assumed to be complex and internally related, while being structured. Thus, structure is only one important characteristic of economic reality among others, which counteract regularities. Furthermore, the processual and open character of economic reality renders any type of time enduring universal regularity impossible. Lawson, therefore argues that regularities or demi-regs alone are not explanatory. In order to explain economic phenomena, he suggests combining dialectics with regularity explanation.

---

[5]See also Loasby (2003), drawing on Potts (2000).

[6]Chick (2004: 5) argues that the particular set of connections and absence of connection, "is what differentiates one system from another and gives them a sense of both character and order", and concludes: "A system is a network, a structure with connections, within which agents act, mostly in ways which reproduce and reinforce the system, but sometimes in ways which lead the system to evolve."

A demi-reg is an occasional actualization of a mechanism or tendency over a definite region of time and space. Therefore, it is not a universal law and yet a short of regularity that may be used to explain some definite economic phenomena.[7] Yet, Lawson (1997: 204) admits that "[t]he patterning observed will not be strict if countervailing factors sometimes dominant or frequently co-determine the outcomes in a variable manner. But where demi-regs are observed there is evidence of relatively enduring and identifiable tendencies in play." It is the aim of this approach to explanation to identify demi-regs, which are able to explain contrasts between social phenomena. Even though it is impossible to control the environment of economic phenomena in a way like laboratory experiments; it is according to Lawson (1997) possible to identify some rather stable empirical facts that do hold at a sufficiently large number of cases. Then you look for departures from these regularities, which are unanticipated or surprising in order to identify contrasts, which give insights in the underlying structures and tendencies. The aim of this method is to identify differences.[8]

Based on these contrastive social demi-regs causal hypothesis about the structure of social phenomena may be formulated. Again, the only way to assess the explanatory power of these hypotheses, is to test them on the basis of empirical phenomena and look for contradictions. This may support the hypothesis, contradict it or lead to a new hypothesis about the underlying structure of some economic phenomena.

It should have become clear that the suggested method of contrastive social demi-regs is an everlasting process, which will never reach an end. It incorporates the idea of social reality being in a constant process. Therefore, any hypothesis formed based on this method is partial as well as time and substance dependent. Universal theory, stable regularities and laws of economics are therefore out of reach under this account.

9.2.3 Degrees of Uncertainty

Acknowledging uncertainty leads to nihilism, is a common hypothesis among economists (Lucas 1972; McKenna and Zannoni 2001; Colander et al. 2009). The underlying argument is, that if we allow for Fundamental Uncertainty in our

[7]Lawson (2003: 79): "According to the concept I defend, social reality is open in a significant way. Patterns in events do occur. But where the phenomena being related are highly concrete (such as movements in actual prices, quantities of materials or outputs, and most of the other typical concerns of modern economic modellers), such patterns as are found tend to take the form of *demi-regularities* or *demi-regs*, that is, of regularities that are not only highly restricted but also somewhat partial and unstable." Italic is in the original. See also Lawson (1997: 204–221).

[8]Lawson (1997: 210) argues: "In each case, an explanation considered to be satisfactory will identify at least one systematic difference between the causal history of the primary component and that of the chosen contrast, or which would appear to be essential for the contrast if (...) it is only an imagined situation. In each case, the set of causal factors is responsible is likely to be different."

Table 9.3 Degrees of uncertainty, authors' own table

Degree of uncertainty	State of the world	State of knowledge	Theory	Method
Certainty	Determinism, if a then b	All possibilities are known	Rational choice	Utility maximization
Risk	Probabilistic determinism, if a then probably b	All possibilities are known as well as their probability of occurrence	Expected utility	Probability calculation/ hedging
Ambiguity	Probabilistic determinism, if a then probably b	All possibilities are known and their probability of occurrence can be estimated	Rational expectations	Probability estimation/ hedging
Fundamental uncertainty	Indeterminism, if a then probably b or something else	Possibilities are unknown or partially unknown, no probabilities can be estimated or calculated	Complex open systems with demi-regs	Identifying structures and looking for departures

economic theories and models, we have to assume indeterminism. This renders any kind of scientific analysis meaningless. This argument ignores, that acknowledging uncertainty does not imply that anything needs to be uncertain. It may be the case that scientific analysis is impossible in stages of Fundamental Uncertainty. Yet, many stages of the economic realm are only fundamentally uncertain to certain degrees. I argue that we have to distinguish four stages of the world, which vary in their degrees of uncertainty. The transitions between the stages of the world are indistinct. Furthermore, it might be the case that an economic situation might include facets of all four states. Particularly, the case of Fundamental uncertainty is underrepresented in economic theory. There are no sufficient methods yet, to deal with these elements that are fundamentally uncertain. This is the lacuna of modern economics. The following parts of this book aim to give an account of how this lacuna could be closed (Table 9.3).

9.3 Non-randomness, Performativity and Uncertainty

The Neoclassical Uncertainty Paradigm assumes perfect randomness of economic action. Yet, empirical observations suggest that economic action is non-random and therefore, predictable to a certain extend. Particularly Esposito (2007, 2011, 2013) argues, that non-randomness is the source of uncertainty in the economy.[9] She

[9]Esposito (2013: 104–105) argues: "Economic decisions are never random. They are guided by motives and projects. They often disappoint and behave unpredictably. This unpredictability, however, can be expected."

argues, that acknowledging uncertainty and non-randomness does not create a more chaotic or unpredictable situation. Instead, it allows explaining profit, change, innovation and surprise and even more important identifying structures that operate in economic reality, which limit its openness and therefore the unpredictability of the future. The precondition, however, is that we abandon the key concept of randomness. If we assume randomness, any economic phenomenon is a coincidence, which came about for no reason and which consequently, can neither be explained nor predicted. Esposito (2013: 120) highlights the importance of reason for explaining and understanding economic phenomena:

> Randomness is the presupposition of classical economics (the idea of the efficient market and the random walk hypothesis). One could say, paradoxically, that it is only if randomness exists that markets can be perfect that is, it is only if they rely on disorder that they can be ordered. The origin of the movements of markets must not be reason (which their efficiency would have already nullified), and their movements must therefore be random. So, understood, randomness becomes the opposite of uncertainty. If one starts from uncertainty, then one must abandon randomness. The idea of uncertainty does not imply (like randomness) a lack of reason, but the impossibility of control. There is always a reason. In fact, there are many reasons and they all have consequences.

Non-random uncertainty reintroduces reason into economic theory and at the same time keeps the non-controllable character of the economy. Esposito, assumes that agents act for some reason, without having full information[10] about the actions and intentions of other market participants. Consequently, their choices are not arbitrary. Contrarily, we can assume that these reasonable choices bring about or create the future.[11] Still, the future is unknown and unpredictable under this

[10]Imperfect information is the physiological condition and reason of markets Esposito (2013: 110). The most relevant information does not relate to the features of goods, but to the orientation and expectations of others. This information is not contained in prices, but is produced by the behaviour of operators who are oriented to prices Grossman (1976, 1989), Grossman and Stiglitz (1980), and Stiglitz (2003). This information cannot be known in advance because it does not yet exist. E.g.: Esposito (2013: 111): "The critical reflections within economics, however, say more. They introduce elements of complexity that the theory of performativity failed to highlight with the same clarity, in a certain sense radicalizing criticism, as an attempt to offer a way out of the stalemate of their own discipline. The key word is uncertainty, understood in a positive sense as a resource. Uncertainty is the basic resource of economic behaviour and of the possibility for obtaining profits. The world of the economy, Shackle (1970: 164) says, feeds on uncertainty. It is an unavoidable and uncontrollable uncertainty, one that is produced by the very behaviour of operators. Without uncertainty, the economy could not function or exist. In a world of rational and efficient markets, one would not be able to earn or invent anything, because any novelty would be neutralized in advance by the perfect distribution of information. However, a genuine entrepreneur produces surprises, invents novelties which could not be predicted in advance because they introduce a point of discontinuity, a 'crucial moment' in history that creates opportunities which did not exist previously. These possibilities cannot be planned, and they produce the persistent uncertainty of time as well as the creativity and dynamism of economic behaviour."

[11]Cf. Esposito (2013: 112): "A decision does not only choose between pregiven possibilities, establishing which ones are the most convenient, but creates new opportunities which prove unobtainable from the available data."

approach. Yet, the future is not random, but, the consequence of the decisions of all economic agents.[12] These agents are reliable for the future and not Fortuna.[13]

From a methodological perspective, introducing non-random uncertainty, implies that it becomes possible to identify structures that bring about certain phenomena (Marzetti and Scazzieri 2011). Even tough, we cannot control the structure, we may use it to explain and also manipulate the course of events.[14] Similar, to the ontological approach discussed before, non-random uncertainty, presupposes decent knowledge about some economic phenomenon, its structure and the motives and reasons that drive economic actors. Indirectly, Esposito's approach neglects the possibility of a general theory in economics. Instead she suggests local case analysis, which takes into account general knowledge about the economy, as well as institutional knowledge. Furthermore, she takes individual motives into account and suggests a constructivist perspective, in the way that she assumes that if there is a compliance of motives, the future will unfold in accordance with these motives. Esposito calls this process reflexivity. She grounds her theory of reflexivity research conducted in the field of finance by MacKenzie (2006a, b). It questions the independence of economic reality from economic theory and reveals that the theories and practices of finance produce its own objects (Esposito 2013: 4). One prime example is the LIBOR (the European interest rate at which banks borrow funds from other banks), which only exists based on the mutual expectations of banks and on the offers of other banks. This index is a creation of the market participants and therefore it does not exist independent of them. The same holds for any kind of derivatives. Derivatives are financial products designed to mediate the uncertainty of tomorrow's risks. Esposito (2013: 5) writes, "In the context of derivatives, dealing with objects that directly reflect the expectations of the operators, objects which are measured and constructed on the basis of expectations of others, the performative component is absolutely evident", and continues (p. 6) "The object does not exist but for the intervention of the observer, an intervention that is doomed to affect it." To her, performativity therefore means that even though the future does not yet exist; the present expectations about the

[12]Cf. (ibid.: 110): "The decision exploits uncertainty, without which there would be no freedom, and at the same time reproduces it, regenerating the unpredictability of the future Davidson (1978: 5 and 10), Snowdon et al. (1994: 300 ff.). Uncertainty, we could say, is the other side of creativity and innovation. This fact should be both understood and appreciated."

[13]This conceptualisation has a dramatic impact on the concept of the individual in economics, which becomes morally responsible.

[14]Cf. (ibid.: 112): "There is always a reason. In fact, there are many reasons and they all have consequences. However, this does not mean that things will go as one wishes. Without a reference to motives, predictions and expectations, one cannot explain what is going on (even when such goings-on deviate from these expectations) and cannot prepare to react properly. If there are reasons, however, then there is no randomness. People do not decide by chance, they decide on the basis of the available information. How can we abandon randomness without giving up structures, describing a world that is unpredictable without being random, which is produced by the motives and decisions of operators but is always surprising? Can we describe the economy by starting from uncertainty and its forms?"

future contribute to its production.[15] In this way economic theories are performative and yet future economic reality remains open and unpredictable, as the expectations of the economic agents can never be known entirely. Expectations are rather fragile, which had already been highlighted by Keynes (1936) and therefore performativity may turn into counter-performativity (MacKenzie 2006a, b: 75f., 184f., 259f.), which means that the future can come about different from the expectations as a result of these expectations. Esposito (2011: 189) and Rebonato (2001) refer to this ambiguity as "model risk", pointing to the fact that even though a model is valid, and may even have worked in the past, there is no certainty that it will also work in the future. Economists have to expect that their theories proof and at the same time refute themselves, due to their own performativity.

All in all, performativity means that economic theories are shaping economic reality and thereby they are reducing and at the same time producing uncertainty. Consequently, economics is included within the object it describes under Esposito's approach (p. 8). She (2013: 7) therefore warns, that economists have to reflect on their relationship as an observer of economic reality with economic reality and with their theories.[16] If performativity is introduced, abstract economic theories, models or hypothesises become empty (Esposito 2013: 8), as they do not reflect their own impact on the actual realisation of reality and therefore systematically produce misleading information.

Nevertheless, performativity also implies a certain predictability (though not in the fashion of mainstream economic theories) in the face of uncertainty. Uncertainty is the precondition and the consequence of performativity. And at the same time, performativity allows to identify the structures of uncertainty and thereby takes away some of its ambiguity. Furthermore, the theory of performativity implies that by analysing the expectations and motives of economic agents, one can develop reasonable predictions about the future, while knowing that they may not be realised due to the reflexivity described. And yet, these predictions can be

[15]Beside the LIBOR, Esposito (2013: 6) also discussed the performativity of the Black-Scholes formula (the formula calculates the uncertainty of the future though the indirect calculation of the implied volatility and builds the basis for option pricing). She writes: "The Black-Scholes formula promises to calculate the reality that it had itself produced, and not reality as such. This is shown by the fact that, in the beginning (when the formula was proposed in 1973), the procedure appeared utterly implausible, based on a series of absolutely unrealistic assumptions about the functioning of markets (as the authors themselves remarked). It was admittedly a flawed formula, which became valid when the markets (...) began to adopt it, "believing" in the future reality promised by the formula, and, thereby, making it real in the present. The formula produced the reality which validated the formula."

[16]According to Esposito (2013: 7) dominant theories of uncertainty in mainstream economics, such as the Efficient Market Hypothesis Fama (1970) or Random Walk Hypothesis Malkiel (1999), Lo and MacKinlay (1999) fail to reflect is own reflexivity and proceed as if economic reality is independent of economic theory. These economic theories treat economic reality "as if" they describe it and neglect the fact that they are unrealistic and performative and therefore anything but descriptions of economic reality. Instead they are analytical instruments Hausman (1992), which have to be used with caution, as they have an impact to the phenomenon they analyse.

used as a guide to action in an uncertain environment and according to Esposito they are more likely to be valid than any mechanistic predictions of standard theories of uncertainty.

A methodological precondition for this approach, however, is according to Esposito (2013: 8 f.) that economics distances itself from its positivistic research agenda, which aims at positivist descriptions and predictions (Smelser and Swedberg 1994). Instead economics needs to become more complex, in the way that the economist becomes "(a)n internal observer who is aware of his influence on the subject he describes is lost in circularity and can no longer give univocal indications."[17] Consequently the task of economics is self-limited in advance and it would become necessary for economists to compare the conclusions of different theories on one problem, as they all might contribute to solve the problem. Esposito, argues on the basis of uncertainty and performativity for an end of general theories[18] in economics and calls for more responsibility and caution on the side of the economist, when she writes (p. 9): "It must observe the economy from the inside, and this as though it were an external observer."

Now, we can turn to Esposito's conception of uncertainty as a resource. This part of her approach particularly draws back on Hayek critique. She argues (p. 10): "Hayek (1937: 44) said that the state of equilibrium is "admittedly fictitious", but still presupposed because it allows us to build a reliable theory, one free from uncertainties, one where subjective factors coincide with objective ones (and we could, therefore, disregard subjectivity, i.e. the role of the observer). Such a theory has no surprise (Hicks 1979: 101), no novelty, no time."[19] Even though such an uncertainty-free theory, is highly rigorous, it fails as a basis for economic research, as it describes a reality, which is not economic to Esposito and many others. To her the source of any economic problem is uncertainty. In an uncertainty-free economy there would be no potential for investment or invention, because any novelty or arbitrage potential would be neutralized by the perfect distribution of information. These thoughts are in line with Shackle (1972), who had argued that the economy feeds on uncertainty. To them uncertainty is the fundamental resource of the economy, which brings about novelty and dynamics and demands for creativity

[17]See also Baecker (1988: 52–53).

[18]E.g.: "The trend towards mathematization rests on imprecise assumptions and leads researchers to lose sight of the complexity and interdependencies of the real world. [. . .] Economics would be plagued by an excess of formalism without theory, which makes it all the more abstract and detached from its object. The result is the "crisis of vision" of an "esoteric" theory speaking about an imaginary hypothetical reality which does not face the data of reality, but merely demonstrates that the real world confirms its predictions Blaug (1992). The detachment from reality is explicit, given that economic theories refer to variables that must be few in number, homogeneous, permanent, and isolated from the rest of the universe, which never is the case Shackle (1979: 74 ff.) These theories are inevitably subject to errors and ambiguities Hicks (1979: Chap. 1), if they are not outright false Zamagni (1982: 13), only serving to remove or neutralise the social factors which generate uncertainty and instability, putting rigor before relevance." Heilbroner and Milberg (1995: 101–105).

[19]See also Shackle (1955: 91), Rizzo (1979: 5) and Clark and Juma (1987: 5).

of the economic actors (Witt 2007). Furthermore, uncertainty is the source of freedom and allows at least hypothetically for equal opportunities on a free market, which is the core of the free market philosophy. In this way the free market presupposes uncertainty.

To Esposito (p. 11 ff.) uncertainty means, that first of all no one ever knows how things actually transpire. Different to standard economic theory, this is not interpreted as a failure, but as precondition for a market economy. Therefore, the economic problem is an unsolvable information problem (Clark and Juma 1987: 90). Consequently, economic success or failure is determined by the individual exploitation of uncertainty.

Finally, Esposito argued for a new economic methodology, which is based on the assumptions:

1. Uncertainty is the inexhaustible source of all economic problems.
2. Economic phenomena are non-random and therefore structured.
3. Economic phenomena are internally performative and economics creates a second order performativity, which feeds the general uncertainty.

Counterintuitively, Esposito argues that an economic methodology, which is based on these three assumptions does not lead to a more chaotic and unpredictable situation, as it allows economists to identify structures, which are not perfectly deterministic, but control or guide the way in which the future of an open system economy unfolds (p. 25). According to her it is the task of the economist under this conception to identify an order that may explain economic phenomena and investigate the motives and expectations of economic actors in order to identify a path in which the economy may develop, while reflecting that their theorizing itself manipulates the way in which the economy develops. This approach, is much more realistic in the sense of Critical Realism, as it takes into account important ontological aspects of the economic reality, than Positive Neoclassical Economics. At the same time it allows for similarly imprecise predictions.

However, the key advantage of this approach compared to Positive Neoclassical Economics is that it allows understanding why economic predictions, can and should never be perfectly right. If they were (apart from accidently right predictions or temporarily perfect performativity), we would live in an unfree market economy. Beyond that Esposito's approach remains rather sketchy. She neither describes how individual expectations and motives should be analysed, nor is she explicit on the use of performativity in explaining concrete economic phenomena. I suspect, that Esposito has a case based approach in mind, in which economists analyse the institutional structure, as well as agent's motives and expectations on some particular phenomenon, while reflecting on the performativity of their investigation, the applied theories and the phenomenon itself. Yet, this procedure is not described in Esposito, so that her approach remains uncertain. The strength of her approach clearly is the precise analyse of economic ontology and the synthesis of thoughts on uncertainty that have been proposed by Knight, Keynes, Hayek and Shackle.

9.4 Conclusion

Realism demands not for realisticness, but for an ontologically realistic theory. For economics, this implies that uncertainty need to be incorporated as it is a substantial part of economic ontology. Therefore, Critical Realists suggest an open and complex system approach in economics that allows for explanation on the basis of structure and demi-regularities. Though, the account rejects general predictability it allows for explanation and understanding. Reason and critical analysis of individual economic phenomena becomes central to the methodology of economics. Furthermore, Espositos idea of non-randomness and performativity, shows that economic explanation in the face of uncertainty is not arbitrary and needs further investigations.

References

Baecker D (1988) Information und Risiko in der Marktwirtschaft. Suhrcamp, Frankfurt am Main
Blaug M (1992) The methodology of economics: or how economists explain. Cambridge University Press, Cambridge
Boylan TA, O'Gorman PF (1995) Beyond rhetoric and realism in economics. Towards a reformulation of economic methodology. Routledge, London
Chick V (2004) On open systems. Braz J Polit Econ 24(1):3–16
Chick V, Dow SC (2005) The meaning of open systems. J Econ Methodol 12(3):363–381
Clark N, Juma C (1987) Long-run economics: an evolutionary approach to economic growth. Pinter Publisher, London
Colander D, Föllmer H, Haas A, Goldberg M, Juselius K, Kirman A, Lux T et al (2009) The financial crisis and the systemic failure of academic economics. Institute for the World Economy, Kiel
Davidson P (1978) Money and the real world. Palgrave Macmillan
Dow SC (2012) Uncertainty-denial. University of Victoria Department Discussion Paper DDP1204, November, pp 1–33
Esposito E (2007) Die Fiktion der wahrscheinlichen Realität. Suhrkamp, Berlin
Esposito E (2011) The future of futures: the time of money in financing and society. Edward Elgar, Cheltenham
Esposito E (2013) The structures of uncertainty: performativity and unpredictability in economic operations. Econ Soc 42(1):102–129
Fama EF (1970) Efficient capital markets: a review of theory and empirical work. J Fin 25 (2):383–417
Friedman M (1953) The methodology of positive economics. In: Friedman M (ed) In positive economics. Chicago University Press, Chicago
Grossmann SJ (1976) On the efficiency of competitive stock markets where traders have diverse information. J Fin 31(May):573–585
Grossmann SJ (1989) The informational role of prices. MIT Press, Cambridge
Grossman SJ, Stiglitz JE (1980) On the impossibility of informationally efficient markets. Am Econ Rev 70(3):393–408
Hands WD (2001) Reflection without rules: economic methodology and contemporary science theory. Cambridge University Press, Cambridge
Hausman DM (1992) The inexact and separate science of economics. Cambridge University Press, Cambridge

Hausman DM (1998) Problems with realism in economics. Econ Philos 14(2):185–213
Hayek FA (1937) Economics and knowledge. University of Chicago Press, Chicago
Heilbroner R, Milberg WS (1995) The crisis of vision in modern economic thought. Cambridge University Press, Cambridge
Hicks JR (1979) Causality in economics. Basil Blackwell, Oxford
Keynes JM (1936) The general theory of employment, interest and money. Palgrave Macmillan, London
Klamer A (2007) Speaking of economics: how to get in the conversation. Routledge, London
Lawson T (1995) A realist perspective on contemporary "Economic Theory". J Econ Iss XXIX (1):1–32
Lawson T (1997) Economics and reality. Routledge, London
Lawson T (2003) Reorienting economics. Routledge, London
Lawson T (2004) A conception of ontology. Cambridge Ontology group, (December), 1–24.
Lawson T (2009) Contemporary economics and the crisis. Real-World Econ Rev 50:122–131
Lawson T, Collier A, Bhaskar R, Archer M, Norrie A (1998) Critical realism: Essential readings. Routledge, London
Lo A, MacKinlay C (1999) A non-random walk down wall street. Princeton University Press, Princeton
Loasby BJ (2003) Closed models and open systems. J Econ Methodol 10(3):285–306
Lucas RE (1972) Expectations and the neutrality of money. J Econ Theor 4:103–124
MacKenzie D (2006a) Is economics performative? Option Theor Construct Derivat Market 28:29–55
MacKenzie D (2006b) An engine, not a camera: How financial models shape markets. MIT Press, Cambridge
Mäki U (1988) On the problem of realism in economics. Fundamenta Scientiae 9:343–362
Mäki U (1989) On the problem of realism in economics. Ricerche Economiche 43(1–2):176–198
Mäki U (1994) Reorienting the assumptions issue. In: Backhouse RE (ed) New directions in economic methodology. Routledge, London, pp 236–256
Mäki U (1998) Is Coase a realist? Philos Soc Sci 28(5):31
Mäki U (2002) The dismal queen of the social sciences. In: Mäki U (ed) Fact and fiction in economics: realism, models, and social construction. Cambridge University Press, Cambridge, pp 307–321
Mäki U (2008) Method and appraisal in economics: 1976–2006. J Econ Methodol 15(4):409–423
Mäki U (2009) Realistic realism about unrealistic models. In: Kincaid H, Ross D (eds) The Oxford handbook of philosophy of economics. Oxford University Press, Oxford, pp 69–98
Mäki U (2012). Economics for real: Uskali Mäki and the place of truth in economics. Routledge
Mäki U, Dilworth C (1992) On the method of isolation in economics. In: Idealization IV: intelligibility in science. Poznan Stud Philos Sci Humanit (special issue) 26:319–354
Mäki U, Mooslechner P, Schuberth H, Schurtz M (2004) Some truths about truth for economists, their critics and clients. In: Economic policy-making under uncertainty: the role of truth and accountability in policy advice. Edward Elgar, Cheltenham, pp 9–39
Malkiel B (1999) A random walk down Wall Street: the time-tested strategy for successful investing. W.W. Norton, New York
Marzetti S, Scazzieri R (2011) Fundamental uncertainty: rationality and plausible reasoning. Palgrave Macmillan, New York
McKenna EJ, Zannoni DC (2001) Post-Keynesian economics and nihilism. J Post Keynesian Econ 23:331–347
Mearman A (2014) How should economics curricula be evaluated? Int Rev Econ Educ 16(Part B):73–86
Mirowski P (2012) From Mandelbrot to Chaos in economic theory. South Econ J 57(2):289–307
Potts J (2000) Uncertainty, complexity, and imagination. In: Earl P, Frowen S (eds) Economics as an art of thought: essays in memory of G.L.S Shackle. Routledge, London, pp 162–184

Rebonato R (2001). Theory and practice of model risk management. Quantitative Research Centre (QUARC) of the Royal Bank of Scotland Oxford Financial Research Centre – Oxford University
Rizzo MJ (1979) Time, uncertainty, and disequilibrium. Lexington Books, Lexington
Shackle GLS (1955) Uncertainty in economics and other reflections. Cambridge University Press, Cambridge
Shackle GLS (1970) Expectation enterprise and profit: the theory of the firm (studies in economics). Allen & Unwin, London
Shackle GLS (1972) Epistemics and economics: a critique of economic doctrines. Cambridge University Press, Cambridge, p 162
Shackle GLS (1979) Imagination and the nature of choice. Columbia University Press, New York
Smelser NJ, Swedberg R (1994) The handbook of economic sociology. Princeton University Press, Princeton
Snowdon B, Vane H, Wynarczyk P (1994) A modern guide to macroeconomics. Edward Elgar, Aldershot
Stiglitz JE (2003) Globalization and its discontents. W. W. Norton & Company
van der Lecq SG (2000) Money, coordination, and prices. Edward Elgar, Cheltenham
Witt U (2007) Novelty and the bounds of unkowledge in economics. Papers on Economics and Evolution 7
Zamagni S (1982) Saggi die filosofia della scienza economica. NIS, Roma

Part III
Methodology of Uncertainty

In contemporary modern economics, such as financial theory, still the Neoclassical Uncertainty Paradigm gets used to model rational behaviour under conditions of uncertainty. In the previous parts of this book we have seen that this subjectivist Bayesian approach is insufficient, both for modelling choice and uncertainty in economic theories. The Paradigm removed the clear distinction between risk and uncertainty, in the way that situations of uncertainty, which are ontologically fundamentally different from situations of risk, can be modelled as if they were similar. This is an illegitimate simplification, which veils important aspects of the economic problem, which, as it had been shown in Part II of this book, is grounded in different degrees of uncertainty. Furthermore, the Neoclassical Uncertainty Paradigm neglects the actual and meaningful act of choice. Rational Choice under conditions of uncertainty is a black box. The approach assumes, that if objective probabilities are not given, they can be replaced by subjective probabilities, so that problems of decision under uncertainty can be reduced to problems of decision under conditions of risk. Underlying this transition is the assumption that all agents have probability beliefs over any source of uncertainty and that they update these beliefs according to Bayes rule, while using them as a basis for expected utility maximization. Even though these probability beliefs have to apply to Savage's four axioms (completeness, transitivity, independence and sure thing principle) it is not clear how these beliefs should be formed, if agents are confronted with uncertainty, which might imply that agents, cannot know all possible states of the world, or that they have no utility function. In short, the Neoclassical Uncertainty Paradigm is meaningless in situations of uncertainty, because situations of uncertainty are characterised by the absence of what Savage's axioms demand (1954).

Nevertheless, the Neoclassical Uncertainty Paradigm had been extremely successful. Since the 1950s it dominates mainstream economics and pushed alternative approaches, as they have been discussed in Part II of this book to the margin. The reasons here fore are very widely[1]. Yet, I argue that one of the most important reasons is that the economic research agenda or expressed differently, the dominant philosophy of the science of economics, neglects the problem of uncertainty and therefore favours methodologies, which do not touch upon this aspect of economic reality. Thus, if one wishes to legitimise theories of true or Fundamental Uncertainty in economics and to close the identifies lacuna, one has to adjust the philosophy of economics to the conditions of the twenty-first century and put uncertainty at its core.

My line of argument in the last part, therefore, proceeds in two steps. In the first step I argue for a new philosophy of the economics science, which accepts uncertainty as a fundamental of economics and therefore aims at understanding and local prediction instead of general theories and general predictions. The central scientific criteria are plausibility and credibility instead of validity and rationality.

In the second step, I suggest a model of reasonable behaviour under conditions of uncertainty. This theory of choice under conditions of uncertainty draws back on the concepts of fiction and reflexivity. It brings together aspects from different philosophies of uncertainty discussed in Part II of this book and unifies them in a theory that conceptualises choice as a local and dynamic process in an open system reality. The last chapter sums up and gives an outlook of what a New Uncertainty Paradigm could imply for the science of economics.

This last part of this book is preliminary in character. It sketches a kind of fictional economics and seeks to explore its opportunities and limitations. Particularly, in the last chapter I delineate a vision for the future of economic research. It shows the point of departure for further research in the field of new economic thinking.

References

Gilboa I, Postlewaite AW, Schmeidler D (2008) Probability and uncertainty in economic modelling. J Econ Perspect 22(3):173–187

Mirowski P (1989) The probabilistic counter-revolution, or how stochastic concepts came to neoclassical economic theory. Oxf Econ Pap 41:217–235

Savage L (1954) The foundations of statistics. Dover Publications, New York

[1]See for example, Mirowski (1989) and Gilboa et al. (2008).

Chapter 10
Extending the Boundaries of Economics

The latest financial and economic crises have undermined the confidence in the economic science and its methods, fundamentally. Now, the discipline of economics is looking for a new methodological guiding principle. Neuroeconomics, or Imperfect Knowledge Economics, emerged from this search for a New Economic Paradigm. Both schools of economic thought are highly methodology driven and limited in scope. Therefore, they cannot be used as a blueprint for a new philosophy of economics, which is able to replace the Positivist Research Paradigm. Even worse, the analysis of this thesis and the economic turbulences of the last decade, have shown that pure positive economics is impossible. This, however, does not also imply that only normative economics is possible. Nor does it imply that economics is not a science. Rather it is the case that the methodology and particularly the aims and the expectations concerning the generality of economic conclusions have to be revised.

Positive economics is underlying a value free research agenda. It was the primary aim to build theories or hypothesises that describe economic phenomena in a deductive-nomological way. This implied that positive economics is neither concerned with the question of how nor why an economic phenomenon was brought about. Its primary aim was to describe that it exists and what its characteristics are, in order to predict in which way a change in the circumstances would bring about a change in the observed phenomena. The prime criteria for discriminating between theories or hypothesises were the scope and correctness of the predictions it yields.

The neutrality of the economist remains under the fictional view of economics, however, the aims of the science of economics change fundamentally. The main reason therefore is that, fictional economics is based on realist ontology. If we acknowledge uncertainty, performativity, and complexity, as fundamental characteristics of the economic nature, precise predictions become impossible. At the same time science, does not become impossible, however more difficult. While positivist economics neglects large parts of the fuzzy nature of economic phenomena in order to save itself as a predictive science, fictional economics acknowledges

J. Köhn, *Uncertainty in Economics*, Contributions to Economics,
DOI 10.1007/978-3-319-55351-1_10

the fuzzy and ambiguous nature of economic problems and aims to understand them, instead of making necessarily imprecise predictions. Fictional economics aims at scientific knowledge, while critically reflecting that reaching absolute and general knowledge is impossible. Positive and fictional economics share the aim that they want to provide a scientific basis for making economic decisions, without anticipating which conclusions are attainable, and which are not, thus without being normative in the way Friedman (1953) had described it. Fictional Economics rejects ad hoc assumptions and predictability, instead, it aims at understanding economic phenomena and evaluates economic theories on the basis of their plausibility, which is a key concept in the theory of fiction and their coherence (Rist 2011).

Positive Economics lacks almost any ontological basis. The link to the nature of economics is nonexistent, so the position that Positive Economics is purely analytical (Hausman 1992) is rather easy to defend. The assumptions concerning the nature of the economy underlying positive economics are likewise abstract and absurd. Positive economics assumes rational behaviour, rational expectations and purely efficient, meaning random, markets. I believe that almost any economist would agree, that neither of these assumptions describes the nature of the economy. Instead they provide an analytical framework for applying a certain mode of explanation (deductive-nomological) and a particular methodology (abstract mathematical models and empirical testing).

In Fictional Economics, the nature of economic phenomena builds the point of departure. Unlike the realist approach the reason therefore is, not to be more realistic, but to provide better explanations. Therefore, Fictional Economics does not aim to be more realistic in any dimension. Rather, it is the case that Fictional Economics aims to acknowledge the essential features of economic nature, because they are crucial for understanding economic phenomena and for enabling researchers, politicians and economic actors to make reasonable decisions. A deeper and more precise understanding of more or less stable economic mechanisms should be the aim of modern economic thinking. Therefore, economic phenomena need to be analysed in the environment in which they occur and not in isolation.

Among the essentials of economic reality are uncertainty, reflexivity, and complexity. Neither, of the three gets acknowledged in positive economics, and yet the analysis of this thesis has shown that they are crucial for understanding important economic phenomena, such as profit, slump or irrational behaviour. These are not anomalies of the economic realm, instead they are the standard case (Rosenberg 2013).

This chapter is organised in four sections. I begin with an analysis of a most recent essay by Georg Soros, in which he suggests a new ontological foundation for the philosophy of economics. The next section builds on Soros' thoughts and goes beyond them. I argue that there are at least three levels of reflexivity in economics. Conjointly, with complexity they produce both epistemological and ontological uncertainty. In the third section I further condense Soros' approach and suggest that economic ontology can best be described by means of an uncertainty corridor. The epistemological consequences of this concept will be discussed in the fourth section. As suggested by Tony Lawson, assuming uncertainty does not lead to nihilism, instead acknowledging and analysing the structure of uncertainty reveals the structure of economic reality. This knowledge can lead to a more precise and conscious science of economics.

10.1 Ontological Foundations of a New Philosophy of Economics

We have learned throughout the analysis presented in this essay, that positive economics blanks out the ontology of economic phenomena and uses scientific modes of research (deduction) and methods (stochastic modelling) inappropriate to the phenomenon under study. The reason here fore is, the economist's conviction, that economics can only be acknowledged as a science, if it imitates the natural sciences. Unlike the natural sciences, economics, not only deals with phenomena emergent from a natural ontology, but is also emergent from a social ontology. Therefore, the science of economics is fundamentally different from that of physics, and yet, similarly scientific, if it includes the social and human origin of the economic problems. I, therefore suggest to step away from the old dichotomy of positive and normative and natural and social in economics. Economics is an inclosing science, with normative, positive, natural and, most importantly, human or social elements. Economics is a human science, after all. Therefore, it needs a differentiated ontological and epistemological foundation, which acknowledges its speciality and at the same time allows for a scientific analysis of economic phenomena. Here, I suggest an ontology of economics that differentiates between natural ontology and social ontology. Both types of ontology are sources of uncertainty, which complicates research in the economic sciences, compared to natural sciences.

Economic phenomena arise at the intersection between objective and subjective reality, which open a spectrum with different elements. Objective reality includes anything that exists independent of the human actor, while the economic agents create subjective reality. The source of objective reality is nature, while that of subjective reality is the human being. Classically, the natural sciences analyse objective reality, which exists independent of the scientific analysis, and which can only be analysed and, for the most part, not manipulated by the researcher.[1]

Consequently, there are some parts of economic reality about which we can make true statements, which can be tested empirically and which are stable over

[1]E.g.: Soros (2013: 317): "In natural sciences, the outside observer, is engaged only in the cognitive function, and the facts provide a reliable criterion by which the truth of the observers' theories can be judged. So the outside observer can obtain knowledge about the natural phenomena she is observing. Based on that knowledge, nature can be successfully manipulated. That manipulation can change the state of the physical world, but it does not change the laws that govern that world."

time. However, even in the natural part of economic reality there are sources of uncertainty that hinder researchers in obtaining universally true knowledge about the economy that can be used for prediction. I call this, following Soros (2013), the natural uncertainty principle.

For the part of the subjective reality of economics, it becomes even more difficult or even impossible to identify the knowledge or stable regularities, as social reality is lacking an independent criterion of truth. We know from the correspondence theory of truth that a true statement represents knowledge and a statement is true if it corresponds to the facts. Yet, in the social realm, all facts are dependent on the observer of the fact. Therefore, it is always impossible to prove a social fact true, as there are potentially as many truths as there are individuals. Consequently, it is impossible to create knowledge about the social realm, similar to that of the natural realm. This, however, does not mean that we are ignorant about social reality. It rather implies that our knowledge about social phenomena is less reliable than that about natural phenomena. This is, following Soros (2013), the human uncertainty principle. In his 2013 paper, Soros perceives economic reality as a reflexive and complex system, in which objective and subjective reality are interrelated. I find his account of the economic ontology particularly informing. It shows the complexity of economic reality and explains, why a general and abstract science of economics is necessarily impossible. Before, I discuss the natural and human uncertainty principles which are constitutive for economic reality, let me briefly introduce the (Soros 2013) reflexive system model of economic reality.

10.2 A Reflexive System and Fallibility

Soros assumes that there is an objective natural reality, about which we can have objective knowledge. Besides that, there is a subjective reality, in which the individual actor can obtain only subjective knowledge. Now, in order to act in this economic realm, agents combine subjective and objective knowledge. Starting from the agent's subjective reality, the agent conceives the objective reality. The agent's perception of the objective reality is influenced by the agent's intentions. So, that the collected information about objective reality is manipulated by the subjective intentions and biases of the agent. Soros therefore distinguishes between the manipulation and the cognitive function and thereby rejects determinism (p. 313). Both the manipulative and the cognitive function only exist in situations with thinking participants (p. 311). The cognitive function describes the thinking individual's attempt to understand the world. The process of cognition involves a passive recognition of objective reality, which is coloured by the thinking individual's cognitive capacities and experiences. The manipulative function on the other hand describes the individual's attempt to change objective reality intentionally. Soros (p. 311) writes: "In the cognitive function, the participant is cast in the role of a passive observer: the direction of causation is from the world to the mind. In the manipulative function, the participant plays an active role: the direction of causation is from the mind to the world."

According to him, economic action is dependent on human intentions, which can be influenced more or less consciously by the individual's free will. Therefore, economic agents possess the power to change economic reality. In this model, it is the individual who shapes economic reality[2] and not economic reality that shapes human economic action. Underlying Soros' account of reflexivity[3] is the assumption that agents change the future in the way that it resembles their expectations by the actions they take. Thus, actions are not, as assumed in Rational Choice Theory, the consequence of some present state of the world, but dependent on some desired future state of the world. Furthermore, actions are not independent. Rather the contrast is the case, actions alter the possible states of the world as well as agent's expectations and preferences. Preferences play an important and highly normative role in this process. If we follow Soros, agent's build the future in the way they want it to be. Naturally, the human uncertainty principle prevents agents from resembling the world in the way they want it to be. Consequently, there is a constant circularity between expectations, preferences, actions and the realised future, which again influences expectations, preferences and actions. Soros writes (2013: 310): "[T]hese imperfect views can influence the situation to which they relate through the actions of the participants. For example, if investors believe that markets are efficient, then that belief will change the way they invest, which in turn will change the nature of the markets in which they are participating (though not necessarily making them more efficient)."

Or expressed a bit more technically, each agent has two functions: the cognitive and the manipulative function, which are both subject to fallibility (Soros 2013: 311). These two functions connect the thinking agent (subjective reality) with the state of affairs (objective reality) in a circular way. The cognitive function helps the agent to understand the word, in the way that the agent observes or experiences the world. The manipulative function, however, is intentional. The agent uses his subjective reality (state of mind), created by experience and observation and applies it to the objective reality. Thereby the agent manipulates the objective reality, as (s)he colours it with her/his subjective views. Both processes (cognition and manipulation) operate at the same time and interfere, as both operations are dependent on each other (Soros 2013: 311). The independent variable of the cognitive function is the dependent variable of the manipulative

[2]Economic reality is thought of as a reflexive system that consists of natural unchangeable parts and human changeable parts.

[3]George Soros (2013) had argued that reflexivity is one of the major sources of uncertainty in economics that causes the unpredictability of economic outcomes. Elena Esposito (2011, 2013), sharing the view that reflexivity is an important force driving economic progress, however, argues that reflexivity can be used to better understand economic phenomena or even exploit reflexivity in order to foresee fundamental changes.

function, namely subjective and objective reality. Consequently, the relationship is circular or recursive and objective reality becomes subjectively manipulated.[4]

This reflexive and infinite process itself creates ambiguity and prevents economists from gaining stable knowledge about economic structures and actions (Herrmann-Pillath 2011). Beside this economy's inherent uncertainty, Soros discusses the uncertain implication of complexity, time, and our human sensorial and computational limitations, which prevent us from comprehending the world in all its details. He calls this the human uncertainty principle and argues that it seduces economic actors and economists to draw back on methods of simplification like generalizations, metaphors, decision rules, moral judgements (Soros 2013: 313), or we use fast and frugal heuristics (Gigerenzer and Gaissmaier 2011).

This, however, leads to fallibility of human reasoning and economic theory. Soros (2013: 311) argues that these mental concepts then take on a subjective existence of its own, which further complicates the situations, as they are not necessarily sufficient. Also, the way in which our brain functions prevents us from understanding a situation in the way it actually is. It mixes expectations, experience, reason and desire, so that an objective representation of the facts is impossible.

The human brain is unable to compute all information available. The latest findings from neuroscience show, that it is almost unable to conduct information without emotion (Damásio et al. 1996; Virlics 2013). Consequently, there is good reason to believe that a rational deterministic decision is impossible. At the same time, the selection mechanisms of the human brain are highly efficient and they save us from becoming mad, confronted with an overdose of information. Brain science shows that misinterpretations and distortions cannot be avoided, when our brains compute millions of sensory data under high time pressure. The human understanding of the world we live in is therefore inheritably imperfect (Soros 2013: 311). This human fallibility causes uncertainty and at the same time is the result of uncertainty, as there is no option to check the facts in a world, which is constantly changing, in a way we cannot know. Figure 10.1 displays his idea, about which Soros (p. 311) concludes:

> Fallibility pervades our attempts to understand both natural and social phenomena, but it is not fallibility that distinguishes the social from the physical sciences. Rather, [. . .], the distinction comes from the fact that in the social system fallible human beings are not merely scientific observers but also active participants in the system themselves.

[4]The label 'objective reality' is from my point of view misleading, as it suggests that there is some real and true objective reality. I fear this is not the case. There is something like a purely observer-independent and therefore objective natural reality. This natural reality is unattainable for us human beings, as we always perceive it with some subjective colour. Consequently, objectivity is always out of reach. Nevertheless, we can agree on facts and knowledge about this reality, which are in some way objective, and yet not universal. In the course of time our agreement about the facts and knowledge may change, due to new observations, interpretations or changed subjective realities. Thus, Soros' objective reality, should not be confused with nature and furthermore, it is constantly changing and highly dependent on our subjective realities.

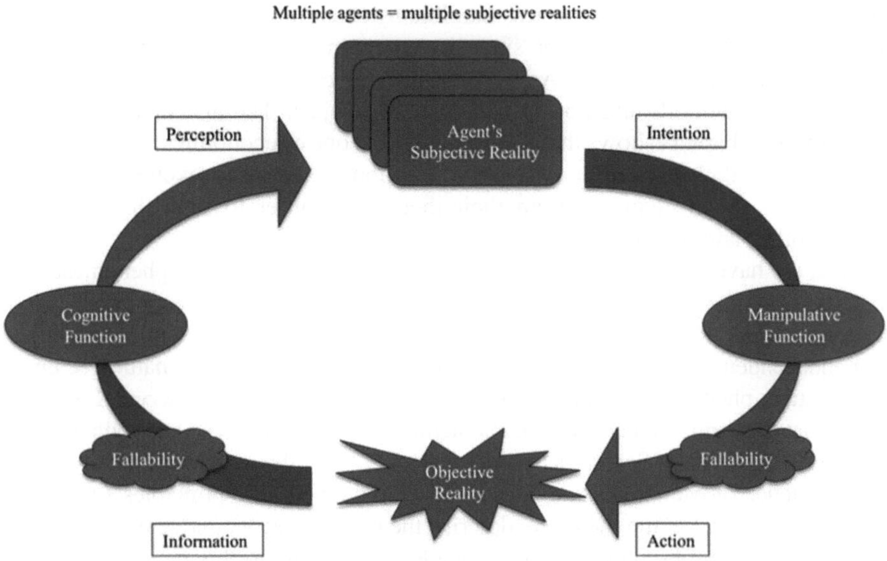

Fig. 10.1 Soros' reflexive system (Soros 2013: 314) (The original source of publication was the Journal of Economic Methodology by Taylor & Francis Ltd. (www.tandfonline.com). I am grateful for their kind permission to use this figure)

All in all, Soros' reflexive system model of economic reality and his description of the necessary fallibility of human actors is a reasonable account of the essentiality of uncertainty in economic reality. Furthermore, his account offers a starting point for a philosophy of science of economics that respects uncertainty as an economic essential. Given Soros' account of economic reality, deterministic economic models are necessarily insufficient and the old aims of the economic sciences of simplicity, generality, and predictability are fundamentally flawed, as they are in contradiction to the human and therefore uncertain nature of economics. However, Soros' account of economic reality, while containing a variety of thoughts on uncertainty presented in this essay, is not comprehensive. In order to build the basis of a new ontologically grounded philosophy of the science of economics Soros' concept needs further clarification and extensions.

10.3 Levels of Reflexivity

The science of economics lies at the intersection between the natural and the social sciences. Natural science and some elements it touches upon, are stable and objectively true. However, most elements, which are subject to economics, are socially constructed. These elements are not part of an objectively given nature. Instead they emerged and evolved over time in a social process, which is complex and reflexive to different degrees. Consequently, the science of economics studies phenomena, which are more or less tangible by scientific means. This speciality of the science of economics, ever since its emergence, caused disputes about the scientificness of economics. As a consequence, economics became defined by means of its methods and not by means of its subject. The analysis presented in the previous chapters shows that this limited the scope of economics fundamentally, and misguided the scientific discipline. Economics came to exclude almost all human and social elements from their theories in order to save their scientific acceptability and methodological strength.

Yet, we have seen from the arguments presented, that economic phenomena only emerge from the interactions of human individuals in an objectively given nature. Economics and the phenomena it studies can neither exist independent of the human, nor independent of nature. This distinguishes economics from the natural sciences, which study phenomena that are more or less independent of the observer. I therefore argue that economics studies human interactions in a naturally given environment. This implies in the sense of Soros, that economic reality is a reflexive system. If we aim at a better science of economics, we have to develop methods and principles adequate to economic reality. Let me therefore, describe the nature of economic reality, before we move to the scientific methods and principles appropriate to this nature. As already indicated, George Soros' model of the reflexive economic reality is the departure point of my open complex system account of economic reality.

Economic reality consists of the natural environment and human individuals with all their natural needs, capacities and desires. Unlike other individuals, humans are capable of acting strategically[5] and possess' images of potential future realities. This fundamental structure presupposes different levels of reflexivity. Hereby, reflexivity is defined as double feedback mechanism between two elements.

10.3.1 First Order Reflexivity

The first and most obvious type of reflexivity is that between objective and subjective reality. Each agent has a subjective reality of its own. Now, if the agent observes objective reality, his subjective reality influences, and yet not determines, his perceptions. These perceptions of reality on the other hand shape the subjective reality. The feedback mechanism between objective and subjective reality is continuous and circular (Soros 2013: 312). Figure 10.2 illustrates first order reflexivity.[6]

[5]By strategically I mean that humans are able to act against their natural instincts and decide consciously which action to take. Nevertheless, human actions are also driven by natural instincts and emotions. Yet, humans have an opportunity to turn against these instincts and emotions.

[6]Rosenberg (2013: 439) critically reflects Soros human uncertainty principle in the following way: "In the biological domain, uncertainty and reflexivity are held in check by environments that change with geological slowness. This produces long-lived local equilibrium outcomes. In the human domain, the environment is cultural. It is composed of nested sets of strategies that are all affected by both reflexivity and uncertainty. The result of their operation is at most short-lived

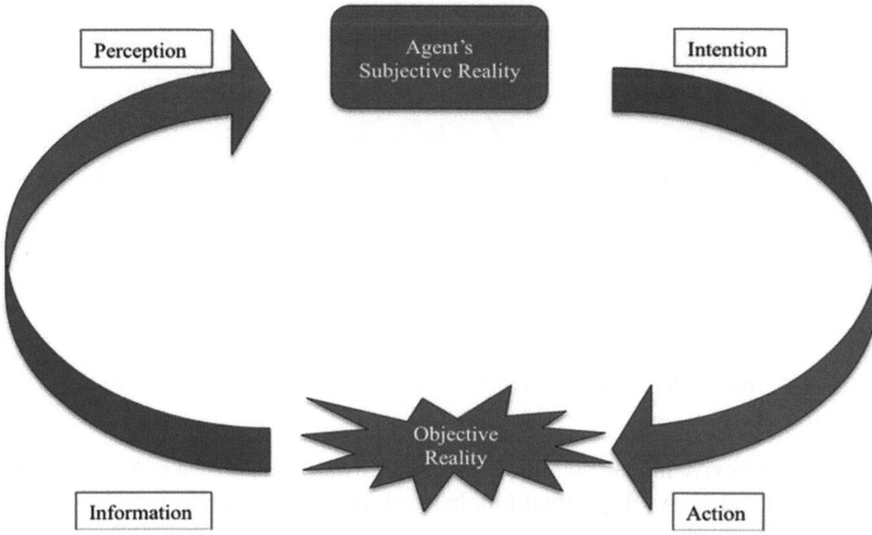

Fig. 10.2 First order reflexivity, authors' own figure

10.3.2 Second Order Reflexivity and the Structure of Events

Using the cognitive function, the individual observes the world. As Soros, had argued, this process is basically passive, in the way that the observer does not aim to manipulate the world. Instead, the observer seeks to understand it. This, however, means that the observer categorises the perceived information and puts them in relation to other information. Though, this process is for the most part not conscious, it describes a reflexive feedback mechanism. Old information shapes the way in which individuals perceive new information. Thus, an objective observation of reality is impossible for the individual. Furthermore, the structure of reality even complicates this reflexive process. The individual is, besides observing reality also capable of memorising the past and imagining the future. Reality therefore has a continuous structure, which feeds back on itself through the observing individual. Consequently, the images of a possible future reality, which are shaped by our perceptions of reality and memories of the past, influence our observations of the present. Thus, the cognitive function described by Soros is itself a reflexive system. Furthermore, second order reflexivity, connects past, present and a not yet realised

local equilibria, broken up by radical environmental change. The source of this radical environmental change in human cultural processes is obvious. It is the iterated, unsynchronised combinations of reflexivity and uncertainty in strategy variation. As the rate of change in the cultural environment increases, the lifetimes of local equilibria shorten, until in many cases they disappear altogether. Human affairs appear chaotic because many of them are far from equilibrium, even if there are any equilibria to which they may temporarily be heading."

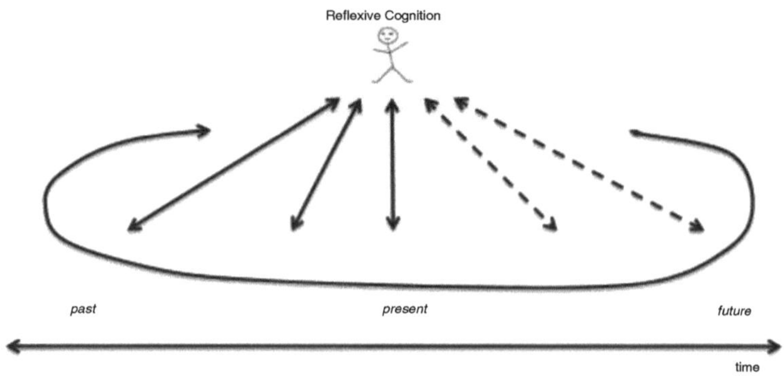

Fig. 10.3 Second order reflexivity, or reflexive cognition of reality, authors' own figure

future in a reflexive human cognition. Figure 10.3 outlines the idea of Second Order Reflexivity and shows the mutual link between past and future.

10.3.3 Third Order Reflexivity

I argue, in the sense of Keynes' beauty contest (1936: 156) that the interactions between agent's subjective realities also have an impact on the perception and intention, and therefore, they also influence the objective reality. In this way, economic systems are double reflexive. As Fig. 10.4 shows there is reflexivity between objective reality and agent's subjective reality and there is reflexivity between agent's subjective realities and other agent's subjective reality. Thinking or imagination and communication create this double feedback mechanism. Thinking agents construct a perception of the objective reality, by their actions and utterances, they communicate directly or indirectly, with or without intentions, their subjective reality to their fellow agent's. These fellow agents interpret and verify the communicated agent's subjective realities and integrate them in their personal agent's subjective reality. By this communicative process, agent's subjective realities influence other agent's subjective reality. Naturally, this communicative function is similarly fallible as the cognitive and the manipulative function. Unlike to the cognitive function, the communicative function is observable, as it not only takes place inside the brain, but shows itself in objectively observable actions and verbal communication. Furthermore, there is a feedback mechanism between the agent's subjective realities, as agents are able to clarify meanings or reach consensus, so that we can in some cases speak of shared subjective realities. And I would argue that the more agents agree on a particular shared subjective reality, the more influential this subjective reality will become on objective reality. These shared subjective realities can be used to identify potential future objective realities and they themselves can be manipulated, in order to create shared subjective

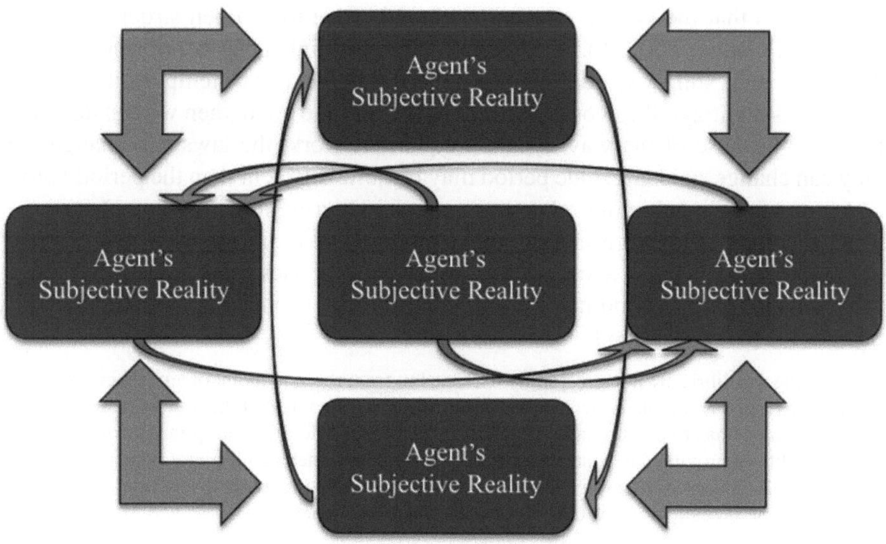

Fig. 10.4 Third order reflexivity, authors' own figure

realities that favour a particularly welcome potential future. In this way reflexivity, can be used for mild forms of prediction and manipulation.

10.3.4 Complexity

Combined with the network structure of economic reality, reflexivity causes complexity in economic reality. Complexity implies that there are dynamic relationships among the elements of the network, which change the network itself in a way that cannot be forecasted, as the relationships are not deterministic, but reflexive. According to Colander (2002: 3) complex systems, like the economic system, are characterised by emergent patterns, which are subject to more or less sudden and predictable changes. Furthermore, the reductionist view that macro-phenomena are brought about by the microstructure of the system gets rejected. Colander (2002: 3) argues: "As complex systems evolve, new patterns can emerge, and these patterns can take on an existence and life of their own." Consequently, complex systems are open systems and its elements are chaotic, reflexive and indeterministic. However, the patterns brought about by the system are not arbitrary. It is possible to analyse the structure of their emergence on the basis of their local background. This idea is similar to Lawson's demi-regs. In a well-defined part of the complex system, regularities and patterns can be identified and explained. Yet, the knowledge is necessarily local and cannot be transferred from one part of the system to another, nor is it possible to argue that the pattern holds for the system itself. The reason therefore, is that the system changes constantly, due to its open structure. Consequently (Colander 2002: 6), "(i)n complexity economics one is not searching out the truth; one is simply searching for a statistical fit that can be temporarily useful in our understanding of the economy. If these fits become good, then we can develop a law, but, because of the way dynamic equations work, the laws can change, and they can change suddenly. One period may be quite different than the period before, and, instead, be much more related to a much earlier period."

The complexity interpretation of economic reality is not new. Particularly, Schumpeter (1954) was sympathetic to this point of view and argued that due to the complexity of economic reality, equilibrium economics is fundamentally flawed. He (p. 969) argued:

> Multiple equilibria are not necessarily useless, but from the standpoint of any exact science the existence of a uniquely determined equilibrium is, of course, of the utmost importance, even if proof has to be purchased at the price of very restrictive assumptions; without any possibility of proving the existence of (a) uniquely determined equilibrium, or at all events, of a small number of possible equilibria, at however high a level of abstraction, a field of phenomena is really a chaos that is not under analytical control.

Following Schumpeter's line of thought, complexity, reflexivity and performativity are serious challenges to the old positivist principles of the science of economics. Yet, they are constitutive for the subject of economics and therefore cannot be ignored, regarding the scientific status of economics. Rather the opposite is the case, if economics keeps on ignoring its subject matter, it loses the status of a science, no matter how elegant its methods are.

If economics is thought of as a complex and reflexive open system, uncertainty is a constant companion of economic phenomena. Furthermore, the science of economics faces two types of uncertainty. The first type of uncertainty is that which comes from the nature of economic reality. While the second type of uncertainty emerges from the science itself. By investigating economic phenomena, economists shape the economy, in a way that cannot be predicted. Economic theories and models are part of economic reality und scientists have to expect that they change the world they analyse by analysing it (MacKenzie 2006a, b).

10.4 The Uncertainty Corridor

The analysis in part two of this book had shown that economists recognised that economic situations are characterised by different degrees of uncertainty. These different ontological states raise different epistemological challenges for the science of economics. Now, we are in the position to describe and understand the nature of these different degrees of uncertainty and the challenges associated with them. I have argued that uncertainty in the economic realm arises from the interactions of human individuals, which are characterised by different degrees of reflexivity and complexity.

Beinhocker (2013: 336) had suggested a spectrum of complexity in economics, which I find particularly useful. He argues that complexity reaches from a simple mechanic system to a complex reflexive system. The more complex the system gets the more open it becomes in the sense of Chick and Dow (2005). To Beinhocker a simple mechanic system is a ball rolling down a frictionless plane in a vacuum. In terms of economics a simple system could be a single good market with only one rational buyer and one rational seller. A simple statistical system is slightly more complex, and according to Beinhocker, comparable to an ideal gas. In economics, the efficient market hypothesis is constructed as a simple statistical system that assumes stock prices to be purely random. If the assumption of randomness gets relaxed, one ends up in a non-linear dynamic system (e.g. turbulent fluid), which can no longer be described by statistical means. An example for a non-linear dynamic system in economics could be the development of an enterprise value. It constantly changes over time in a non-linear way. These kinds of systems can only be simulated and unambiguous solutions become impossible. Beyond non-linear dynamic systems, there are complex systems, like climate change. These systems are a complicated network of diverse interrelations and they are characterised by feedback mechanisms between its parts, non-linear relationships, emergent properties, which cannot fully be explained by the microstructure of the system, non-reductionism, which implies that changes in the microstructure need not cause changes in the macrostructure and the other way around, openness and path dependency. From an economics perspective, any market can be interpreted as a complex system with emergent properties, such as prices. Beinhocker (2013: 337) sees complex adaptive (e.g. human brain) and complex reflexive systems as the most complex structures. They differ from complex system in the way that they adapt over time, by changing their structure or building new elements. These types of systems resemble the economy as a whole, which constantly changes its own framework, due to innovations or new institutions, which again lead to new changes in the complex system. Therefore, the economy is both an adaptive and reflexive system.

Complexity is one part of uncertainty in economics, the other is, reflexivity. While any natural system may be complex to different degrees (e.g. bacterium's gaining food), they cannot be reflexive, as reflexivity is inseparably linked to intelligent actors, which are, in the case of economics: humans. So far, we have distinguished three types of reflexivity in economics, which add on to each other. We start with simple feedback mechanisms on the one side of the spectrum and end up with third order reflexivity, according to which, economic research influences its subject under study in an unforeseeable way. If one puts complexity and reflexivity in relation, one gets an uncertainty corridor for economics. The corridor describes the level of uncertainty of economic phenomena in relation to its complexity and reflexivity. Besides illustrating the degree of uncertainty, the researcher is confronted with, the measure also gives an idea of how robust the conclusions of the analysis, no matter which methods get used, might be.

Uncertainty, per se, is not problematic. We have learned by Hayek, Knight and Keynes, that it is the source of innovation and dynamics. Yet, for the science of

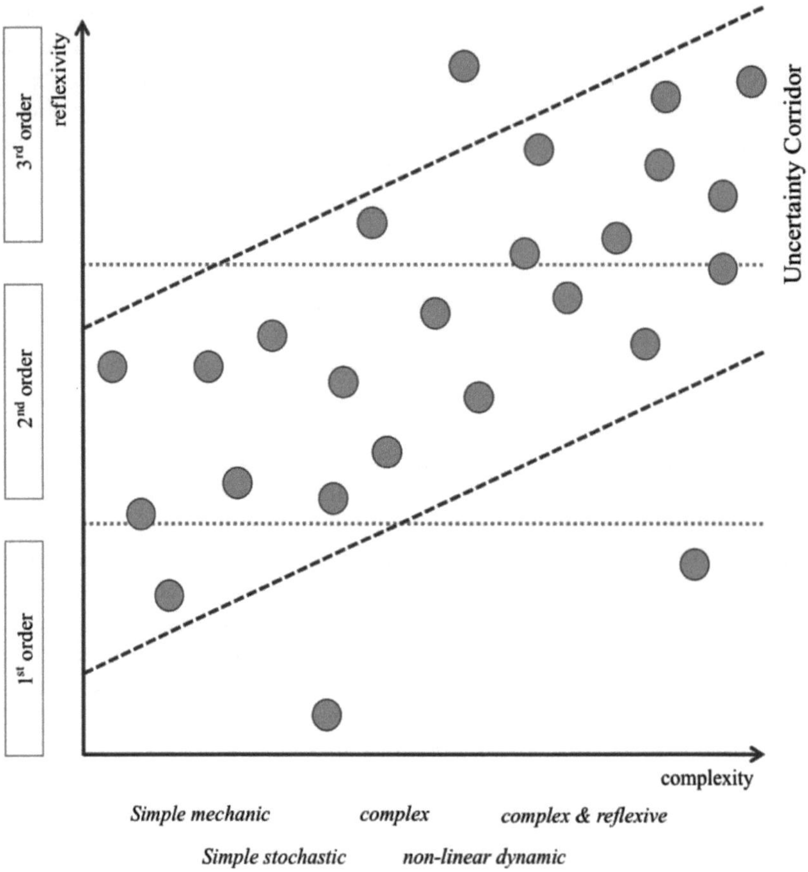

Fig. 10.5 The uncertainty corridor, authors' own figure

economics, uncertainty is highly problematic as it prevents economics from reaching rigor and unambiguous conclusions in the sense of a positive science. As Fig. 10.5 shows, the more uncertain an economic phenomenon gets, the more ambiguous becomes economic research. Therefore, the corridor of uncertainty in Fig. 10.5 also describes the epistemological challenges associated with a particular measure of uncertainty.

On the lower left corner, the epistemological challenges are few, while there are many, not yet solvable by the methods of economics, in the upper right quadrant. The uncertainty corridor describes the different levels of uncertainty that can be found in economics in general. In addition to that, each economic phenomenon, depending on the level of analytical precision follows this corridor. Consequently, the different aspects of an economic problem might be uncertain to different degrees and therefore subject to different epistemological challenges. I mean that it might be legitimate to use simple statistical models to analyse one element of an economic phenomena and at the same time complement the statistical findings with other more uncertainty-robust methods. The uncertainty corridor explains why methodological pluralism in economics is not arbitrary but necessary. Acknowledging uncertainty in economics does not imply that all present economic methods are meaningless or wrong (including highly abstract mathematical models and statistics). It just shows that they only cover small parts of economic reality and therefore need to be complemented. These complementary methods are naturally (due to the level of uncertainty under which they get used) less rigorous and explicit in the sense of positive economics. Still, they are not meaningless and help to gain insights in a highly uncertain reality.[7] Beinhocker (2013: 338), concludes: "Success for a theory is always highly contingent and subject to future refutation while failure is generally fatal. This asymmetry is true for any evolutionary epistemological system where objective truth is inaccessible but increasingly successful approximations are possible."

10.5 Epistemological Implications for the Science of Economics

Uncertainty is fundamentally linked to economic phenomena and the science of economics. It prevents a positivist philosophy of economics with purely rigorous methods and unambiguous results. The analysis has shown, that modern economics, which acknowledges uncertainty as an economic fundamental needs new principles of research, in order to explore also highly uncertain elements of economic reality, without becoming speculative and unscientific (Kirman 2011a, b; Hermann-Pillath 2011, 2013). I suggest logical coherence and validity to replace simplicity and predictive power as prime principles of economics. Furthermore, we need a pluralism in economic methodology, including statistical models, computer simulations and verbal elaborations. However, at the end this will not save us from necessarily ambiguous conclusions and temporal theories, which need constant rethinking and a responsible economist. The reason, herefore, is that uncertainty brings back free will and moral responsibility into economics.[8] Through reflexivity, economic

[7]This conclusion is not new. However, during the last decade's economists pushed this insight aside. E.g.: Box and Draper (1987: 424): "Essentially, all models are wrong, but some are useful."

[8]Cf. Beinhocker (2013: 338): "I should also briefly note that while complex reflexive systems present a challenge due to their Knightian uncertainty, there is also an upside-their inherent indeterminacy creates space for novelty and creativity. In a perfectly deterministic system, there is no room for novelty to emerge. In a perfectly random system, there is insufficient coherence for novelty to matter. Complex reflexive systems are somewhere in between—they are hard to forecast and fallibility is inevitable, but there is nonetheless pattern and structure. This creates a space for novelty, experimentation, and in human systems creativity. One may even argue that there is a link between reflexivity and free will—reflexivity makes free will both possible and necessary."

theories are performative (Esposito 2011) and change economic realities. This makes economics particularly powerful compared to the natural sciences, which cannot not change their subject under study. On the other hand, performativity calls for a conscious and mindful economists profession, as economists have the power to change the world we live in.

For Positive Economics Friedman (1953) had suggested choosing between alternatives hypothesises on the basis of their predictive power (fruitfulness) and according to their simplicity. This implies, the less complex a theory is, the more desirable it is for economics. If we acknowledge uncertainty, predictive power becomes a meaningless concept. In the present, when a scientist or practitioner has to choose between alternative hypotheses, the future is unknown, therefore it is impossible to know which theory is more accurate in terms of predictive power. Even if there is evidence from the past that suggests that one hypothesis is more powerful than the other, we cannot expect, that the same will hold in the future. If predictability would be accepted as an instrument for evaluating hypothesises, it would only be possible to evaluate them, when the future is already realised. Therefore, the concept of predictability cannot be used as a basis for evaluating theories in the present, as it only reveals itself in the not yet known future.

Simplicity is a pragmatic ideal, which aims at generality.[9] In economic epistemology under conditions of uncertainty, simplicity is only a minor criterion. If there were two similarly plausible theories and one were simpler than the other, it would be sufficient for matters of practicability to prefer one over the other. Yet, in economics of uncertainty it will rarely be case that two theories with similar conclusions are competing with each other. It rather is the case that theories with different conclusions are competing with each other.

Truth, is also not suitable as a criterion for good theories and models. Under conditions of uncertainty, there is no universal truth. Truth is as impossible as objective observations of reality in a complex and multi-reflexive system. Instead of true theories and models, we can find more or less stable regularities, mechanisms or powerful heuristics (Byrne 2007; Sugden 2009; Hermann-Pillath 2011; Priddat 2014b). Fallibility and different degrees of uncertainty leave us with approximations of knowledge. These approximations help us to understand and act in an uncertain reality. While muddling through reality, economists will find, that some approximations are better than others and some approximations may even be falsified. This implies that economic epistemology under conditions of uncertainty

[9]Friedman (1953: 5–6) defines: "A theory is "simpler" the less the initial knowledge needed to make a prediction within a given field of phenomena; it is more "fruitful" the more precise the resulting prediction, the wider the area within which the theory yields predictions, and the more additional lines for further research it suggests. Logical completeness and consistency are relevant but play a subsidiary role; their function is to assure that the hypothesis says what it is intended to say and does so alike for all users—they play the same role here as checks for arithmetical accuracy do in statistical computations."

is a dynamic evolutionary process. Models and theories are temporal in character and yet they are not arbitrary (Boldizzoni 2011; Hermann-Pillath 2011).

I suggest interpreting economic theories or models as temporal and dynamic fictions. These fictions guide our perception of economic reality and help us to find our way through a reflexive and complex reality via heuristics, approximations and plausible explanations. Fictions are neither true nor false, instead they are plausible. Plausibility is a quality criteria used in fictional literature, according to which a story, or in our case, an economic hypothesis, is plausible, if it is believable by a group of other people (Campe 2002; Arrow 1978, 2013; Morgan 2013: Chap. 12; Priddat 2014b). This is only the case, if the hypothesis, does not violate the laws of logically valid reasoning. Furthermore, the hypothesis becomes more believable the more precise it is. Thus, unlike positive economics, fictional economics in not only interested in the conclusion, but also in the details and the underlying structure of the theory, as it makes the hypothesis more believable. Nobody would believe in a fiction that says, that billiards will become an Olympic discipline. Whereas, the fiction becomes more believable if the author explains as precisely as possible, how billiards becomes an Olympic discipline. Fictional economics is interested in the microstructure that brings about some phenomenon. The reason therefore is, that only if the microstructure is known, the black box of explanation can be opened and it might become possible to understand, how the economic system might have brought about some phenomena. As we take an open system point of view in fictional economics, we cannot expect to identify universally true causal relationships, yet we might be able to identify regularities, demi-regs or mechanisms or plausible storylines that might be able to make sense of the observed phenomena. In this way, Fictional Economics, as I suggest it, has more to offer than Positive Economics. Positive economics only aims at explanation and prediction via the deductive-nomological mode of explanation. The mode is not interested in understanding, how a phenomenon was brought about. Consequently, the law like regularities identified by positive economics do not allow for understanding economic phenomena.

The methods of research used to understand economic phenomena is not restricted by Fictional Economics. In this way, fictional economics offers a truly pluralist research agenda. Statistical inference, field or laboratory experiments, equally to pure analytics, historical analysis or mathematical models are similarly welcome in fictional economics. However, independent of the applied method, the researcher has to offer a plausible meaning comprehensible and believable, story of how some phenomena was brought about or why we have to expect some particular phenomenon in the future. The researcher is similar to the author of a fiction novel, and he or she uses some particular method, in order to identify evidence that convinces the recipient of the potential truth of the story. At the same time both author and recipient know, that the story told is only potentially true, and the recipient has the freedom to decide to what extend he or she believes in the fictional story (Heinzelman 1980; Eco 1994; Kleeberg 2009; Künzel 2014). This view is pretty similar to that offered by Deirdre McCloskey in her "Rhetoric's of economics". Methods, models, theories, mathematics and graphs are used by economists in order to convince their readers. They are rhetorical devices used to fuel the ethos and the pathos of the author (Klamer 2007). Fictional Economics makes this implicit structure of economic persuasion explicit and acknowledges, that this rhetoric or fictional point of view, is the only one possible. It also implies, that economics is not about identifying some universally true relationships, but about the art of persuasion or plausible storytelling (McCloskey 1983, 1985, 1997, 1998, 2009; Byrne 2007; Klamer 2007; Beckert 2008, 2011; Kleeberg 2009; Esposito 2011, 2013; Bianchi 2014; Künzel 2014; Priddat 2014a). Furthermore, economics is about future creation.

Fictional Economics is underlying an evolutionary epistemology. It assumes that the users of theories have the freedom to choose between alternative fictions in economics. Depending on their interests and convictions, one theory might be more plausible to them, than another. Furthermore, the underlying evolutionary epistemology presupposes, that the plausibility of each fiction is dependent on the time in which it is presented. While the fiction of efficient financial markets might have been plausible in the 1970s, when the analytical instruments were less precise, the same fiction is implausible to large parts of their recipients today. There is large evidence (good reason to believe) that the theory (though it is elegant) is misguiding. The fiction of financial markets was neither true in the 1970s, nor today. Therefore, the fictional theory cannot be falsified in the sense of Popper (1934). Since, something that is by definition not true, can also not become false. The quality of economic fictions lies outside the categories of true and false. Nevertheless, there is an evolutionary process in economic epistemology, which causes fictions that have been accepted at some point of time to become refused at another point of time (Bolizzoni 2011; Hermann-Pillath 2011). The evolutionary economic epistemological system operates on selection via plausibility. This implies that the evaluation of economic theories is a discursive process, in which users of economic theories decide which theory is more plausible than other. While the audience and the evidence changes over time in a dynamic and complex process, one and the same theory will be evaluated differently. Consequently, an uncertain economic ontology that presupposes an evolutionary epistemology proves axiomatic principles, as they have dominated economics since the marginal revolution, impossible. Economic reality is subject to change and innovation; and so are economic theories.

In the course of time, new methods became possible, for different reasons (computerization, big data, new techniques, such as complexity modelling, …) (Pentland 2014; Bianchi 2014). This new evidence rendered old fictions implausible and fostered new fictions, which will become implausible sooner or later, as mankind develops. For economics, this implies that there are no wrong methods in the same way as there are no wrong theories. Modern fictional economics presupposes competing methods and competing theories. Theory and methodology selection is a temporally limited decision, which needs to be corrected sooner or later. In discriminating between methods and theories, economists, politicians and any economic actor needs to balance the arguments and evidence and single out the theory or methods most plausible to him or her at a specific point in time.

10.6 Conclusion

Economics is a human science after all. The nature of economics is reflexive and complex to different degrees. This renders economics particularly complicated. On the other hand, economists do not have to fear the uncertainty that originates from the reflexive and complex nature of economic reality. Uncertainty in economics is structured. The suggested conceptualisation of uncertainty in economics via the uncertainty corridor differentiates between different epistemological and ontological problems. The analysis shows that most economic phenomena can be understood, though it needs more than abstract economic theories. Economic science needs a methodological toolkit that is as flexible and dynamic as the subject it aims to study. Furthermore, economics must acknowledge its performative power and the responsibility that comes with it.

References

Arrow KJ (1978) The future and the present in economic life. Econ Inq 16:157–169
Arrow KJ (2013) Knowledge, belief and the economic. WIFO Monatsberichte 12:943–951
Beckert J (2008) Fictional expectations in the economy. Working Papers, pp 1–32
Beckert J (2011) Imagined futures fictionality in economic action. Max-Planck-Institut für Gesellschaftsforschung Discussion Paper 8, pp 1–30
Beinhocker ED (2013) Reflexivity, complexity, and the nature of social science. J Econ Methodol 20(4):330–342
Bianchi M (2014) The magic of storytelling: how curiosity and aesthetic preferences work. Economics Discussion Papers Kiel Institute for the World Economy 23
Boldizzoni F (2011) Poverty of Clio. Princeton University Press, Princeton
Box GEP, Draper NR (1987) Empirical model building and response surfaces. Wiley, New York
Byrne RMJ (2007) The rational imagination. MIT Press, Cambridge
Campe R (2002) Spiel der Wahrscheinlichkeit. Literatur und Berechnung zwischen Pascal und Kleist. Wallstein Verlag, Göttingen
Chick V, Dow SC (2005) The meaning of open systems. J Econ Methodol 12(3):363–381
Colander D (2002) Complexity and the history of economic thought. Routledge, London
Damásio AR, Damásio H, Christen Y (1996) Neurobiology of decision-making. Springer, Berlin
Eco U (1994) Im Wald der Fiktionen: Sechs Streifzüge durch die Literatur. Deutscher Taschenbuchverlag, München
Esposito E (2011) The future of futures: the time of money in financing and society. Edward Elgar, Cheltenham
Esposito E (2013) The structures of uncertainty: performativity and unpredictability in economic operations. Econ Soc 42(1):102–129
Friedman M (1953) The methodology of positive economics. In: Friedman M (ed) In positive economics. Chicago University Press, Chicago
Gigerenzer G, Gaissmaier W (2011) Heuristic decision making. Annu Rev Psychol 62:451–482
Hausman DM (1992) The inexact and separate science of economics. Cambridge University Press, Cambridge
Heinzelman K (1980) The economics of the imagination. University of Massachusetts Press, Amherst

Herrmann-Pillath C (2011) Economics of identity and creativity. University of Queensland Press, Brisbane
Herrmann-Pillath C (2013) Foundations of economic evolution: a treatise on the natural philosophy of economics. Edward Elgar, Cheltenham
Keynes JM (1936) The general theory of employment, interest and money. Palgrave Macmillan, London
Kirman A (2011a) The crisis in economic theory. Rivista Italiana degli Economisti, SIE—Societa' Italiana degli Economisti 16(1):9–36
Kirman A (2011b) Complex economics: individual and collective rationality. Routledge, London
Klamer A (2007) Speaking of economics: how to get in the conversation. Routledge, London
Kleeberg B (2009) Gewinn maximieren, Gleichgewicht modellieren. Erzählen im ökonomischen Diskurs. In: Klein C, Martínez M (Hgs) Wirklichkeitserzählungen. Felder, Formen und Funktionen nicht-literarischen Erzählen. Metzler, Stuttgart, pp 136–159
Künzel C (2014) Imaginierte Zukunft: Zur Bedeutung von Fiktion(en) in ökonomischen Diskursen. In: Balin I, Zilles S (Hrsg) Literarische Ökonomik. Fink, Paderborn
MacKenzie D (2006a) Is economics performative? Option Theor Construct Derivat Market 28:29–55
MacKenzie D (2006b) An engine, not a camera: How financial models shape markets. MIT Press, Cambridge
McCloskey DN (1983) The rhetoric of economics. J Econ Lit 21(2):481–517
McCloskey DN (1985) A conversation with Donald N. McCloskey about rhetoric. East Econ J 11 (4):293–296
McCloskey DN (1997) The rhetoric of economics, revisited. East Econ J 23(3):359–362
McCloskey DN (1998) The rhetoric of economics (Rhetoric of the human sciences). University of Wisconsin Press, Madison
McCloskey DN (2009) Rhetoric matters: ethical standards in a humanistic science of economics. Challenge 52(4):25–31
Morgan J (2013) Forecasting, prediction and precision: a commentary (Ch. 12). In: Kabalak A, Priddat BP (Hrsg) Ungewissheit als Herausforderung für die ökonomische Theorie: Nichtwissen, Ambivalenz und Entscheidung. Metropolis, Marburg
Pentland A (2014) Social physics: how good ideas spread—the lessons from a new science. Penguin Press, New York
Popper KR (1934) The logic of scientific discovery. Taylor & Francis, New York
Priddat BP (2014a) Economics of persuasion. Ökonomie zwischen Markt, Kommunikation und Überredung, Metropolis
Priddat BP (2014b) Prognose als narrative Plausibilität. In: Cevolini M (Hrsg) Die Ordnung des Kontingenten. Springer, Berlin, pp 251–280
Rist G (2011) The delusions of economics: the misguided certainties of a hazardous science. Zed Books, London
Rosenberg A (2013) Reflexivity, uncertainty and the unity of science. J Econ Methodol 20 (4):429–438
Schumpeter JA (1954) History of economic analysis: with a new introduction. Oxford University Press, Oxford
Soros G (2013) Fallibility, reflexivity, and the human uncertainty principle. J Econ Methodol 20 (4):309–329
Sugden R (2009) Credible worlds, capacities and mechanism. Erkenntnis 70(3):3–27
Virlics A (2013) Emotions in economic decision making: a multidisciplinary approach. Procedia Soc Behav Sci 92(10):1011–1015

Chapter 11
Uncertainty and Fiction

The economic theory of choice denies uncertainty to a large degree. In my previous chapters I have argued that this denial is both illegitimate from a philosophy of science perspective and misdirecting economics. Uncertainty is fundamental to economic phenomena and economic actions. However, so far it is not sufficiently represented in economic theories. Therefore, the conclusions of economic theories are not applicable to real political questions. In what follows, I suggest a theory of reasonable[1] economic action under conditions of uncertainty. The theory describes how choice could be conceptualised under conditions of uncertainty.

The chapter is organized in three sections. I begin by presenting the co-evolution of probability and fiction. I argue that though probabilistic reasoning became dominant in the sciences, the concept of fiction has more to offer for economics, as it does not neglect its uncertain nature. The second section analyses the use of fictionalism in economics and describes its analytical strength for the science of economics. In the third part I suggest an evolutionary fictional choice approach as an alternative to expected utility thinking. The chapter shows the advantage of fictionalism for economics and delineates a New Research Paradigm.

11.1 The Co-emergence of Fiction and Probability

Drama, as today's most important form of fictional literature[2] and the theory of probability both developed in the seventeenth century as an attempt to deal with the increasing complexity and uncertainty of reality. The collapse of the clerical

[1]The concept of reasonableness is contrasted to the standard economic concept of rationality, which describes the marginalist ideal of utility maximization by means of numerical probabilities (objective probabilities under conditions of certainty and risk and subjective probabilities under conditions of uncertainty).

[2]Much older forms of fictional literature are Epic and Lyric.

J. Köhn, *Uncertainty in Economics*, Contributions to Economics,
DOI 10.1007/978-3-319-55351-1_11

sovereignty of interpretation during the enlightenment left apparent chaos, arbitrariness and contingency (Bernstein 1998). Consequently, people were looking for a new guide to action. And as a consequence, the theory of probability and fictional literature developed (Campe 2002; Priddat 2014c). Today, we often contrast fiction and stochastic. According to our perception, stochastic belongs to the valuable instruments of the hard sciences, while fiction is an artistic and non-serious concept. Therefore, stochastic is argued to be about the real nature of things, while fiction is about non-existing things. The common origin of the two concepts, however, suggests that fiction and stochastic share much more than what distinguishes the two.

Both concepts were designed to bring back apparent order and to systematically explore the possible in a time in which categories like reality, knowledge and fact became more and more ambiguous. While the theories of probability used different methods of calculation as a guide to action in the face of uncertainty, fiction helps oneself with the power of imagination in order to explore the possibilities of reality. The consequence of these different approaches is that theories of probability provide unambiguous numerical results in the face of uncertainty, while imagination obtains the ambiguity of an uncertain reality. The reduction of complexity and uncertainty is thus weaker if one uses imagination instead of calculation. Furthermore, probabilistic treatments of uncertainty only apply to epistemological uncertainty, while fictions allow us to explore the possibilities of ontological uncertainty. Imagination allows exploring possible worlds or possibility spaces and thereby produces no certainty and no explicit result. Each imagined fiction of reality might well be wrong or right, however nobody can tell. The same is true for any kind of non-objective probability measure. However, its numerical appearance conceals its ambiguity and leaves us with the illusion of certainty and correctness.

There are different linguistic, philosophical and sociological theories of fiction, which cannot all be discussed in depth here. Nevertheless, I will draw attention to some aspects of these theories, which are important to the argument I make in favour of fictionalism in economic theory. I will focus on linguistic and philosophical theories of fiction.

The term "fiction" derives from the Latin word "fictio" and means "forming". As Beckert (2011: 5) argues based on Bunia (2009) and Vaihinger (1911: 129) the verb "forming" itself derives from the term "fingere", which means "to shape", "to form" or "to make up". From this origin, it can be seen that the main characteristic of fiction is that it is created by someone. Instead of being about reality, "fiction creates a world of its own" (Beckert 2011: 5). This "world of its own" in principle need not correspond to reality. Fiction thus described an imagined reality, which is different from reality. This however does not imply generally that fiction is "non-serious" as Searle (1969, 1975, 1996, 1999, 2011) had argued. Fictions are based on reality to different degrees. The author of a fiction is not allowed to create a fantastic world, which has nothing to do with reality and at the same time fiction allows the author to create a world, which is only slightly different from reality or describes a way in which reality could develop, however has not yet developed. Beckert (2011: 5) puts it this way: "The worlds created through fiction are based not on an empirically observable truth but on the author's imaginings. This does not imply that there is no correspondence to realty. On the contrary, the assertions made in fictional texts achieve their credibility often because they could very well be true or because they are closely interwoven with elements that are indeed nonfictional." This non-fictionality of fictional literature serves to build up mutual trust between recipient and author. Albeit the author of a fictional text should reveal the fictionality of the story, the author aims to make the recipient believe that the story could be true. In this way author and recipient of fictional literature enter into a quasi-contract.

Initially, the author signals and reveals that he writes a fictional text and at the same time commits itself to realisticness, in the way that the described world is like the real world in its basic structure (Beckert 2011). Any difference between the real world and the fictional world will be pointed out explicitly by the author. As a consequence fictional texts always contain a mixture of fictional and factual representations (Esposito 2007). The factual representations included in a fictional text need to be right. So, if a fiction refers to some historic date or the results of some scientific experiment, the recipient can be sure that the representation is actually true. Any violation of this rule destroys the credibility of the author. The fictional representations on the contrary can neither be true nor false. It should become obvious that a fictional text therefore can never contain any false elements. Instead fictional representations are invented and therefore they can only be coherent and sound. Furthermore, authors of fictional literature commit themselves only to invent fictional representations, which could be true, in the way that there is resemblance between reality and fiction. The less the author complies with this rule, the more fantastic and therefore less credible the story gets.

The recipient, on the other side agrees by entering the quasi contract, that the story is not true, however possibility true as it contains no lies and false statements. Coleridge (1985) speaks in this context of the "willing suspension of disbelief". While being aware of its fictional elements, the recipient agrees to believe in the possibility of the story. This commitment affects the way in which the recipient uses the fiction and the conclusions or findings derived from it. If the recipient thinks the fiction is true, or behaves as if it were true, the quasi contract is cancelled. Fiction thus demands mindfulness in dealing with it, as it always operates on the borderline between reality and fantasy (Eco 1994).

Especially, when it comes to the use of fictions in science the disclosure of fictionality or unrealisticness becomes particularly important for the use in scientific findings. Yet, it is often the case, particularly in economics that it is not made explicit that the theory is based on unrealistic assumptions or even does not correspond to the real world in important ways. At the same time, fictional reasoning is particularly important in the sciences as it allows for scientific progress in a world in which knowledge is limited (Krüger 1989). Simplifications, are key to analytical precision and success. Hans Vaihinger (1911: XII) for example had argued that scientific categories and theories are based on "consciously false assumptions.[3] This implies that in the sciences the objects described often do not possess the characteristics ascribed to them (Beckert 2011: 7). Therefore, they are treated "as if" they would possess these characteristics. In this way, scientific theories could be interpreted as fictions, as they imagine the objects of their theory in a way that is not realistic, however corresponds to the way in which the objects actually are in reality.

We now turn to the temporal aspect of fiction. Initially, a fiction is timeless. Past, present and future fictions are equally possible. Of course most of our images of fictions are about the future. A fictional novel, for example, often takes place in the future. It imagines how things could develop. Yet, the future orientation of fictions is not constitutive for fictions. It is equally possible to imagine a fiction about the past. Such a fiction novel imagines, how things also could have been. Even though they have been different. Thus, fictions do not need to be about the future. It rather is the case that fictions need to be possibly true. Stories about some reality, either past present or future, can be classified as a fiction only if they describe a realm that is possible and yet not real, given the knowledge we have at the moment the fiction gets developed.

Esposito (2007: 17) introduces the concept of acceptability. According to her, a fiction needs to be acceptable in the way that it describes a world that is as plausible as if it were true and yet, it is not true. In order to apply to this criterion a fiction needs to be realistic. Quiet contradictory fictions are necessarily not true or not yet true and, at the same time, they need to be realistic. In a way, they are believable untruth, which derive their legitimation from the promise that they could be true and that people agree that they could be true. In this way, the label fiction is a quality criteria for an untrue story, which proves, that other people think, given the knowledge we have that this story could be true (Byrne 2007; Bianchi 2014). This intersubjectivity marks the boundary between fiction and fantasy. A fiction needs to be approved by some public that agrees that the story could be true, while it is not true and therefore acceptable. Fantasy, neither needs to be possibly true, nor does it need to apply any objective standards. Fantasy is a purely subjective category, while fiction is not (Booth 1961, 1990; Mendlesohn 2008).

Here from quality criteria for fictions can be derived. It seems to be the case that credibility is the highest quality criteria for a fiction. Esposito (2007: 13) had argued that a description of a possible world becomes acceptable as a fiction, only if this possible world is as plausible that it could be true. Any violation of the laws of logical reasoning renders a fiction a phantasm. Thus, fictions are neither true nor false, yet they have to be potentially true. Or as Esposito (2007: 13) puts it, fictions are "believable untruth". Beside potential truth and nearness to reality or realisticness and coherence are other elements of the credibility of fictions.

After we have explored some of the key literary aspects of fictions, we will now turn to the philosophical debate about fiction. Fictionalism is a branch of philosophy, which uses the concept of fiction as an analytical instrument to elicit those aspects of reality, which are not obvious. Therefore, fictionalism is a theoretical approach in which

[3] See also Beckert (2011: 7).

fictions are used as analytical instruments. The truth value of the fiction is less important than the analytical function of the fiction. Similar to the literary conception of fiction, fictionalism is not an arbitrary concept (Boyd 2009). Operating on the basis of thought experiments one imagines possible worlds, which are coherent and sound and yet not real. In this way, a possible world is a hypothetical situation that describes non-actual but possible objects and incidents. A possible world is thereby neither true nor false, instead it is logically possible, which implies that it is not necessarily false, disregarding whether it is actually true or false (Booth 1961). Analytical progress on the basis of possible worlds should take the form of a possibilistic discourse, in which the authors of a possible world make their recipients belief that the world they have imagined is actually possible and helpful as an analytical instrument (Nolt 1986: 440; Walton 1990).

11.2 Uncertainty and Fiction in Economics

In a world in which knowledge is limited, it is necessary to imagine fictions (fictions, which are possibility true given the knowledge one possesses and not contradictory to reality) about those elements of reality about which knowledge is incomplete: and yet needed in order to act, and act as if these fictions were actually true, while knowing that they might be wrong.[4]

Economists (Earl 1983, 2011; McCloskey 1994, 1998; Akerlof and Shiller 2009: 51ff.; Klamer et al. 2014) have emphasised the importance of fictions for economics and economic actions. I argue here that that fictions have four different, however related, functions in economics:

1. Gaining and storing knowledge.
2. Explanation by understanding with the help of fictions.
3. Assessment of the future.
4. Guide to action.

In what follows I will shortly elucidate the functions of fictions in economics.

11.2.1 Fictions and Knowledge

There is also evidence (Landy 2004) that fictions and fictiontelling are fundamental to human knowledge and human action. Memories, for example, are built and stored

[4]Beckert (2011: 7): "Since the future cannot be known, expectations are images of future states of the world which are taken by actors *as if* they were true. These are "Placeholders" in the decision-making process through which the unknowability of future states of the world and courses of events is *overlooked* for the moment." See also Riles (2010).

with the help of fictions. People tend to remember long-since-forgotten details from the past, when they tell a fiction about some past events or when somebody else reminds them of a fiction by telling a fiction itself. Conversations, for example, are often a source of memory, as they tend to take the form of reciprocal fictiontelling (Akerlof and Shiller 2009: 51). Somebody tells a fiction, which reminds somebody else of an in-some-way similar experience, of which (s)he then tells a fiction. This fiction then fuels the memory of the other person. In this way, fictions help us to remember who we are and what we experienced and therefore know. Beside this knowledge function, fictiontelling also works as an instrument for understanding and by assessing the future.

11.2.2 Fictions and Understanding

Economic models and theories are coherent fictions of some specified part of the economy and it's functioning, which can be used as analytical tools (Hausman 1992). As such economic theories and models are contingent instruments, which have been derived from a fiction about the functioning of the economy that is coherent and more or less believable to the recipient. The author of the theory had made up a believable fiction through the use of imagination, which is not contradictory to sense data and the recipient's perception of reality.

Through fictiontelling, we try to give ourselves and others reasonable accounts of why things happened in the way they did. Occurrences that could have happened on a random basis, become ordered and linked in a way that we are able to understand. In this way, we create understanding via fictions. We do this in ordinary life, but also in the sciences. In science, fictions are replaced by theories and models as modes of explanation and persuasion (Klamer 2007; McCloskey 1983, 1997, 1998). Already in 1983 McCloskey had argued that economic modes and theories need to be interpreted as rhetoric devices used by economists in order to persuade their audience and make them believe in the validity of the argument (Priddat 2014a). He (McCloskey 1983: xx) defines with reference to Booth (1974: xiii, xiv, 59, 137). Rhetoric is "the art of probing what men believe they ought to believe, rather than proving what is true according to abstract methods" it is "the art of discovering good reasons, finding what really warrants assent, because any reasonable person ought to be persuaded", it is "careful weighing of more-or-less good reasons to arrive at more-or-less probable or plausible conclusions-none too secure but better than would be arrived at by chance or unthinking impulse"; it is the "art of discovering warrantable beliefs and improving those beliefs in shared discourse"; its purpose must not be "to talk someone else into a preconceived view, rather, it must be to engage in mutual inquiry". It is what economists, like other dealers in ideas, do anyway: as Booth says elsewhere, "We believe in mutual persuasion as a way of life; we live from conference to conference" (Booth 1974: 13). And McCloskey points out, "Rhetoric is exploring thought by conversation." (McCloskey 1983: 482 f.).

With irony McCloskey (1983: 505) argues, "[...] one might acknowledge the metaphorical element in verbal economics about the "entrepreneur, "for instance, or more plainly of the "invisible hand," yet argued that the linguistic hygiene of mathematics leaves behind such fancies. This indeed was the belief of the advanced thinkers of the 1920s and 1930s who inspired the now-received view in economic method. Most economists subscribe to the belief without doubt or comment or thought. When engaging in verbal economics we are more or less loose, it is said taking literary license with our "fiction"; but when we do mathematics we put away childish things.", and finally concludes: "But mathematical theorizing in economics is metaphorical, and literary." Besides the mythological understanding of elements of economic theories recognized as fictions, McCloskey's rhetorical reading of economic theories points to further important elements that characterizes both economic theories and fictions. First, fictions and theories need to be coherent in order to be valid and therefore believable and rational. Second, neither fictions nor economic theories can be verified unambiguously. And even falsifying either of the two is a challenge. We can therefore conclude that both theory and fictions cannot be proven true, without being false at the same time. Mathematical precision and rhetorical tricks may help economic theories and models to appear as if they were axiomatic results of a hard science. Yet, it should have become clear that they are in fact coherent fictions, which help us to understand some happenings in the economy and make sense of them (Morgan 2013; Priddat 2014b, c). If we come to believe that economic theories are very similar to fictions, we also have to acknowledge that the frontier between science and humanities has become indistinct. Then science, and therefore economics, is about facts and opinions, it is objective and subjective, it is positive and at the same time normative, it is precise and vague, about things and ideas, natural and social in nature and therefore extremely complex.

11.2.3 Fictions, Future and Action

Beside this memory of knowledge and understanding functions of fictions, fictions can be used to assess the future imaginatively Beckert (2011: 7), for example, argues that "[...] influential economic actors [...] shape expectations through narratives given an account of the current economic situation and its future developments. Such narratives serve as "analytical bridges to the near future" (Holmes 2009: 389). Instead of just reporting the facts, fictions create "the economy itself as a communicative field and as an empirical fact" (ibid.: 384). Similar to mathematical models, fictions do not have the potential to foresee future events (Morgan 2013; Priddat 2014c). Yet, fictions allow us to assess the future and build images of it, which enable us to act. We do not believe somebody who states that the price of gold will rise about 15% next week.

However, when the same person tells us a coherent and therefore believable fiction that explains why the gold prices will rise next week, we may very well believe it, act based on it, even develop the fiction further and retell it (Svetlova 2009, 2010, 2011, 2012). Fictions shape our expectations of the future and provide the analytical basis to handle it in a reasonable way or even to create it. It has been argued that if a sufficient number of market participants believe in a certain theory or fiction, it may very well become real, because everyone is acting as if it were true. In this way theories and fictions are performative (Beckert 2011; MacKenzie and Millo 2003; MacKenzie 2006a, b).

These elements and capacities of fictions can be used to develop a theory of choice under conditions of uncertainty that is not based on subjective probability beliefs, but on plausible, coherent and at least partially objective fictions.

11.3 Fictional Choice

> The human mind is built to think in terms of narratives, of sequences of events with an internal logic and dynamic that appear as a unified whole. In turn, much of human motivation comes from living though a story of our lives, a story that we tell to ourselves and that creates a framework for motivation. Life could be just "one damn thing after another" if it weren't for such stories. [. . .] Great leaders are first and foremost creators of stories. (Akerlof and Shiller 2009: 51f.)

Decision situations in economic context are characterised by different degrees of uncertainty. Here, I suggest a theory of choice that takes into account the uncertainty accompanying economic choice and the limits of human knowledge and rationality. The theory opens up the black box in the theory of choice and explains how agents could reasonably behave when knowledge is incomplete to different degrees.

I argue that decisions are based on fictions, which are mental representations and imaginations that correspond to the knowledge agents possess and that could possibly be true. I use the literary concept of fiction as the point of departure for my theory. Fictions are imaginations, which can be believed and therefore shared by other actors. Fictional choice theory is therefore a non-purely subjective theory of reasonable individual choice under conditions of uncertainty.

The theory offers a new conceptualisation of economic behaviour, that (1) could be used as a microfoundation for micro and macro-economic models and (2) as an explanation for innovation and dynamics as well as misallocations and crisis in the economy. On the more abstract level (3) it offers an ontological and epistemological meta-theory for economics that allows economists to tackle questions that lay outside the narrow toolbox of Positive Economics.

Let me now, firstly, introduce the fundamental concepts underlying fictional choice theory. Afterwards I will explain the theory on the basis of Fig. 11.1.

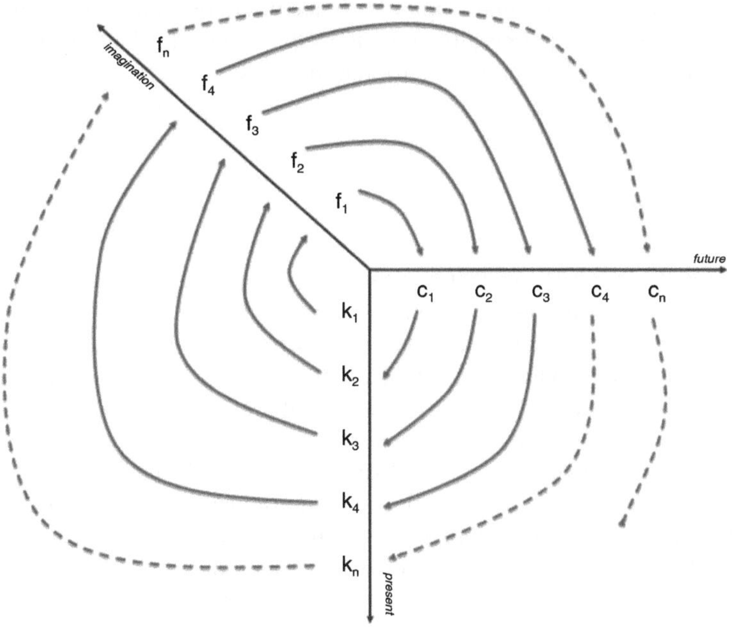

Fig. 11.1 The structure of fictional choice, authors' own figure

11.3.1 Knowledge

We assume that people possess a wide range of background knowledge. This includes knowledge about facts, statistics (relative knowledge) social norms, heuristics, formal institutions, but also observations of the behaviour of other actors. Agents have access to this knowledge in an unstructured way. Some of it is known explicitly and some of it by intuition. Other elements are memories from the past, which might be correct or just facts that were made sense of ex post. Yet, all this knowledge allows no direct inference to the future. From none of this knowledge logically follows a particular generally optimal choice, due to the complex and reflexive nature of economic reality. There are three reasons. First of all, most of our knowledge is not certain but uncertain or ambiguous, which implies, that we cannot trust in our knowledge. And secondly, choice is not only dependent on the knowledge we possess, but also on large parts it is dependent on the knowledge that we not yet possess, namely the knowledge about how things will develop. This is the second dimension, in which the basis for choice is uncertain. In the very moment of choice, it is impossible to know for certain, how the future will unfold. Yet people have images of the future, which are based on their more or less certain knowledge and on their creativity. Thirdly, agents peruse different goals with their choices. Therefore, choice can only be optimal on an individual basis. Furthermore, as soon as the decision was taken, new knowledge becomes available to the decision maker and the originally optimal choice might become non-optimal. Thus, any choice can only be temporally optimal, as the knowledge base is dynamic and reflexive and therefore uncertain to different degrees.

11.3.2 Fictions

Based on the temporarily available background knowledge, agents build images of possible futures in the present, which we call fictions. Fictions are coherent and believable stories of future realities. By imagining possible futures, agents structure their personal scattered knowledge and build fictions, which are *reasonable* to them and *believable* for others. Thus, if the agent would tell his personal narrative about the future to somebody else, the story must be believable to the other person. The agent transfers unstructured memorised knowledge from the past into imagined and structured fictions about reality and some future reality. Internal and external plausibility gets produced. Internal plausibility is reached by the author of the fiction in the way that the fiction does not contradict any piece of personal knowledge. External plausibility, however, is reached if the fiction does not contradict social knowledge. This is the knowledge, which is shared by a certain relevant crowd of people. In a way fictions, therefore, have to be objectifiable. Fictions need to be plausible to its creator and also to its audience or imagined audience (Kleeberg 2009; Priddat 2014c). Though fictions should not contradict reality, they are on the level of imagination and therefore open to the creativity and intentions of its creator.

In this way plausibility is a form of persuasion that creates decidability. By making a story plausible, the story becomes credible and creates apparent certainty. Storytelling, therefore can be interpreted as a certainty creation procedure. Naturally, any certainty is an illusion. Yet, the process of making our stories plausible protects us from naive certainties. It allows us to discriminate between certainties, in the way that one certainty is more plausible than another to a certain group of people. Unlike statistics, this certainty creation procedure is not mechanic but intelligent, as it draws back on the knowledge of many socially interconnected thinking individuals. At the end of this procedure, we come up with socially controlled potential certainties that can be used as a basis for reasonable decision-making.

Certainty creation is a communicative and social process of reinsurance. Similar, to option contracts, it transforms an uncertain reality into a temporarily certain one. This reality is certain, unless nobody starts to doubt the plausibility of the created certainty, which is nothing but a plausible fiction. The fundament of certainty is, thus, the absence of disbelief, which is created by a collective communicative confirmation. In this way certainty leaves the individual subjective level and becomes a collective and objective category in this fiction-framework.

11.3.3 Intentions and Biases

We know that people like and dislike different things. From this fact, we have concluded that agents are different and therefore have different preferences and different capabilities to satisfy these different preferences. It can be shown that people do not choose randomly, but based on their preferences and intentions to satisfy these preferences. In the same way as we can assume that people choose intentionally and we can assume that they create fictions intentionally. Dependent on the capabilities of the agents, they do this more or less consciously. For our purpose, it is irrelevant whether agents act or create fictions consciously or unconsciously according to their intentions. Yet, it is important to note, that the intentions of an agent influence its actions and fictions. One could thus argue that fictions, though they are plausible and objective, they are also biased by the intentions of an agent.[5] Beyond that, we also should take into account the latest findings from behavioural economics and neurosciences, which show, that there is a magnitude of behavioural and psychological biases, which also influence our fictions and actions. We therefore can conclude that agents build biased and yet plausible fictions.

11.3.4 Weight of the Argument

In order to make a choice and take action, agents evaluate these fictions and tend to opt for to the fiction they mostly believe in and which best serves their intentions and capabilities. They evaluate the evidence for the fiction's being possible. The better the evidence is and the more others share this fiction, the more the agent believes in the possibility of the fiction. The more possible the fiction is, the more possible is its realization. We thus apply a pragmatic logical non-mathematical concept of probability here. The possibility of a fiction, thus, can be derived from the evidence for the fiction.[6] Under this definition evidence is a wide concept, which includes personal and social knowledge, similar to intuition and gut feeling. It thus is a purely personal measure; however, it is not arbitrary. Similar to the plausibility of a fiction, the possibility of a fiction is also dependent on a collective communicative conformation procedure. Possibility beliefs of the collective about some fiction, feedback on the possibility beliefs of an individual. Collective beliefs are integrated in individual beliefs via a belief confirmation procedure that involves all kinds of evidence. Thus, individual possibility beliefs are not random. Instead they are partially based on the objective confirmation procedure and include them. Possibility beliefs include subjective and objective perspectives. Therefore, the

[5]This is what Soros (2013) had subsumed under the label of human fallibility.

[6]See Shackle (1979).

assessment of the future via fictions is always a special and intersubjective procedure. Individual, fictional assessments of the future are impossible.[7]

11.3.5 Dynamics

Now the agent can choose the fiction, which satisfies his intentions the most and which is at the same time most probable as a basis for action.[8] Yet, at the very moment the choice was made and the action was taken, we have to assume, that both the personal and the social knowledge changes. Agents gain new insights by acting and their actions will be observed by others, which again take their conclusions and actions, which again can be observed by the agent, who initially took the action. In the new present, knowledge thus changed, which makes it necessary to build new fictions. Even though the decision maker made his choice very carefully, it is non-optimal. In the very moment, it was made, the decision itself reveals new knowledge, which might have changed the decision makers opinion, if (s)he had known it beforehand. If we follow this conception of choice in an uncertain environment, choice is a dynamic process that will never allow for an optimal choice.

Yet, choice is not arbitrary under this theory. Choice is based on even partially objective fictions. At the same time, it allows for novelty and creativity. Introducing the dimension of imagination breaks up the linearity between past and future.

11.3.6 The Process of Choice

Under fictional choice theory, choice is conceptualised as an endless process. The process begins in some point in time (this point in time is assumed to be the temporal present), in which the decision maker possesses some knowledge k_1. Based on this knowledge the decision maker imagines possible futures and builds believable and coherent fictions f_1. (S)he then evaluates these fictions based on the agent's intentions and capabilities and the evidence that supports the possible truth of the fictions and acts upon it. The consequence is choice c_1. As described above, knowledge changes in the very moment the decision was taken, therefore new knowledge k_2 emerges. Consequently, the process restarts.

Conceptualised in this way, economic decision-making is a reflexive and complex communicative process that can reach local stability. Furthermore, the process

[7]The question of fiction selection is crucial for a theory of fictional choice and needs further research.

[8]The process of choice is strongly influences and determined by feelings and intuitions and therefore cannot be interpreted as purely free will.

provides an analytical framework, for what Esposito calls performativity. If our choices are dependent on our knowledge and on the fictions, which might be economic theories we developed, then we are creating the future by our actions in a way we imagine it to be (performative action). Esposito (2013: 108) defines performativity as the intervention of the observer in the market in which (s)he operates. For economic theory, this means that a theory is performative if it changes the structure of its observed phenomena. Both kinds of performativity hold for most economic actions and theories (e.g. McKenzie 2006a, b). Now, fictional choice theory integrates both levels of reflexivity, performative actions and performative theory. This implies that choice becomes a performative action, which might be based also on performative theories. By making a performative choice the boundaries between past, present, future and imagination fade and in the words of Esposito (2013: 112) performativity becomes radical. To Esposito (p. 113) this radicalism is desirable, when she argues: "If every economic operation is performative, then the difference between theory and practical operations is diluted and the boundary between the place where science is produced and the 'outside' society weakens." This means that economics is dependent on the economy and the economy is again dependent on the science of economics, which is nothing but third order reflexivity. Yet, Esposito, goes beyond reflexivity, she rightly points out that if economic choice is performative, economic models, imaginations and memories shape economic reality (Esposito 2013: 114):

> Every economic transaction, according to Shackle (1972: 96), is a decision—that is, a choice between alternatives. However, these alternatives are not the elements of a closed list given in advance. The decision-maker generates the options he hopes to achieve with his choice, with guesses and imagination, options, which did not exist before his decision. Production and innovation (practice and theory), then, are part of the same process, as each economic action produces information which is used by producers and consumers to conceive new possibilities. (Clark and Juma 1987: 96)

This finding has strong implications for the science of economics. First of all, Esposito's account states that economics performs the economy (p. 114). Therefore, economics is anything but a positive science, which implies that on the one side economic theories are influential and on the other side that economic theories always have a normative implication. If economic theories perform the economy, the economic scientist has to be even more careful with its models and theories, as they shape reality.

Secondly, if Esposito is right, then uncertainty is non-random, as the future reality follows more or less directly from present decisions. Still, the future is unknowable in the present and uncontrollable. Yet it is not random, as most of modern economics assumes. Randomness implies a lack of reason (p. 120). However, if choice is performative, then the future is not realized by accident, but because of the choices of economic actors. Their imaginations are the reason for an unpredictable future. The source of uncertainty in the economy is reflexivity and complexity and not chance. Thereby, uncertainty loses its arbitrariness and becomes more assessable, though not controllable. The more detailed information one possesses about the knowledge and imaginations of the decision maker, as well as the knowledge and imaginations of the decision-makers relevant to the choice under question, the more precise fictions can be developed, which will become reality in one way or another. Now, it is up to the economists, to find the reasons driving the economy. Due to the complexity and reflexivity involved, this analysis can only be local and of temporally limited validity. The same holds for individual economic choices as conceptualised in Fig. 11.1. The more precise the background knowledge is, the closer the imagined fictions might be to future reality and the more optical the choice might become. Yet, as soon as the future reality is realised, the system is destabilised and a new reality gets created. Under this conception, only local and temporally limited validity is possible, both on the theory level and in day-to-day choice.

11.4 Conclusion

Now we have seen that uncertainty in economics is the result of a complex and reflexive economic ontology. Randomness only plays a minor role in economic uncertainty. Therefore, the theory of fictional choice neglects stochastic or statistical means. Instead, reflexivity and complexity are at the core of the theory. The theory emphasises complexity, as it incorporates the open system reality, as the knowledge of the decision-making agent is dependent on the knowledge of other agents. The same holds for the imagined fictions. Furthermore, the theory is a constant and multidimensional reflexive feedback loop of future and past, between the imaginations of different agents, and between knowledge and fictions. All in all, diction-making can be visualised as an infinite spider web, that changes constantly, in a way the decision-making spider at the centre of the web, cannot fully understand, however, imagine. Fictions build the intellectual bridge between present and future. Similar, to their original function in eighteenth century literature, fictions create temporal and intersubjective certainty in a naturally uncertain environment.

References

Akerlof GA, Shiller RJ (2009) Animal spirits: how human psychology drives the economy, and why it matters for global capitalism. Princeton University Press, Princeton

Beckert J (2011) Imagined futures fictionality in economic action. Max-Planck-Institut für Gesellschaftsforschung Discussion Paper 8, pp 1–30

Bernstein PL (1998) Against the gods: the remarkable story of risk. Wiley, New York

Bianchi M (2014) The magic of storytelling: how curiosity and aesthetic preferences work. Economics Discussion Papers Kiel Institute for the World Economy 23

Booth WC (1961) The rhetoric of fiction. University Of Chicago Press, Chicago

Booth WC (1974) Modern dogma and the rhetoric of assent. University of Chicago Press, Chicago

Booth WC (1990) The company we keep: an ethics of fiction. University of California Press, Berkeley

Boyd B (2009) On the origin of stories: evolution, cognition, and fiction. Harvard University Press, Cambridge

Bunia R (2009) Was ist Fiktion? Kunstform 202:46–52

Byrne RMJ (2007) The rational imagination. MIT Press, Cambridge

Campe R (2002) Spiel der Wahrscheinlichkeit. Literatur und Berechnung zwischen Pascal und Kleist. Wallstein Verlag, Göttingen

Clark N, Juma C (1987) Long-run economics: an evolutionary approach to economic growth. Pinter Publisher, London

Coleridge ST (1985) Biographia literaria: the collected works of Samuel Taylor Coleridge, biographical sketches of my literary life & opinions, vol 7. Princeton University Press, Princeton

Earl P (1983) The economic imagination. Sharpe, New York

Earl P (2011) From anecdotes to novels: reflectice inputs for behaviorial economics. N Z Econ Pap 45b(1):5–22

Eco U (1994) Im Wald der Fiktionen: Sechs Streifzüge durch die Literatur. Deutscher Taschenbuchverlag, München

Esposito E (2007) Die Fiktion der wahrscheinlichen Realität. Suhrkamp, Berlin

Esposito E (2013) The structures of uncertainty: performativity and unpredictability in economic operations. Econ Soc 42(1):102–129

Hausman DM (1992) The inexact and separate science of economics. Cambridge University Press, Cambridge

Holmes DR (2009) Economy of words. Cultural Anthropol 24(3):381–419

Klamer A (2007) Speaking of economics: how to get in the conversation. Routledge, London

Klamer A, McCloskey D, Ziliak S (2014) The economic conversation. Palgrave Macmillan, Basingstoke

Kleeberg B (2009) Gewinn maximieren, Gleichgewicht modellieren. Erzählen im ökonomischen Diskurs. In: Klein C, Martínez M (Hgs) Wirklichkeitserzählungen. Felder, Formen und Funktionen nicht-literarischen Erzählen. Metzler, Stuttgart, pp 136–159

Krüger L (1989) The probabilistic revolution. MIT Press, Cambridge

Landy J (2004) Philosophy as fiction: self, deception, and knowledge in proust. Oxford University Press, Oxford

MacKenzie D (2006a) Is economics performative? Option Theor Construct Derivat Market 28:29–55

MacKenzie D (2006b) An engine, not a camera: How financial models shape markets. MIT Press, Cambridge

MacKenzie D, Millo Y (2003) Constructing a market, performing theory: the historical sociology of a financial derivatives exchange. Am J Sociol 109(1):107–145

McCloskey DN (1983) The rhetoric of economics. J Econ Lit 21(2):481–517

McCloskey DN (1994) Knowledge and persuasion in economics. Cambridge University Press, Cambridge

McCloskey DN (1997) The rhetoric of economics, revisited. East Econ J 23(3):359–362

McCloskey DN (1998) The rhetoric of economics (Rhetoric of the human sciences). University of Wisconsin Press, Madison

Mendlesohn F (2008) Rhetorics of fantasy. Wesleyan University Press, Hanover

Morgan J (2013) Forecasting, prediction and precision: a commentary (Ch. 12). In: Kabalak A, Priddat BP (Hrsg) Ungewissheit als Herausforderung für die ökonomische Theorie: Nichtwissen, Ambivalenz und Entscheidung. Metropolis, Marburg

Nolt J (1986) What are possible worlds? Mind 95:432–445

Priddat BP (2014a) Economics of persuasion. Ökonomie zwischen Markt, Kommunikation und Überredung, Metropolis

Priddat BP (2014b) Prognose als narrative Plausibilität. In: Cevolini M (Hrsg) Die Ordnung des Kontingenten. Springer, Berlin, pp 251–280

Priddat BP (2014c) Entscheidung als notwendige Fiktion. Über eine fundamentale narrative Struktur in der Ökonomik: Wahrscheinlichkeit und Erwartung. Witten Working Papers, Witten
Riles A (2010) Collateral expertise. Curr Anthropol 51:1–25
Searle JR (1969) Speech acts: an essay in the philosophy of language. Cambridge University Press, Cambridge
Searle JR (1975) Indirect speech acts. University of California, Berkeley, CA
Searle JR (1996) Construction of social reality. Penguin Books, London
Searle JR (1999) Mind, language and society: philosophy In the real world (masterminds). Basic Books, New York
Searle JR (2011) Making the social world. Oxford University Press, Oxford
Shackle GLS (1979) Imagination and the nature of choice. Columbia University Press, New York
Soros G (2013) Fallibility, reflexivity, and the human uncertainty principle. J Econ Methodol 20 (4):309–329
Svetlova E (2009) Do I see what the market doesn't see? Counterfactual thinking in financial markets. Hist Soc Res 34(2):147–157
Svetlova E (2010) Plausibility check of consensus: expectation building in financial markets. J Financ Econ Pract 10(1):101–113
Svetlova E (2011) Understanding crisis: on the meaning of uncertainty and probability. In: Dejuán Ó (ed) The first great recession of the 21st century: competing explanations. Edward Elgar, Cheltenham, pp 42–62
Svetlova E (2012) On the performative power of financial models. Econ Soc 41(3):418–434
Vaihinger H (1911) Die Philosophie des Als Ob. In: System der theoretischen, praktischen und religiösen Fiktionen der Menschheit auf Grund eines idealistischen Positivismus. Vdm Verlag, Saarbrücken
Walton KL (1990) Mimesis as make-believe. Harvard University Press, Cambridge

Chapter 12
Human After All

I aimed to understand the nature of uncertainty in economics. During my research, I discovered a variety of different approaches, theories and methods that deal with the problem of uncertainty in economics. I was unable to give the same attention to all of them, due to their complexity and scope. The comprehensive discussion of the problem of uncertainty in economics points to its significance for the science of economics and its challenging character. The problem of uncertainty has historic, political, methodological, epistemological, ontological and theoretical implications that prevent a generally accepted concept in economics. As a consequence, the Neoclassical Uncertainty Paradigm emerged as a methodology-wise elegant compromise. Today, this compromise has become untenable. Still, large parts of mainstream micro- and macroeconomics and especially Modern Financial Economics is built on the fragile fundament of this outdated Paradigm, which deemphasises the significance of uncertainty for economic phenomena and the science of economics.

At this point the reader would expect a concluding summary of my argument. I will not deprive the reader of a short summary, and yet, I will leave the classical framework and ask, what my analysis would imply for the way forward in new economic thinking.

My analysis has shown, that uncertainty is one of the fundamental sources of economic phenomena.[1] If anything could be known, economics would be a science of optimal organisation and not a science of innovation, novelty, progress and emergent properties. There would be no need for markets, as the price of a good does not need to be discovered. The price would simply be known. The classical economists were sensible to Fundamental Uncertainty, yet, the economist's desire for becoming acknowledged as a scientific discipline, pushed the problem of Fundamental Uncertainty to the margin of the discipline, until it had been almost

[1]Beck (1986) came to a similar conclusion and also emphasized that most of this uncertainty and the associated risk is created by the modern society and modern economics.

J. Köhn, *Uncertainty in Economics*, Contributions to Economics,
DOI 10.1007/978-3-319-55351-1_12

erased from the economic research agenda. The main reason was that Fundamental Uncertainty did not fit the newly developed Positivist Research Paradigm. Instead of analysing uncertainty in its fundamental form, it became reinterpreted as a form of subjective probability that can be treated similar to risk. Therefore, it became possible to integrate uncertainty under the subjective probability interpretation into the Positivist Research Framework.

Nevertheless, the analysis in Part II has shown that Fundamental Uncertainty cannot be expressed in terms of probabilities. Consequently, probability calculus is insufficient for managing the bounds of knowledge. Although, subjective probability theory is a brilliant intellectual achievement, subjective probabilities are mere subjective beliefs that cannot be falsified. Therefore, subjective probability theory falls short on one of the key criteria that distinguishes science from religion.

We have seen that uncertainty has its origin in different levels of reflexivity that comes from the human nature of economics and the complexity of the open economic system. Therefore, uncertainty is fundamental to the nature of economics and, in addition to that, an insurmountable epistemological challenge. I have suggested the use of coherent and believable fictions as the bridge between present and future. Fictional choice theory offers an approach of non-probability based, reasonable and dynamic choice in situations of Fundamental Uncertainty. The process of plausibility testing based on knowledge and social communicative reinsurance is the guide to reasonable action and not rational but meaningless calculations. The theory implies that choice is a dynamic and individual procedure that places the highest demands on the discipline of the mind of the decision-making agent. It requires the believable and coherent imagination and evaluation of different possible future states of the world. Decision-making becomes a scenario analysis of a coherent possibility space. The development of possible fictions is as crucial in this approach as the evaluation of the fictions. Both are human cognitive processes, which is subject to error and surprise. The theory places the highest demands on the decision-making agent, who is held responsible for the decision. At the same time, the approach acknowledges the reflexivity of economic action and choice as well as its performativity. This leaves us with the conclusion that economic choice is never optimal and often subject to surprise, no matter how hard one tries to make up a coherent and believable fiction. Fictions are the guide to reasonable and yet never optimal actions.

The second aim of my inquiry was to understand the implications of uncertainty for the principles of the science of economics. I suggest that uncertainty calls for a fundamental reformation of the principles of the science of economics. The old principles of positive economics neglect Fundamental Uncertainty and favour theories that are insufficient for modelling or acknowledging uncertainty. Consequently, we need a new philosophy of economics and new methods. Fictional choice theory is a first attempt, which needs further critical refection and development. Furthermore, we need a new attitude to deal with economic theories. They are fictions, but theories. After almost a century of abstract, mechanic and barbarous economics, economics has the opportunity to become a human science, after all. Economics of uncertainty is not a question of mathematics and statistical yes or no's. It rather shows that they are just instruments and not theories, which state any truth. It is completely legitimate to use statistical methods in order to model ambiguous situations, yet, one should not believe that these models say anything about the truth.

Now, let me turn to the part of my concluding chapter that goes beyond. I want to ask, what kind of implications my conclusions could have for the science of economics. My answer is trinomial and not conclusive. First of all, I want to highlight that a pluralist methodology in economics becomes compulsory. Secondly, economics is a human science. Thirdly, we need a normative theory of evaluation and awareness for surprise.

12.1 Pluralism

We have learned that the economy is often thought of as a causal and deterministic structure in which more or less stable laws should be discovered. This is the ideal of Positive Economics and an evidence-based science (Cartwright and Stegenga 2011). Furthermore, only stable and manipulatable causal relationships are explanatory and can be exploitable by policy makers (Hendry 2004: 39, 2013). In fact, the famous Lucas et al. (1976) critique points to the failure of received macroeconometrics to model causal relationships. His critique and the Positive Ideal of Economics fostered a methodological monoculture in economics, which i, both philosophically illegitimate and practically dangerous as it ignores the fundament of the economy and economic action. The question we have to ask is, what kind of science would be possible if knowledge is almost impossible in economics?

I emphasise the scientific claim of economics. Yet, I do not believe that any particular methodology can render economics scientific. Quite the opposite is the case. It is negligent to assume that any method, however sophisticated and complex it is, could legitimise a science. Using one and the same instrument in any situation is like a magic trick. The magician uses a sophisticated and exactly planned trick in different situations in order to impress its audience. The situations are different, the technique remains the same and we applaud. If a surgeon, however, would use one and the same tool for any disease, we would call it careless. Nothing else accounts for economics. The economy is a system as complex and reflexive as the human body, and therefore it is as negligent and unscientific to apply the same method to all its diseases. This is charlatanism and not science. Particularly, if we must assume that the economic reality is constantly evolving and therefore unstable. It is almost fraudulent to stick to one method and neglect others.

Furthermore, the evolutionary and complex open system ontology of economics renders any claim of a general and objective principle impossible. Thus, if general and rational economics is impossible and the methodology is not constructive for a science, why should we retain the scientific status of economics?

Like the Critical Realists and physicians, I would suggest a research process with the aim of understanding and critically rethinking as the core of science. We should start by identifying the problem and investigating its nature. At this stage, it will already become clear how precise our conclusions can be. The more the phenomena are subject to uncertainty, the less robust will our conclusions be. Only then, we can start to identify methods for analysing the phenomena. Each method will highlight other aspects of the phenomena, and only combined with one another the conclusions become meaningful. In selecting methods appropriate to the problem, again the uncertainty corridor might help. It shows that methods appropriate to highly complex phenomena might be meaningless for less complex problems. After having analysed the problem from different perspectives with different methods, we can draw conclusions and critically rethink them. We should ask, what if the conclusions are wrong or is it possible that things are different? How confident am I? Would I act on this? How uncertainty-sensitive are my conclusions? Why am I convinced about my findings? And finally, we should put our findings in relation, to what sort of finding is possible given the nature of the phenomena under study. Only then are we to implement our insights in business or politics. Yet, we must keep in mind that our conclusions are performative, therefore the final question is essentially normative. Would I want my conclusions to become a general principle of the economy for some period of time?

12.2 Humanism

Uncertainty is based on human fallibility and complexity, reflexivity, as well as performativity of economic reality. Furthermore, the economic realm is in part natural and in part social. All in all, this declassifies economics as a deterministic and predictive, purely positive science. On the other hand, economics is also not non-science, as it can follow a scientific research procedure and also to establish more or less robust conclusions. Still, it is also not a social science, as it is not only focused on the description of social phenomena. Economics is a science that calls for judgement. It is normative, positive and ambiguous. Therefore, it can best be described as a human science.

The fundamental aim of economics is to provide the best possible living conditions to the largest group of people. The human individual is thus at the centre of economics, and it is the individual that acts, while considering more or less consciously the economic circumstances as well as the decisions of others. If Economics is subject to uncertainty, no optimal solutions can be calculated in this everlasting striving for the greatest good for the greatest number of people. It is up to the individual and socially organised individuals to decide (for example in a democratic and constitutive constitution), which economic institutions are desirable and which are not. The human being creates the economy and its rules. Thus, we are not following some abstract economic principles, but the rules, which have evolved over time based on human action and thought. Keynes once said that his greatest fears were the thoughts of some unworldly thinkers, because their thoughts might become real guiding principles. My analysis of uncertainty in economics suggests that Keynes' fear is particularly legitimate.

Economists created the daemon of the General Principles of Economics that are driving intellectual life in economics and human life today. Beyond that, the conclusion that economics is a human science, also suggests that the human individuals have the power to change the principles of economics and by that the economy. Humans are not following some universal economic laws, but the laws that they have imposed on themselves with the help of economists.

The analysis of this book has shown that economics has the power to create the future. Only complexity, reflexivity, and human fallibility prevent us from creating the future in the way we imagine it. Still, a performative economics has the obligation to critically reflect on their conclusions. Particularly performativity calls for the responsibility of the human for the conclusions of economics. It is our responsibility to decide, if we want a particular idea to influence economic reality or even shape it, as financial markets do. Uncertainty is a driving force of human live and human progress. We should use this force instead of banning it from our thinking. Uncertainty calls for wise human judgement.

12.3 Normativity

Fictionality in economics uses fictions to assess the future and to manipulate it, while knowing that it is impossible to create it. This approach is thought of as a continuous case study analysis for various economic problems. It presupposes a conscious handling of uncertainty, a theory of persuasion and microanalysis of structures, motives, and expectations on the individual, as well as on the institutional level. Furthermore, fictionality suspends the dualism between theory and practice in modern economics and constitutes economics as a normative science. Economics is normative in the way that it presupposes value judgements, considerations and evaluations; and economics is a science, as it aims for universal understanding and uses structured analytical procedures. Let me briefly sketch how such a fictional normative science of economics could look like. Fictional Economics is built on three pillars: firstly, micro-grounded case analysis, secondly, unity of theory and practice and thirdly, a theory of evaluation. Fictional Economics is an endless reflexive scientific process that oscillates between normative and positive as well as between economic reality and economic theory.

Let me now elaborate on the details of this suggested concept, outlined in Fig. 12.1. I begin with the micro-grounded case analysis. We have learned throughout this essay that general theory is impossible. Furthermore, each economic problem is subject to different degrees of uncertainty. Theories, motives, expectations, and institutional structures are the breeding ground for possible and believable fictions, which build the bridge between present and future. Consequently, analysing these microstructures underlying our fictions allows us to understand the structure of economic reality and to evaluate possible future economic realities. In general, this could work for the economy as a whole, yet different levels and degrees of uncertainty necessarily hinder us. Therefore, we should look at economic problems in isolation, while reflecting on

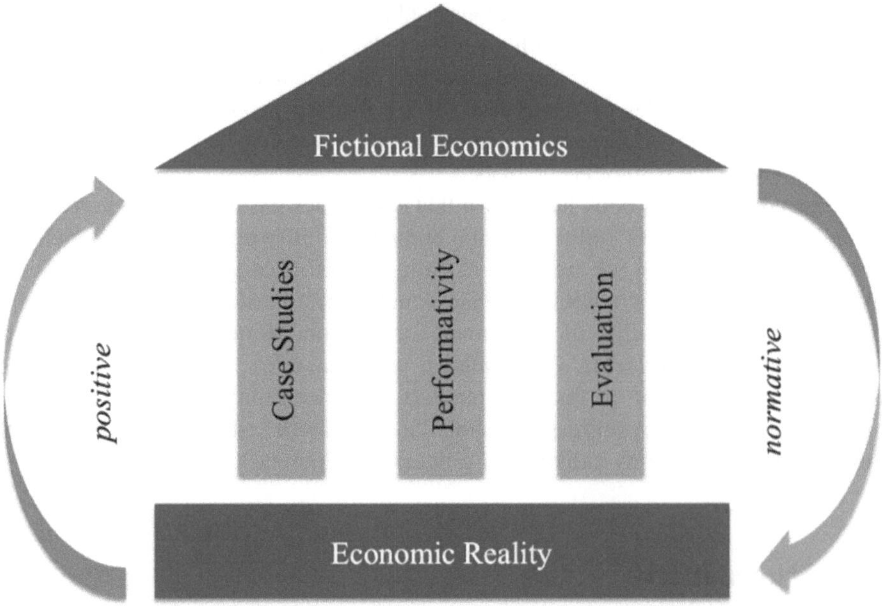

Fig. 12.1 Fictional economics as a reflexive process. Authors' own figure

its interconnection with the economy as a whole. For example, if I wanted to know whether the European Central Bank should raise the base rate, I firstly have to clarify the circumstances and the associated degree of uncertainty. Then, I could look for existing theories and analyse their conclusions based on their assumptions. Then, I would have to ask myself, how reliable these conclusions might be, given the degree of uncertainty associated with this question. The underlying questions are: How plausible and believable are these fictions? Afterwards, I would have to go deeper into the structure of the phenomena and analyse the breaking points of my fictions. It would become necessary to ask experts and talk to normal people to determine what they think about the plausibility of my fictions. I have to inquire about their motives and expectations. Only then, in the light of all the various sources of information, could I start to critically rethink and determine the best course of action regarding the base rate. It is possible that, my analysis has shown that the base rate is not the problem. Instead it might be the case, that the commercial banks refuse to lend money because of particular accounting standards. If I would have started with one particular approach, a conclusion of this kind would have been impossible. Besides not prejudging particular outcomes, this micro-grounded case analysis allows us to understand the structure of the problem, which is essential to building a wise policy suggestion.

Secondly, fictional economics neglects the difference between theory and practice. We have learned that economic theories are performative. This means that economic theories shape the way we understand the economy. On the other hand, it means that the economy works the way our theory suggested it. Thus, any theory, no matter how isolated from economic reality it had been developed, is affecting the economy.

Therefore, it is neither fruitful nor legitimate to think of economics as an isolated science that can only be performed in high-class universities. Rather the opposite is the case, economic reality, which is the economy, the market place, or individual actions are the benchmarks for a good economic science and not university rankings or journal scores. If we take performativity seriously, then our best theories and economists are those, which are successful in everyday lives and not in an idealist science fiction league. We should expect that their science fictions might become reality. No morally responsible individual can want that. It should become the aim of a fictional economics to develop theories that create conditions for a better economic future, in which nobody is suffering or gets exploited.

Finally, the analysis has shown, that rationality analysis does not go deep enough to analyse an uncertain economy. Fictional economics needs evaluation principles, which go beyond rationality analysis. In fictional economics, we have the obligation to choose. Thus, on the one hand we are free to choose and on the other hand the concept shows, that it is our responsibility to create a desirable future with our actions, while knowing that the process is endless and always only temporally optimal. It is also our responsibility to balance possible futures in everyday lives, but also in politics. In this process uncertainty and surprise in omnipresent, consequently, we should develop an evaluation procedure that accounts for non-optimal choice.

I suggest, that we should evaluate fictions by firstly, analysing the degree of uncertainty associated with it. The underlying question thus is, how much certainty is possible? Then we can ask, how much certainty is necessary, given what is possible, to take a reasonable course of action? Afterwards we can start to analyse what we know until we have reached the certainty we need. The final control question should always be, what if I am wrong? Can I live with the consequences? Is there anything I can do to get prepared for unpleasant surprises?

To me, this is the only reasonable way to act in a necessarily uncertain economic environment and in the science of economics. Our handling of uncertainty should get much more explicit and conscious. Economics is a human and uncertain science. Let us face it!

References

Beck U (1986) Die Risikogesellschaft: Auf dem Weg in eine andere Moderne. Suhrkamp, Frankfurt am Main

Cartwright N, Stegenga J (2011) A theory of evidence for evidence-based policy. Proc Br Acad 171:289–319

Hendry J (2004) Between enterprise and ethics: business and management in a bimoral society. Oxford University Press, Oxford

Hendry J (2013) Ethics and finance: an introduction. Cambridge University Press, Cambridge

Lucas RE, Brunner K, Meltzer AH (1976) Econometric policy evaluation: a critique. In: Brunner K, Metzler AH (eds) The Phillips curve and labor markets, Carnegie-Rochester conference series on public policy, vol 1. Elsevier, Amsterdam, pp 19–46

MIX
Papier aus verantwortungsvollen Quellen
Paper from responsible sources
FSC® C105338

If you have any concerns about our products,
you can contact us on
ProductSafety@springernature.com

In case Publisher is established outside the EU,
the EU authorized representative is:
Springer Nature Customer Service Center GmbH
Europaplatz 3, 69115 Heidelberg, Germany

Printed by Libri Plureos GmbH
in Hamburg, Germany